YOSEMITE'S TIOGA COUNTRY

Best wishes,
Gene Rose

Yosemite's Tioga Country

A History and Appreciation

by Gene Rose

YOSEMITE ASSOCIATION

YOSEMITE NATIONAL PARK, CA

Publication of this book was made possible by generous grants from James McClatchy, the McClatchy Foundation, and Mike and Lennie Roberts.

Yosemite Association
Box 545
Yosemite National Park
California 95389

Since 1923, the Yosemite Association has initiated and supported interpretive, educational, research, scientific, and environmental programs in Yosemite National Park, in cooperation with the National Park Service. Authorized by Congress, the Association provides services and direct financial support in order to promote park stewardship and enrich the visitor experience.

To learn more about our activities and other publications, or for information about membership, please write to the address above, call (209) 379-2646, or visit www.yosemite.org.

Unless otherwise noted, the photographs in this book are from the Yosemite Research Library collection, maintained by the U.S. National Park Service in Yosemite National Park.

Book design by Robin Weiss Graphic Design, San Carlos, California.
Project coordination by Steven P. Medley.

Printed in Singapore.

Contents

ACKNOWLEDGMENTS

In compiling this book I was assisted by a number of exceptional individuals. The traits they shared are their love for and devotion to the high country of Yosemite National Park and the Tioga Pass Road—one of the most remarkable routes in America.

Many of these individuals belong to the "extended Tioga tribe," a select group of mountaineers who hail from the greater Sierra family. Within their ranks are many dedicated guardians and admirers of the area—people whose very identities and reputations have been inextricably linked to the special world of Tioga Pass.

Some of those devoted pathfinders left the high country long ago, but they passed on their legacies to the rest of us. In words, pictures, and deeds, they helped define the high country scene I write about in this book. And it was their spirit that led me on. Those elders include Chief Tenaya, John Muir, John Lembert, Joseph LeConte, William Colby, Edward Parsons, John Bingaman, Forest Townsley, and Ansel Adams. Other mountain memories were provided by Charles McNally (an early Tuolumne Meadows seasonal ranger), Sterling Cramer (a Curry Company executive of many years), and Arthayda Quick (wife and partner of the late veteran ranger, Clyde Quick).

In the fifteen years it took to complete this effort many of classic Yosemite characters have passed on. Their ranks include Leroy Rust, the long-time Yosemite postmaster; Herb Ewing, veteran Mather District ranger; and Tom Sovulewski, grandson of Yosemite's first civilian superintendent, Gabriel Sovulewski.

Other mountain legends helped me with my work. During one brief gathering in the summer of 1991, I managed to corral Ferdinand Castillo, the Tioga Pass entrance station ranger, Carl Sharsmith, the famed NPS naturalist and botanist, and Nic Fiore, acclaimed skimeister and veteran High Sierra Camps manager, at Tuolumne Meadows. It was a memorable event, featuring three Sierra stalwarts with a collective 139 summers (or thereabouts) spent in the Tioga high country. Their stories (and tall tales) were plentiful, and their love of their surroundings was manifest.

Additional guidance for this book came from the late Shirley Sargent,

Yosemite's premier author-historian; Neil Kelly, formerly of the Tioga Pass Lodge; Mavis and Chuck Grover, past operators of the Saddlebag Lake Resort; and Don Banta, Lee Vining native, booster, and businessman, and his father Bill Banta. Wally Woofsen, Nicholas Faust, and Emily Martin of the Inyo National Forest also lent their assistance to the publication. Lily Mathieu La Braque graciously granted the use of passages from her book, *Man From Mono.*

I am appreciative also of my wife Doris; historian Marian Albright Schenck; the assistance of Jay Johnson, Yosemite native and American Indian, who read chapter one; Craig Bates, curator of ethnography for the Yosemite Museum, who also helped with the first chapter; geologist N. King Huber of the U.S. Geological Survey, who added depth to my superficial understanding of geology; former Yosemite park historian Jim Snyder, who offered invaluable counsel at numerous turns along the way; Dr. Edgar Wayburn, the Sierra Club veteran who helped with the history of the new road; Scott Carpenter, former Yosemite park archaeologist; and Ron Mackie, retired Yosemite wilderness ranger.

Many others shared their photographic images or their information. Linda Eade of the Yosemite Research Library; Greg Cox and Miriam Luchans of the Yosemite Museum; Steve Medley, president of the Yosemite Association; Bill Myers of Southern California Edison Company; Vicky Hoover of the Sierra Club; Susan Snyder of the Bancroft Library; Carol Gilbert and Richard L. Kizer of the California Department of Transportation; John R. Gonzales of the California section of the state library; Fern Dame, curator of the National Geographic Society; postcard collector Marilynn Guske; and Marilyn Harper, freelance editor, all provided valuable assistance.

Finally, I would like to specially acknowledge Jim McClatchy and the McClatchy Corporation, as well as Lennie and Mike Roberts for their generous grants to the Yosemite Association in support of the publication of this book.

To these past, present, and other members of the "Tioga tribe," I express my sincere thanks for your help in preserving the unique and rich heritage of the Tioga region.

INTRODUCTION

The Tioga Road, the famed Sierra route that transects the high country of Yosemite National Park, is a remarkable scenic mountain byway. At a sky-scraping 9,941 feet, it is California's loftiest roadway, attracting thousands of vacationers every year. But these fifty-nine miles of asphalt are more than an avenue to the finest high country in the Golden State. In many ways, the Tioga Road is one of the most important highways in America, having helped pave the way for the creation of the national park system, often described as "the best idea this nation ever had."

Running from Crane Flat to Lee Vining, the road winds through one of the most scenic and spectacular sections of California. Along its comparatively short span, travelers can experience a wonderland of deep forests, sparkling lakes, dazzling domes, ephemeral waterfalls, towering peaks, and mountain meadows. From Olmsted Point to Tenaya Lake to Tuolumne Meadows, here is a road that touches the sky. The highway climbs gradually from the west, reaches an altitude of nearly two miles, then begins its precipitous descent through Lee Vining Canyon to the haunting beauty of the Mono Lake Basin and the eastern Sierra.

Besides its spectacular beauty, the Tioga Road offers rich human history, with a heritage that extends back to prehistoric Native Americans, the area's original pathfinders. From the first human migration across this mountain corridor, the Yosemite high country has lured a continuing array of visitors, variously seeking riches, adventures, and recreation.

For many centuries, the Indians ventured back and forth across this high world in search of society, trade, food, and relief from the heat. More recently, Euro-American trailblazers arrived, penetrating the depths of the pristine wilderness hoping to find minerals, pastures for grazing, and better lives. Some visitors, such as John Muir, recognized the value of the Yosemite high country, and helped protect the region as part of one of our nation's finest national parks.

Because it has been protected as an invaluable national treasure, the Tioga Pass region has inspired millions of visitors over the years. The late Ferdinand Castillo of the National Park Service became possessed by the area. Until his death in 1993, Ferdinand reigned as "the keeper of the gate," working in the small entrance station at the top of the Sierra.

"Welcome to Yosemite," Ferdinand would intone as he greeted incoming visitors. Often he added a "travelers' advisory" to his message. "The sun is low. Watch for deer on the road," was a common warning. For those leaving the park and headed toward the Blue Slide area of Lee Vining Canyon, it was "Look out for rocks on the road. Please come back again." Ferdinand truly loved this "high way" and considered it an object of affection that he wanted to share with thousands of his fellows.

Several years ago, a Lee Vining schoolteacher asked her students to write a paper describing their perceptions of "heaven." When the papers came back she discovered an inordinate number depicting the area around Tioga Pass.

This is the story of the special highway that leads through the "heavenly" Tioga region, and of the lives and times the road and high country have touched. I hope that it inspires in you the same love that so deeply affected Ferdinand Castillo and that is discovered anew by untold numbers of travelers to the area each year.

Gene Rose
January 2006

CHAPTER I

EARLY HIGH COUNTRY HISTORY

N o one knows much about the first people to make their way across the crest of the Sierra through what is today the Yosemite high country. There is no written history, only a corridor scattered with arrowheads, midden soils, and obsidian chips to mark the passage of those who long ago topped the high Sierra near Tioga Pass.

Recent studies suggest that there were nearly two dozen locations within the Yosemite area where Native Americans could have crossed the Sierra crest without major difficulty.[1] Early on, the pathfinders apparently followed a series of animal trails that led up from the high desert on the eastern slope or the foothills of the western slope of the Sierra. Over time and through trial and error, a route was developed between the Mono Lake Basin and Yosemite Valley called the Mono Trail. Located about two miles south of 9,941-foot Tioga Pass, the Mono Trail topped a gentler but slightly higher summit, with an elevation of 10,604 feet. Simultaneous with other trails over the centuries, the Mono Trail became an established trade and migration route for those on both sides of the mountains.

Route variations to the Mono Trail in Yosemite developed over time. The Whitney Survey maps of 1864-67 show two Mono Trails, one above and one below Yosemite Valley, meeting in Tuolumne Meadows. These routes grew as the region's upper elevations were increasingly visited by several Indian groups.

It is likely that the use of the high country routes was confined to summer and early fall, when the mountains were free of snow. With the coming of summer's heat, many Indians would leave their lower-elevation villages and camps, and move up slope. Numerous campsites were located along the way, although Dana and Tuolumne Meadows appeared to be the ultimate destinations on this route, affording ample and ideal camping space. Nearly sixty archaeological sites[2] have been documented along the route, the precursor of today's Tioga Road. There seems to have been a major encampment at Tuolumne Meadows, and a number of smaller camping areas, such as at Dana Meadows. Bedrock mortar holes on the

Opposite: Snow-covered Tenaya Lake, the shining centerpiece of the Yosemite trans-Sierra corridor, wears a winter mantle of snow. Photo by author.

western slope of Lembert Dome, for example, bear witness to the fact that the Indians enjoyed a good campsite as much as today's visitors. There are similar pounding rocks near Crane Flat.

Besides camping and trading, the Indians would feast, play games, and dance. They also hunted for deer, rabbits and other small game, and occasionally bear. Obsidian found in many of the surrounding high passes and along the Kuna Crest area could indicate that the Indians were pursuing the bighorn sheep that once were common to Tioga country.

Simple visiting occupied a major portion of time in camp—just as present-day family members will catch up at a large family reunion. Gatherings fostered social contact and even led to inter-tribal marriages. For instance, Chief Tenaya, the last leader of the Yosemite Valley Indians,

This early drawing depicts the Mono Lake Paiutes living on the east side of the Sierra at the time of contact with Euro-Americans. Photo from Picturesque California.

was purportedly born of a Mono mother and an Ahwahneechee Miwok father. The extent of the contacts between the Yosemite, Mono, and other groups is uncertain, however. Ways of life for native peoples on both sides of the Sierra became threatened starting in the late 1700s, when Spanish colonizers, aided by the military, began their missionary work in California. But the first direct contact between the Indians and whites may have occurred when Joseph R. Walker crossed the Sierra in 1833.

The Walker party included fifty men with four horses each, ammunition, trade goods, and a year's supply of food.[3] The party's route led from Utah across the Great Basin, to the Humboldt Sink, and on toward Carson Lake. Near that location, the group encountered a large band of northern Paiute Indians, some of whom apparently were perceived as threatening. Believing themselves in jeopardy, the Walker party opened fire on the Indians, killing nearly forty of them in what some historians now regard as a massacre.

Seeking to put the incident behind them, the party moved quickly southward though the wilderness of western Nevada and along the towering Sierra escarpment. Somewhere near today's Bridgeport —along a river that would one day bear Walker's name—they apparently turned west again and entered the uncharted mountains, probably crossing the crest near today's Virginia Pass. For several days they wandered through a maze of mountains, where even their direction of travel came into doubt. Freezing fall weather then swept over the scene, bringing early snows and cold. In the deep drifts, their progress faltered and the exploration became an ordeal. Eventually their food supplies ran out, and the group slaughtered its own horses.

Walker's clerk, Zenas Leonard, observed that some party members feared that they might never find their way through the impenetrable wilderness, and that they might die in this "awfully sublime" place. Yet they pressed on. Some researchers believe the members of the Walker party made their way to the headwaters of the Tuolumne River near Return Creek and then stumbled onto the Mono Trail as they moved to the west. At one point, an expedition scout encountered a solitary Indian with a burden basket of acorns. Startled to see the white-skinned intruders, the Indian dropped his load and fled into the brush. The scattered acorns were quickly recovered and taken back to camp, where they were "eaten gratefully by the hungry white men" despite the acorns' repulsive tannin taste.[4]

Around October 20, 1833, the Walker party may have come upon one of the great wonders of the western world when it reached the lip of Yosemite Valley. "Here we began to encounter in our path, many small streams which would shoot out from under high snow banks, and after running a short distance in deep chasms where they have through the ages cut in the rocks, precipitate themselves from one lofty precipice to another, until they are exhausted in rain below. Some of these precipices appear to us to be more than a mile high. Some of the men thought that if we could succeed in descending one of these precipices to the bottom, we might thus work our way into the valley below – but on making several attempts we found it utterly impossible for a man to descend, to say nothing of our horses," Leonard wrote in his journal.[5]

At that point, the Walker party fortunes seem to have improved. As the explorers continued west along the Indian trail, the snows that had plagued their path disappeared. And the food supply grew when two fat deer and a bear fell to the party's hunters. On October 30, the group encountered a stand of incredibly large trees, much larger than any person in the party had ever seen. Thus Walker's men became the first known non-Indians to have encountered the giant sequoias—in either the Merced or the

Top: *The first snows of winter bring down the curtain for another season along the Tioga Road. The Kuna Crest and Dana Meadows reflect the seasonal change. Photo by author.*

Bottom: *This boy, identified by the photographer as a Paiute Indian, was captured by camera in the early 1860s.*

Joseph R. Walker led his party across the Sierra Nevada through the high country of Yosemite in 1833.

Tuolumne Grove. From here they continued downhill near the Tuolumne River to its junction with the great San Joaquin River.

Recently, the course of Walker's traverse has been questioned by historians. One revisionist contends that Walker's trans-Sierra route lay to the north, where his hard-pressed group passed through the Calaveras Grove. This researcher questions whether Walker ever saw Yosemite Valley or the Tuolumne Grove of Big Trees. Because there is so little data and no map from the time, the traditional version of this epic crossing still is generally accepted.[6]

With the exception of the acorn carrier, the Indians in the Yosemite area avoided any contact with the Walker party. For the next seventeen years (until about 1850), they remained relatively insulated from the changes that accompanied the Mexican domination of California and the growing Yankee immigration. The native people continued their mountain migrations for a time, unnoticed until California and the West experienced the massive changes accompanying the California gold rush.

Throughout the Mother Lode a tidal wave of gold seekers swept over the foothills, disrupting the peaceful existence of the original occupants. The "forty-niners" devastated not only the Indian lands but also the Indians themselves. When the natives tried to defend their property, they were attacked.

During the gold rush, miners William Penn Abrams and U. N. Reamer were apparently the first Euro-American men to gaze upon Yosemite Valley, making their way into the lower canyon in 1849 while hunting bear. However, it was several years before the secluded valley of the Indians became widely known.[7]

While the invasion by miners came somewhat later to the Yosemite region, it was no less dramatic. Hostilities increased when several raids were made by Indians in the foothills on the trading posts of James Savage, a prospector-turned-merchant and entrepreneur—some time around December 17, 1850. Three employees were killed at Savage's Fresno River store. The attacks were followed by others, and the miners and settlers in the Mariposa area began to band together to retaliate. Savage was promoted to the rank of major in the Mariposa Battalion, to lead the citizen militia mobilized to put an end to Indian hostilities.

Elected major of the citizen militia, Savage and Captain John Boling headed for the mysterious valley of Yosemite with the volunteers from the battalion in late March 1851. According to some neighboring tribes, the Ahwahneechee Indians who resided there were "lawless, like the grizzly bear, as strong. We are afraid to go to this valley, for there are many witches there."[8] From a camp on the south fork of the Merced River, Savage sent a messenger ahead to demand the surrender of the Ahwahneeches and their relocation to the Fresno Indian Reservation near Madera.

The Tioga Road provides another perspective on Yosemite's famed landmark known as Half Dome. Photo by author.

In the 1930s, photographic greats Ansel Adams and Edward Weston regularly used these gnarled trees above Tenaya Lake as subjects for their spectacular images. Photo by author.

Near today's Bishop Creek, the battalion encountered a small band of Yosemite Indians, headed by the Ahwahneechee leader, Chief Tenaya. He resisted initial efforts to move his people to the reservation. "My people do not want anything from the 'Great Father' you tell me about. The Great Spirit is our father, and he has always supplied us with all we need. We do not want anything from white men. Our women are able to do our work. Go then; let us remain in the mountains where we were born; where the ashes of our fathers have been given to the winds. I have said enough!"[9]

Later, Tenaya assembled some seventy people for the trip to the Central Valley, but Savage believed that many of the Yosemites were still in hiding. "My tribe is small—not large, as the white chief has said. The Pai-utes and Monos are all gone . . . young and strong men can find plenty in the mountains; therefore why should they go? to be yarded like horses and cattle. My heart has been sore . . . but I am now willing to go, for it is best for my people that I do so," the venerated chief responded.[10]

Sending Tenaya and his tribe to their camp, Savage and his men pushed on through deep snows, hoping to capture the rest of the tribe. Following the southern section of the Mono Trail—part of which would become the trail from Wawona to Yosemite Valley—the battalion made its way into the incomparable valley on March 27, 1851[11] The group earned the distinction of being the first non-Indians to descend to the valley floor. There, however, they found just one old woman and a remarkable but deserted landscape. After a quick search of the valley, Savage's men torched the Indian dwellings and food caches, then returned to their South Fork camp. Meanwhile, Tenaya's group abandoned its trek to the reservation, escaped its captors, and found its way back to Yosemite Valley by another route.

About two months later, following still more Indian incidents, Captain John Boling forced his way into Yosemite Valley along the same route and captured five Indians. Many of the natives, including Tenaya, fled into the high country. Two of the captured Indians, who promised that they would bring in the chief and his people, were released to follow the escapees. When the three other captives attempted to take flight, they were shot and killed. One of the victims was Tenaya's youngest son.

Boling's unit stayed in the valley for several days in hopes that the Indians would turn themselves in. When the patriarch chief, Tenaya, did so, and he discovered that his son had been slain by the soldiers, he was overcome with grief. As a final measure, Boling's unit then climbed onto the north rim of the valley and began to search along the Mono Trail. On May 22, 1851, they found the remainder of Tenaya's tribe, half-starved and in poor health, near what later became known as Tenaya Lake. Easily apprehended, they were marched off to the reservation.

The Yosemite Indians were not happy in their new home. The proud Tenaya found himself tormented by the other tribes. "The other Indians taunted him with his now lowly position. He begged for a leave from the reservation for he indicated he could not endure the hot sun and was hungry for his acorn diet, which he said he preferred to government rations."[12] In time, Tenaya was permitted to return to Yosemite Valley on

Lafayette H. Bunnell recorded his experiences with the Mariposa Battalion in 1851. His account serves as the basis of much that historians know about the Ahwahneechee people at the time of contact.

Top: Mount Dana towers over Tioga Lake awaiting the warming days of spring. Photo by author.

Bottom: Ellery Lake, named for the engineer who pushed the first road up the eastern slope, holds on to winter late into the year. Photo by author.

the promise that he would refrain from any further violence.

But on May 3, 1852, a group of eight miners, prospecting in the valley, were set upon by Indians, who felt their mountain sanctuary was being threatened. In the melee, two of the miners were killed, while the others fled for their lives.[13] The incident set off a new wave of fear among the foothill miners and settlers. With the Mariposa Battalion disbanded, a unit of the California 2nd Infantry was dispatched from Fort Miller, just northeast of today's Fresno, to suppress what was perceived as another Indian uprising. Led by Lt. Tredwell Moore, the infantry unit established a base camp somewhere in the mountains above Yosemite Valley. On July 1, Moore ordered his next in command, Lt. N. H. McLean, to enter the valley "to destroy the rancherias and provisions there" that had been abandoned by the Indian people.[14]

In the meantime, Moore intercepted half a dozen fleeing Indians in the high country. Discovering clothing from the prospectors, Moore executed all six men and then returned to base camp to await reinforcements. "From information received from the Indian women taken a few days since, I have determined to follow the Yosemites across the Sierras into the Mono County. The Yosemites are on friendly terms with the Monos and have fled to this country thinking that the whites will not follow them across the snow," he wrote.[15] In the ensuing days, Moore picked up the chief's trail at Tenaya Lake and moved eastward. By that time, the Indians already had made their way along the Mono Trail to the east side of the Sierra, where they found refuge with their Mono neighbors.

Once reinforced, Moore's men continued eastward to Tuolumne Meadows, searching the canyons and ravines along the way. They located and crossed Mono Pass, and descended the eastern slope. For several days the unit combed the basin without locating the "cunning chief" and his followers, then gave up the chase. Before heading home, Moore named

Mono Lake and the two major islands that dot its expansive surface. He also named several of the adjacent rivers and creeks in honor of his men.[16] He chose to call the gentle mountain saddle north of Mono Pass "McLean Pass," after his trusted lieutenant. This was the original name for Tioga Pass. He also christened a small stream McLean's River, but that name, too, disappeared with time.

The Yosemite Indians stayed with the Monos until the following summer, when they slipped back into Yosemite Valley.[17] Chief Tenaya was subsequently killed by the Monos as the result of a quarrel over either a game or the theft of some horses; the incident was never documented. In the years that followed, Indian populations declined still further and their lives and cultures dramatically changed. Those remaining continued to use the old trails to make the acorn harvest in Yosemite Valley. Others were drawn into the growing tourist trade as workers in many capacities, mixing the traditional with the new.[18]

Conflicts preceded the mapping of the Yosemite region. In 1853, John B. Trask, California's first state geologist, published an early map of northern California, including the Sierra, entitled, "Topographical Map of the Mineral Districts of California" (see page 34). Many of the area's major landmarks were missing, however, including Yosemite, Mount Whitney, Lake Tahoe, and Mono Lake.

How Trask obtained the information he used to publish such a map is unclear. On his own he had traveled and written extensively about California geology. He had visited many of the gold-bearing locations indicated on his map, especially the Mother Lode areas of Big Oak Flat, Bear Valley, Mount Ophir, and other sites, and had penned several extensive

Lieutenant Tredwell Moore named Mono Lake when he and U.S. troops pursued Indians from Yosemite Valley to the east side in 1852. Photo from Picturesque California.

GEOLOGICAL SURVEY OF CALIFORNIA

J.D.WHITNEY, State Geologist.

MAP
of a portion of the
SIERRA NEVADA
adjacent to the
YOSEMITE VALLEY
from surveys made by
CH.ᴾ F.HOFFMANN and J.T.GARDNER,
1863 — 1867.

Scale 2 miles to 1 inch.

This California
Geological Survey
map based on
the Hoffmann-
Gardiner surveys
of 1863–67 was
the first to use the
name "McLane's
Pass" (also spelled
"McLean's" in other
sources) for what is
now called Tioga
Pass. That name
was used into the
1890s, when the
pass became known
as "Tioga." Map
courtesy of the
Bancroft Library.

reports on the geology of these gold mining areas. He was in many of the mining areas covered by the map as early as 1851, but his travels did not include Mono Pass. His recorded elevation for the pass was only half its actual height.[19] Obviously, he heard about the trail and pass in his travels, perhaps from Indians or other miners, and added them sight unseen.

Just two years later, in 1855, a surveyor under government contract, Alexis W. von Schmidt, crossed the mountains east of the Kuna Crest along part of the Tioga corridor and made a cursory survey of the Mono Lake basin while plotting the Mount Diablo base line. Unfortunately, von Schmidt's map does not show trans-Sierra trails.[20] When members of the California Geological Survey began their work in the Sierra in the early 1860s, they noted few aboriginal people. They did map the northern and southern version of the Muir Trail in Yosemite, the earliest depiction of these well-known Indian routes.[21]

John Muir first visited the region of the Mono Trail in the summer of 1869, when he worked as a sheepherder for rancher Pat Delaney.

By the time John Muir passed over the Mono Trail in the summer of 1869, the presence of Indians along the route was further reduced. Foothill rancher Pat Delaney engaged Muir to oversee two herders who were taking his sheep to the mountains. Muir learned about Mono Pass and began to make plans to visit the historic crossing point. On August 14, he left Tuolumne Meadows bound for Mono Lake and the eastern slope of the Sierra by way of Mono Pass. "At length, as I entered the pass, the huge rocks began to close around in all their wild, mysterious impressiveness, when suddenly, as I was gazing eagerly about me, a drove of gray hairy beings came in sight, lumbering toward me with a kind of boneless, wallowing motion like bears.

"I never turn back, though often so inclined, and in this particular instance, amid such surroundings, everything seemed singularly unfavorable for the calm acceptance of so grim a company. Suppressing my fears, I soon discovered that although as hairy as bear and as crooked as summit pines, the strange creatures were sufficiently erect to belong to our own species. They proved to be nothing more formidable than Mono Indians dressed in skins of sage-rabbits.

"I afterward learned that they were on their way to Yosemite Valley to feast awhile on trout and procure a load of acorns to carry back through the pass to their huts on the shore of Mono Lake," Muir observed.[22]

From this initial meeting, Muir regarded the Indians as unkempt and out of place in his pristine world of peaks and passes. After he made his way down the eastern slope, Muir observed the Monos hunting rabbits and harvesting wild rye grain and the larvae of the fly common to the area.[23] Regardless of his antipathy toward these people, Muir's observations are a valuable record of their culture during this time period.

Another early Yosemite mountaineer, John B. Lembert, who

Time, wind, and weather have shaped and pruned the picturesque trees that line the Tioga Road. Photo by author.

homesteaded in Tuolumne Meadows in 1885—his name now graces the familiar Lembert Dome—reported seeing as many as one hundred Indians passing over Mono Pass and through Tuolumne Meadows during the summers he resided there. The trips were still important for affording the trading of obsidian, pine nuts, and deer skins.[24]

After the Tioga mines were developed about 1880, some of the Indians from Mono Lake made their way by horseback to summer encampments at Tuolumne Meadows. Agnes Castro, the grandmother of Yosemite forestry technician Larry Castro, made such a trip. As he recalled, "My ancestors used to make this trip from Mono Lake, up through Bloody Canyon and over Mono Pass. They could walk from Mono Lake to Yosemite Valley in three days. But they loved the Tuolumne Meadows area and used to camp there so that their travels might take a week or two."[25] A few local Native Americans managed to preserve the tradition of the mountain migration for several years up until World War I, when the arrival of the automobile brought even greater changes to the Tioga scene.

Fragments of this high country heritage surface in the oral histories of Native Americans of the greater Yosemite area. Jay Johnson, a long-time National Park Service employee who has traced his roots back to the 1830s, has heard stories suggesting that the trans-Sierra migrations were for social purposes as well as for trade. "When I was a young boy my mother would point out the places in Tuolumne Meadows where our ancestors camped. The Mono Paiutes were regarded as distant relatives, with whom they enjoyed getting together," he noted.[26]

Current research suggests that the Indian populations and activities were much more extensive and much older than was projected in the early 1900s. Within the boundaries of Yosemite, there are no less than 2,000

Jay Johnson, a local Native American and retired National Park Service employee, traces his roots in the Yosemite area back to the 1830s.

significant Native American sites.[27] Hydration analysis of obsidian flakes and carbon dating of charcoal and other artifacts indicates that the Indian era may have begun more than 6,000 years ago.

Still, comparatively little is known of the early migrations and encampments. Reminders of the Native American era continue to mark the Mono Trail. Some of the place names the Indians applied to the high country landmarks, such as Kuna and Koip, remain.[28] Over time many of the names were Anglicized or changed by those who followed. For instance, Tuolumne, while placed on the map by Western man, is believed to be of Indian derivation. The words Mono, Tioga, and Tenaya all carry widely different Indian origins, and were placed on today's map by the European Americans who explored the area in the second half of the nineteenth century.

Some of the name changes, though well-intentioned, were disturbing and regrettable. The Mariposa Battalion captured Tenaya's band near the lake the Indians called Pyweack. When Bunnell informed the chief that they were naming the lake in his honor, the old man's reaction was disbelief. He pointed "to the group of glistening peaks, near the head of the lake, [and] said: 'it already has a name; we call it Py-we-ack.'"[29] "Upon telling him that we had named it Tenieya [sic], because it was upon the shores of the lake that we had found his people, who would never return to it to live, his countenance fell and he at once left our group and joined his own family circle. His countenance as he left us indicated that he thought the name of the lake no equivalent for the loss of his territory."[30]

In the last quarter century, park archaeologists have identified dozens of archaeological sites along the Tioga corridor west of the crest. Former park archeologist, Scott Carpenter, thought the Mono Trail one of the oldest trails in the area, one that humans have been using for thousands of years.[31]

The quest for a fuller understanding of the Indian place in the history of the Tioga region continues. In all likelihood, the complete story will never be known. Perhaps it is just as well, as it leaves today's travelers free to ponder the ways of those elders who roamed the mountains before them.

NOTES

1. Ron Mackie, interview by author, Yosemite National Park, 4 February 1991.

2. Scott Carpenter, telephone conversation with author, 7 February 1991.

3. Bil Gilbert, *Westering Man - The Life of Joseph Walker* (New York: Atheneum, 1983), 4-5.

4. Carl P. Russell, "Yosemite Indians," *Fresno Bee*, 24 May 1925.

5. Gilbert, *Westering Man,* 135-36.

6. Scott Stine, professor of history at California State University, Hayward, telephone conversation with author, 12 March 2004.

7. Douglas E. Klye, *Historic Spots in California* (Stanford: Stanford University Press, 1990), 186.

8. Lafayette H. Bunnell, *Discovery of the Yosemite and the Indian War of 1851 Which Led to That Event* (Yosemite: Yosemite Association, 1990), 38.

9. Ibid., 49.

10. Ibid., 55.

11. Robert Eccleston, *The Mariposa Indian War, 1850-51*, ed. C. Gregory Crampton (Salt Lake City: University of Utah Press, 1957), 59.

12. Ester Henderson, "Saga of Chief Tenaya, Last of the Yosemites," *Fresno Bee*, 11 February 1968, B-4.

13. Linda Wedel Greene, *Historic Resource Study, Yosemite*, vol. 1 (Washington, D.C.: U.S. Department of the Interior, National Park Service, 1987), 25.

14. Thomas C. Fletcher, *Paiute, Prospector, Pioneer* (Lee Vining, Calif.: Artemisia Press, 1987), 19.

15. Ibid., 21.

16. Ibid., 104.

17. Greene, *Yosemite Historic Resource Study*, vol. 1, 25.

18. Craig D. Bates and Martha J. Lee, *Tradition and Innovation* (Yosemite: Yosemite Association, 1990), 25-38.

19. John B. Trask, *Topographical Map of the Mineral Districts of California* (San Francisco: Britton & Rey, 1853). See pages 30–31.

20. California Division of Mines, *Bibliography of the Geology and Mineral Resources of California*, Bulletin 104 (Sacramento, March 1932), 27.

21. William Brewer, *Up and Down California,* ed. Francis Farquhar (Berkeley: University of California Press, 1964), 408-15.

22. John Muir, *The Mountains of California* (Berkeley: Ten Speed Press, 1977), 92.

23. John Muir, *My First Summer in the Sierra* (Boston: Houghton Mifflin, 1916), 226-27.

24. William E. Colby, interview by Hal Roth, 1961. Bancroft Library, University of California, Berkeley.

25. Larry Castro, conversation with author, Yosemite National Park, 18 February 1990.

26. Jay Johnson, conversation with author, Yosemite National Park, 4 February 1990.

27. Scott Carpenter, telephone conversation with author, 23 March 1990.

28. A. L. Kroeber, "California Place Names of Indian Origin," *University of California Publications in American Archaeology and Ethnology* 12, no. 2 (1916): 31-69.

29. Bunnell, *Discovery*, 213.

30. Ibid., 213-14; Erwin Gudde, *California Place Names* (Berkeley: University of California Press, 1969), 234-35.

31. Scott Carpenter, telephone conversation with author, 7 February 1991.

CHAPTER 2

GEOLOGY AND GIANTS: MUIR, MATTHES, AND HUBER

Long before Native Americans made their way into the Tioga Pass country, the forces of nature were at work, pushing up the peaks and carving away the canyons. The Indians had legends to explain the evolution of the features of their mountain world. When the first European men came upon the scene, a few began to ponder Yosemite's geological genesis. It was, not surprisingly, the Indians' trans-Sierra Mono Trail to which the geologists turned to unravel the secrets of these mountains.

To travel the Tioga Road today is to take a short but complex course on the vast world of Sierra geology. It has been interpreted by the likes of John Muir, François E. Matthes, King Huber, and other geologists who became fascinated with the Yosemite landscape. More than a century after the geological question was first posed, the story continues to evolve and be refined by new generations.

The first serious effort toward understanding Yosemite's geologic past came in the early 1860s, after the California legislature established the State Geological Survey. As its main task, the survey had the staggering responsibility to map and identify the resources of the decade-old state. Headed by Josiah Dwight Whitney, the distinguished Yale geologist, the survey did not reach Yosemite until June of 1863. After a brief visit to Yosemite Valley, the four-person party "came up the terrible hill" out of Yosemite Valley and made its way along the Mono Trail. "We camped at Porcupine Flat, a pretty, grassy flat, at an elevation of 8,550 feet, surrounded by scrubby pines, and tormented by myriads of mosquitoes," observed William H. Brewer, the field supervisor of the survey.[1]

When survey members gained an unrestricted view of the towering Sierra, their spirits soared. "A group of mountains so high, of which absolutely nothing is known" unfolded before the party; Whitney became so excited that he "could hardly sleep that night." As they moved eastward the next day, they saw a huge mountain rising to the north of the trail. "We climbed a peak over eleven thousand feet high, about five miles from camp, which we named Mount Hoffmann after our topographer [Charles

Opposite: John Muir carried on a long-term love affair with the Yosemite high country. He became the first president of the Sierra Club and is considered to be California's most venerated citizen.

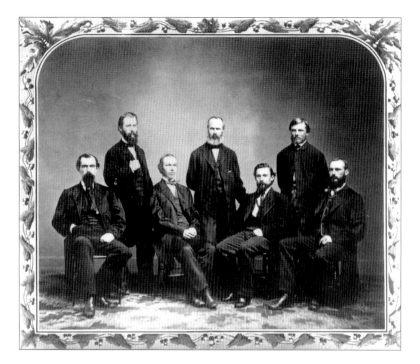

Left: This portrait of the Whitney Survey party included, from left, Chester Averill, William Gabb, William Ashburner, J. D. Whitney, Charles Hoffmann, Clarence King, and William H. Brewer.

Right: William H. Brewer was the field supervisor for the California Geological Survey party that extensively explored the Sierra Nevada.

F. Hoffmann]," Brewer wrote in his field notes for June 24, 1863. The following day they reached Tenaya Lake, "a most picturesque alpine lake. . . Its clear waters are very blue and very deep. . . Above rise domes of granite, many of them naked, while patches of snow lie around on every side."[2]

Moving eastward, the survey party established a base camp at a large meadow—"a most lovely spot" near Soda Springs—with the uncharted crest of the Sierra stretching out in the distance. Brewer noted that another small party was also camped nearby, composed of individuals who were "exploring for a road," and had shared a newspaper that carried disturbing reports of the Civil War. Over the next few days the survey members climbed and named several of the peaks in the region, including Mount Dana, so designated to recognize one of the foremost geologists of the times.[3] From the summit of Mount Dana, Brewer noted that whatever direction he turned, the view provided "the wildest mountain desolation." The survey members ranged far and fast, and placed names on tens of mountains, lakes, and other features. They chose to call the big meadow where they had established base camp Tuolumne Meadows.

From the summit of Mount Dana, Brewer spotted a string of mules making its way over Mono Pass, en route to the nearby Esmeralda mining district. Brewer recognized the low saddle to the north as McLean's Pass—a place name that Lt. Tredwell Moore likely had applied a dozen years earlier. One day it would be known as Tioga Pass.

After a week's stay and with supplies running low, Whitney returned to Big Oak Flat, accompanied by a packer who was to re-stock the party. With Whitney's departure, Brewer and Hoffmann turned toward the magnificent mountains that rose to the south of the Indian trail at Mono Pass. Hoping to climb even more summits, the two hiked up Lyell Canyon and camped the night of July 1 at its head. "Sharp granite peaks rise behind to about 13,000 feet, with great slopes of snow, and pinnacles of granite coming up through, projected sharply against the deep blue sky. It was most picturesque, wild and grand. And what an experience! Two of us alone, at least 60 miles from civilization on either side, among the grandest chain of mountains in the United States," Brewer observed.[4]

The following morning, the two mountaineers began an arduous climb over rocks and snow and finally emerged above the last trees. "We cross great slopes all polished like glass by former glaciers," Brewer waxed. For hours they struggled through the deep snow toward the highest summit. Some 150 feet from the top, the two encountered an obstructing pinnacle of rock that made their goal unattainable. At 13,000 feet, only a few feet short of the summit, they abandoned their quest, but they did use the opportunity to name the peak. "As we had named the other mountain Mount Dana, after the most eminent of *American* geologists, we named this Mount Lyell after the most eminent of *English* geologists."

When the packer returned with additional supplies, the three men left their Tuolumne Meadows camp and moved eastward. As they made their way over Mono Pass and down Bloody Canyon, Brewer observed that it was a "terrible" trail. "You would all pronounce it utterly inaccessible to horses, yet pack trains come down, but the bones of several horses or mules and the stench of another told that all had not passed safely. The trail comes down 3,000 feet in less than four miles, over rocks and loose stones, in narrow canyons and along by precipices."[5]

Along the shores of Mono Lake, the survey members observed Indians collecting *kutsavi* (the pupae of brine flies), which Brewer described as worms that develop into flies. "The Indians gave me some; it does not taste bad, and if one were ignorant of its origin, it would make fine soup. Gulls, ducks, snipe, frogs and Indians fatten on it," he added.[6] The California Geological Survey trio made its way to the mining camps around Aurora before it headed back over Sonora Pass, its 1863 introduction to Yosemite at an end.

Other events touched the Yosemite scene that would soon overshadow the survey's initial work and eclipse the geological discussion. A growing number of people was becoming concerned that Yosemite Valley was being ruined by settlers and commercial development. A call went up for governmental protection of what was recognized as a world-class wonder. In response, U.S. Senator John Conness introduced legislation in 1864 to cede to the State of California "the cleft or gorge in the granite peak of the Sierra Nevada Mountains . . . for public use, resort and recreation." Shortly thereafter, at the height of the Civil War, Congress and President Lincoln approved the Yosemite Grant, marking a new era in the preservation of the nation's natural wonders.

In the summer of 1864, Frederick Law Olmsted arrived in Yosemite. At that time, Olmsted was already on his way to becoming the nation's foremost landscape architect. In the late summer he ventured onto the Mono Trail with his twelve-year-old son, John, accompanied by the geological survey's William Brewer and his packer, Stephen Cunningham.

Frederick Law Olmsted, one of our nation's foremost landscape architects, met William Brewer in Yosemite's high country in 1864.

Mount Gibbs was named by the Brewer survey party for Harvard professor Oliver Wolcott Gibbs. Photo by author.

Brewer, of course, had been to the Yosemite high country the year before. But the land of lakes and domes was something Olmsted had never witnessed, and he was moved by the sublime scenery. In a subsequent letter to his father, he wrote that the wilderness vista was "of a very peculiar character and much the grandest that I have ever seen."[7]

The party rode up to Tuolumne Meadows and on to Mono Pass. There the group paused to name one prominent peak for Olmsted's friend, Oliver Wolcott Gibbs, a professor of science at Harvard and a long-time crony of Whitney. Along the way, Brewer saw additional evidence of glaciation, but dismissed its consequences because he could not locate an active glacier.

Olmsted apparently had other things on his mind. At the time of the creation of the Yosemite Grant a few months earlier, Olmsted had been singled out as someone who could help guide the new state reserve. Soon after he returned from his first visit to Yosemite, Olmsted was appointed chairman of the commission that was to oversee the grant. It was a responsibility that was every bit as staggering as the land itself.

In his first official act with the commission, Olmsted hired Clarence King and James Gardiner, of Brewer's survey party, to delineate the boundary of the new reserve. The task became a race with winter and a legislative deadline to complete the survey before December. After they enlisted a crew and secured supplies, King and Gardiner established a base camp near Black's Hotel in Yosemite Valley. They took over two vacant cabins for an office and quarters, and refined their plans. On October 8, they began the field survey for the grant, using a large solitary pine on El Capitan as a monument. For the next week, Gardiner pushed the survey line to the east, trying to skirt the ridges and other natural obstructions along the north rim of the great abyss.[8]

Meanwhile, King, though ostensibly scouting the boundary line, was just as busy scouting peaks to be climbed (and climbing them). He scampered to the top of the highest of the Three Brothers. Then he topped North Dome and many of the secondary peaks along the north rim of Yosemite Valley, venturing to both sides of the Mono Trail. King was in his element. With his prior success on Mount Tyndall in the southern Sierra, he had become a confirmed mountaineer, "bagging summits." On Mount Hoffmann, King marveled at the geological forces that had created the peaks and canyons. Then he ventured down into the depths of Tenaya Canyon, and was similarly impressed. Along the way, he observed glacial polish and trails of ancient glaciers, but either he did not realize the extent to which glaciers can modify the landscape or he dismissed these signs as insignificant.[9]

King continued to climb as the surveyors moved along. When the party turned to the south rim, he found more inviting mountaintops. Admittedly these high places afforded excellent vantage points for surveying, but other forces drove the brilliant and bold adventurer. Despite the changing fall weather—the first snows arrived in late October—the survey continued. Ever the mountaineer, King set his sights on the Obelisk, a peak he would subsequently rename Mount Clark in honor of Galen Clark, the Yosemite pioneer and pathfinder. Fighting fatigue and the weather, King and his survey assistant Richard Cotter made their way to the base of the mountain only to be turned back by another storm. Despite the weather and self-imposed distractions, King and his associates completed the survey by the December deadline. Gardiner got caught in an early storm and barely made it out of the Sierra.

King could not forget the high summits of Yosemite. In July 1866, he returned to the slopes of Mount Clark with Gardiner. The two found a route up the spire in an ascent that was one of the epics in mountaineering history. In August, King's party made one of the early explorations of the Ritter Range and the Minarets. The group's attempt to climb 13,157-foot Mount Ritter was unsuccessful. Returning to Clark's Ranch (present-day Wawona), they then circled back to Tuolumne Meadows using the Mono Trail. Still pursuing adventure, King's

Clarence King enjoyed a fabled mountaineering career, with several first ascents and many remarkable adventures.

Left: Scottish wanderer John Muir first came to the Yosemite area in 1868 and quickly became fascinated by the geology of the region.

Right: Muir, whose geologic explanation for Yosemite's creation was eventually vindicated, died in 1914.

group ventured down the Grand Canyon of the Tuolumne River until it had gone to a point that was impassable to "any creature without wings." King climbed Mount Conness in early September before crossing Mono Pass, descending Bloody Canyon, and returning east.

Clarence King made many Sierra entrances and exits. He was daring and dashing, and, in the words of his biographer Thurman Wilkins, "was the representative American for the era that saw the final westward expansion of the United States." He used Yosemite and the High Sierra as his proving ground.

Two years years later, in 1868, an unknown Scottish-born wanderer by the name of John Muir made his way across the San Joaquin Valley and hiked into the mountains, where he beheld the beauty of Yosemite. The introduction was something akin to love at first sight. Muir looked for work so that he might sustain himself in the area. The next spring, 1869, Snelling rancher Pat Delaney hired Muir to oversee the herders taking his sheep to the mountain meadows northeast of Yosemite Valley. Since the job afforded Muir the opportunity to roam and explore the high country, he accepted it. The journey followed to a large extent the meadows bordering the Mono Trail.

Muir had briefly studied geology at the University of Wisconsin, and he soon began to make his own observations of the natural scene. During his first summer in the Yosemite region, he noted evidence of what he felt was glacial action. He wandered higher and higher, looking and learning. In September 1869, Muir made the first ascent of Cathedral Peak, gaining a high vantage of the land below. As the big picture gradually emerged for Muir, he sketched and recorded his impressions.

Not long thereafter, Muir began to question the prevailing wisdom regarding Yosemite Valley's geological origin as articulated by Professor

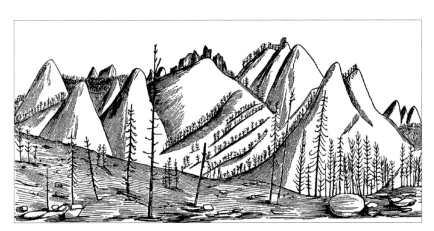

Whitney. In the geological survey's 1865 field report,[10] Whitney held that a singular cataclysmic incident had created the great chasm of Yosemite Valley. The distinguished scholar concluded that the structure beneath that section of the Sierra had collapsed, thereby creating the huge indentation, or valley, in a gigantic, singular event—the so-called "dropout theory."

Muir, unable to find any fissures or collaborating evidence that would support Whitney's theory, advanced an alternate scenario. Muir held that granite—the primary rock of Yosemite—was shaped by glacial action over time. In the process, the remaining bedrock material was exposed to immense pressure, which left cracks and joints. Water seeped into these fissures and froze. The resulting expansion of ice allowed additional granitic material to peel off in a process known as exfoliation. In 1871, Muir's first Sierra article, "Yosemite Glaciers," appeared in the *New York Daily Tribune*.[11]

Muir was not the original critic of Whitney's geological analysis. In 1870, William F. Blake, a geologist from the University of Arizona, had taken issue with the collapse or dropout theory.[12] He speculated that the valley had been carved by water that rushed under the glacier and eroded the land underneath. Other learned men became involved. John D. Runkle, president of Massachusetts Institute of Technology, visited Yosemite in the summer of 1871 and aligned himself with Muir.

The following year, 1872, Joseph L. LeConte, a geologist from the newly-founded University of California and a student of the great Harvard naturalist, Louis Agassiz, accompanied Muir to the mountains for what was apparently a higher education on the subject. In the spring of 1873, LeConte stunned the world of geology by publishing his account of "Muir's discovery," and endorsing Muir's geological conclusions.[13]

The issue resurfaced later that same year at a meeting of the Boston

Above: Muir, who explored the Sierra Nevada far and wide, gave lectures about the origin of Yosemite Valley, offering evidence for his glaciation theory.

Opposite: Geologist François Matthes made investigations in the Yosemite area that supported in large part John Muir's theory of glacial formation.

Society of Natural History, when Muir's findings were presented in what was essentially Whitney's own backyard. The debate initiated, the battle was on. Over the next two years, the geologic origins of Yosemite Valley were argued in back-to-back editions of *The Overland Monthly* (November and December 1874), as well as in other periodicals. Besides supporting his glacial theory, Muir's articles provide the first glimpse of his blossoming literary style. "Two years ago when picking flowers in the mountains back of Yosemite Valley I found a book. It was blotted and storm beaten; all its outer pages were mealy and crumbly . . . but many of the inner pages were well preserved, and though all were more or less stained and torn, those chapters were easily readable," Muir wrote of the glacial scene.[14]

Season after season Muir moved along the Mono Trail, gradually refining his glacial theory. He maintained that the great Yosemite canyon had been scoured by glaciers. In 1876, Muir gave his first lecture. "During five years' observations in the Sierra, I have failed to discover a single fissure of any kind, although extensive areas of clean-swept glacial pavements afford ample opportunity for their detection, did they exist."[15] Muir suggested five great flows of ice had gouged out the Yosemite Valley: the Yosemite Creek, Hoffmann, Tenaya, South Lyell, and Illilouette glaciers. He was convinced that ice, water, and time had been the main sculptors of Yosemite Valley.

"Five immense glaciers from five to 1,500 feet in depth poured their icy floods into Yosemite, united to form one huge trunk, moved down through the valley with irresistible and never-ceasing energy, crushing and breaking up its strongest rocks, and scattering them in moraines far and near," Muir observed in his "Studies in the Sierra."[16]

In many respects, Muir's hypothesis was up against the establishment's. While Whitney, Brewer, King, and other members of the geological survey had recognized the presence of glaciers at an earlier age in the upper Tuolumne River drainage, they concluded that the glaciers no longer existed. They made no serious effort to advance the glacial scenario.

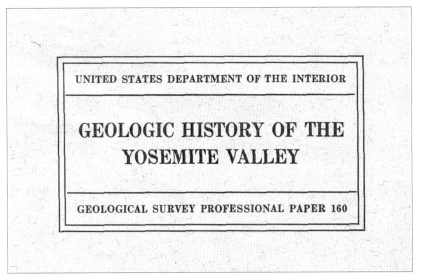

UNITED STATES DEPARTMENT OF THE INTERIOR

GEOLOGIC HISTORY OF THE
YOSEMITE VALLEY

GEOLOGICAL SURVEY PROFESSIONAL PAPER 160

Top: One of the products of François Matthes' comprehensive study of Yosemite's geology was his landmark paper published in 1930.

Bottom: François Matthes using his plane table in Yosemite Valley.

Apparently Brewer and King did not want to be at odds with Whitney, so they all but ignored Muir's glacial perspective.[17]

The debate was joined by others and went on for years. Whitney died in 1896, still clinging to his dropout theory. Gradually Muir's findings found favor, reinforced by his publication of more and more articles on the topic. Further, in 1903, a Dutch-born topographer, François E. Matthes, an employee of the U.S. Geological Survey, made his first visit to Yosemite Valley. He, too, fell under the spell of Yosemite's geologic grandeur.

Matthes began to investigate geologic evolution with an unbridled passion. He traversed the Mono Trail and made his way to the high country, hoping to shed more light on the once-great rivers of ice. In Muir's footsteps, Matthes climbed numerous summits, looking for glacial evidence along the mountain routes.

John Muir, an aged and ailing mountaineer, died in 1914. He had created the preservation movement and the Sierra Club, and helped to establish Yosemite National Park. The grand old man left his adopted and beloved Range of Light and stepped into the darkness of eternity.

By then, Matthes' geologic investigations were well along. In 1923, he made the first known ascent of Vogelsang Peak.[18] Unlike his predecessors, Matthes tended to look at the bigger picture, maintaining that the geology of Yosemite was inextricably linked to that of the Sierra Nevada and the West. With his assistant, Frank C. Calkins, Matthes made detailed studies of Yosemite Valley and prepared large-scale geologic maps. In 1930, with the release of Matthes' *Geologic History of Yosemite Valley*, the debate was resolved.

Although Muir's deductions were not exactly correct, he—not Whitney —had determined the correct geological basics of the situation. Matthes found that while Muir had overestimated the extent of glaciation, Muir had failed to recognize that glaciers entered Yosemite Valley more than once, advancing and retreating over the ages. Matthes found evidence of at least three major glaciations in Yosemite.[19] While Muir's theories of the geological origins of Yosemite were not entirely accurate, Whitney had missed the mark entirely.

There is still much to be learned about Yosemite geology. After more than a century of debate and study, the understanding of the evolution of Yosemite's topography is still being refined, though the influence of glaciers is a given. A lay person could justifiably argue that Yosemite's origin reaches all the way back to the "big bang," when the solar system emerged.

On a planetary level, we now know that the evolution of the continents transcends our earthly measurements of time. The Earth's crust is composed of tectonic plates that are constantly moving, much like fallen leaves on the surface of a pond. The oldest rocks in the Yosemite region were derived from sediment eroded off the western edge of the North American continental plate and deposited on the adjacent oceanic plate. Along with limestone and chert derived from animal life in the sea, this sediment was consolidated into thousands of feet of shale and sandstone. Somewhat more than 200 million years ago, this oceanic plate was subducted or thrust beneath the continental plate. In its new high-temperature environment, the subduction process resulted in the generation of molten magma that rose up within the continental crust to form the embyonic granite that would one day become the Sierra Nevada.

Geologist N. King Huber took over where François Matthes left off, and is considered the modern authority on Yosemite geology. Photo by James Snyder.

Emplacement of the granite within the Earth's crust was probably accompanied by the eruption of volcanoes at the Earth's surface to create a new landscape similar to the present Cascade Range along our northwest coast. Once the magmatic construction of the ancestral Sierra Nevada had ceased, erosion became the dominant force. By about 70 million years ago, the volcanoes had largely been removed and the granite itself was exposed and being eroded to produce a pre-Yosemite landscape of rolling hills and broad valleys. Finally, through a combination of uplift of the Sierran block and down-dropping of the area to the east, beginning some tens of millions of years ago, the Yosemite region acquired a tilted-block aspect with a long, gentle slope westward and a steep eastern escarpment. This heightened declination accelerated the flow of ancestral rivers, such as the Tuolumne and Merced, hastened the process of erosion, and etched deep, V-shaped canyons into the contours of the land.[20]

Periodically, the newborn Sierra Nevada range was tempered by fire and ice. Volcanoes blew their tops, mostly north of Yosemite, adding their lava and mudflows to the scene. With the coming of the Ice Age, a series of vast glacial ice fields formed over the high Sierra and covered all the major landmarks except the highest peaks. The glaciers ground and quarried the ridges and the walls of canyons, widening and deepening them into huge U-shaped troughs. Enormous granitic blocks were shaped into domes and mountains, and rocks with joints and seams were severed by vertical fracturing. The glaciers ebbed and flowed, retreating and advancing, time and again, chiseling here and polishing there.

The most recent glacial period, the Tioga, began 30,000 to 60,000 years ago, and prevailed until about 15,000 years ago. During its reign, the great Tuolumne glacier moved well down the Tuolumne River Canyon, sculpting the walls of the Hetch Hetchy Valley. From one of its sources near today's Saddlebag Lake, the glacier flowed southwest across Tioga Pass leaving the mark of its heavy but creative hand upon the land. In Yosemite Valley, the Merced glacier reached as far as Bridalveil Meadow, where it left a small terminal moraine.[21]

Geologist N. King Huber, an authority on Yosemite geology now retired from the U.S. Geological Survey, believes the geomorphic differences between the Hetch Hetchy and Yosemite Valleys triggered much of the Muir-Whitney debate. He maintains there is little specific evidence of major glaciation in Yosemite Valley today, and that spalling and exfoliation have left pinnacles and other formations that could not have survived the heavy hand of glaciation. "This paucity of direct evidence is probably the basis for Whitney's stand against the glacial origin of Yosemite Valley, noting as he did, the glaciation of Hetch Hetchy Valley."[22]

The quest for a complete explanation of Yosemite's geological heritage continues, with Huber pressing the search. In recent years he has assembled and published a geologic map of Yosemite National Park and saw a geologic map of Yosemite Valley by Frank Calkins, Matthes' assistant, through to publication. When Huber drives the Tioga Road today, he sees both a geological masterpiece and a puzzle. As a leading Yosemite expert who has studied the late Cenozoic uplift of the Central Sierra, he believes the Yosemite area is unmatched in its geologic processes. "So much happened there. There are examples of almost every geologic process known. Uplift, glaciers, volcanoes—the area we know today as Yosemite has had a little of everything," he explained.[23]

Although Muir and Whitney differed in their opinions on the creation of Yosemite Valley, the two men shared a similar response to the view from Mount Hoffmann, the geographic center of the park, at the heart of the Tioga Road corridor. While he was more restrained, Whitney held that "The view from the summit of Mount Hoffmann is remarkably fine," and Muir suggested that to best enjoy Yosemite, one should "go straight to Mount Hoffmann . . . From the summit nearly all the Yosemite Park is displayed like a map."[24]

NOTES

1. William Brewer, *Up and Down California* (Berkeley: University of California Press, 1974), 407.

2. Ibid., 407.

3. Ibid., 411.

4. Ibid., 411.

5. Ibid., 415-16.

6. Victoria Post Ranney, ed., *The Papers of Frederick Law Olmsted, Vol. V. The California Frontier, 1863-65* (Baltimore and London: The Johns Hopkins University Press, 1990), 252-257.

7. Clarence King, *Mountaineering in the Sierra Nevada* (Yosemite: Yosemite Association, 1997), 124-134.

8. Ibid., 134-143.

9. California Geological Survey, *Geology, Vol. I, Report of Progress and Synopsis of the Field Work from 1860 to 1864* (Philadelphia; Caxton Press of Sherman & Co., 1865), 489.

10. *New York Daily Tribune*, 5 December 1871, 8.

11. François E. Matthes, *Geologic History of the Yosemite Valley*, U.S. Geological Survey Professional Paper 160 (Washington, D.C.: U.S. Government Printing Office, 1930), 4.

12. Joseph LeConte, "On Some of the Glaciers of the Sierra," *American Journal of Science*, 3d ser., 5 (1873): 325-342.

13. John Muir, "Studies in the Sierra," *Overland Monthly* 13 (September 1874): 494-95.

14. John Muir, "Yosemite Glaciers, The Ice Streams of the Great Valley," *New York Daily Tribune*, 5 December 1871, 8.

15. John Muir, "1876 Sacramento Lecture," *Sacramento Daily Record*, 26 January 1876.

16. Muir, "Studies in the Sierra," 494-95.

17. Elizabeth Stone O'Neill, *Meadow in the Sky* (Fresno: Panorama West Books, 1984), 19.

18. Hervey Voge, ed., *A Climber's Guide to the High Sierra* (San Francisco: Sierra Club, 1956), 75.

19. N. King Huber, *The Geologic Story of Yosemite National Park* (Yosemite: Yosemite Association, 1989), 46.

20. Ibid.

21. N. King Huber, "Evolution of the Tuolumne River," *Yosemite* 52, no. 1 (Winter 1990): 5; and N. King Huber, "The Late Cenozoic Evolution of the Tuolumne River, Central Nevada, California," *Geological Society of America Bulletin* 102 (1990): 102-115.

22. Huber, "Evolution of the Tuolumne River," 5.

23. N. King Huber, interview by author, Menlo Park, California, 17 July 1990.

24. Josiah D. Whitney, *The Yosemite Guide-Book* (Cambridge: Welch, Bigelow, & Co., 1870), 93; and John Muir, *The Yosemite* (San Francisco: Sierra Club Books, 1988), 149-150.

CHAPTER 3

THE HIGH COUNTRY TRAIL OF GOLD AND GRASS

T he quest for gold had unexpected impacts in Yosemite in the 1850s. It introduced forces that would shape not only the Tioga Road but also the future of Yosemite National Park and the National Park Service itself.

In the aftermath of the 1848 discovery of gold at Sutter's Mill, most mining activity occurred along the foothill belt on the western slope of the Sierra, in an area known as the Mother Lode. As the gold seekers expanded their search, they ranged far and wide, seeking other locales where they might find the precious, alluring metal. The high country above the recently-discovered Yosemite Valley did not escape their interest.

In 1852, after pursuing the Yosemite Indians over Mono Pass, some of the soldiers under Lt. Tredwell Moore began to explore and investigate on their own. At several locations along the Sierra crest they noticed interesting ore and mineral deposits and collected samples.[1] Among those who had accompanied Moore was Leroy Vining, although accounts differ.[2] When Moore and his party returned to the San Joaquin Valley two months later, the Indian "uprising" had all but been forgotten. But when the soldiers displayed samples of sparkling ore—what was presumed to be gold—it set off another wave of interest in Yosemite's highlands.

Vining, recently arrived in the Mariposa area from Laporte, Indiana, quickly organized his own group, including his brother Dick. The party made its way over Mono Pass and down Bloody Canyon, scouring the eastern slopes of the Sierra, looking for promising deposits. But after several unsuccessful efforts to find gold, the miners returned to Mariposa, where Leroy subsequently did hit a rich vein of gold and made a sizeable strike.

While a few argonauts continued to scratch away among the peaks of the high country for the next few years, the initial interest waned. Throughout the Mother Lode, gold seekers deserted the diggings as the privation and hardship, coupled with little remuneration, took their toll. They turned to ranching, logging, and homesteading—anything that would sustain them.

Opposite: For years the stone Great Sierra cabin on Tioga Hill stood as a monument to the folly of those who toiled for gold and silver in the Yosemite high country. The structure no longer exists.

Hetch Hetchy Valley, through which flowed the Tuolumne River, was long occupied by Native Americans before it was entered by Euro-Americans in 1851.

Surveyor Alexis von Schmidt led early mapping efforts in the Mono Lake area.

Among the first of these former miners to venture into the Yosemite high country were Joseph and Nate Screech. They, too, were driven by gold fever. As with other hungry and frustrated miners, the two brothers turned to hunting to sustain themselves. In 1851, while out looking for game, Nate came upon Hetch Hetchy Valley on the Tuolumne River, a favorite and long-time encampment site of the Tuolumne Indians. Later, Joseph moved into the scenic valley and set up camp. Although the historical record is obscure, it is clear that both Joseph Screech and the Native Americans of the area recognized the great natural beauty of the Hetch Hetchy and claimed it for their own.

As the interest in metallic riches persisted, California state officials recognized the need for a map that would define the fledgling state and identify and locate its mineral resources. In early 1850s, not long after California had become a state and Yosemite had been discovered, John B. Trask, the first state geologist, undertook that Herculean task. His resulting 1853 map represented a grand but hardly accurate effort. His drawing of the northern California region was entitled "Topographical Map of the Mineral Districts of California" (see page 34). Although it identified the Sierra Nevada as the "California Range," many of today's prominent landmarks were missing. Despite its many shortcomings, his early map identified a trans-Sierra trail at Mono Pass, albeit with the inaccurate elevation of 5,000 feet. However ill-described, Mono Pass was on the map.[3]

Where Trask led, others followed. Surveyor Alexis von Schmidt, a German-born immigrant, came to California at the height of the gold rush to find riches. Be he soon returned to surveying in order to survive. In 1855, he made the first quasi-official exploration of the Yosemite high country under a government contract. Making his way along the established trans-Sierra migration route of the Indians known as the Mono Trail, von Schmidt crossed the mountains east of the Kuna Crest and made a preliminary survey of the Mono Lake area, while plotting the key Mount Diablo base line.

As the wonders of Yosemite Valley gradually became known, largely through the publicity efforts of James Mason Hutchings, an early promoter of tourism to the region, a growing number of adventurers visited that enchanted mountain scene. By the end of the Civil War, Yosemite Valley had gained both national and international fame. What was at first a trickle soon became a stream of visitors as the images and inspired words of the early Yosemite artists and authors came to the public's attention.

Some of the visitors to the *sanctum sanctorum* traveled over the Mono Trail to reach the ridges and meadows of the high country. At one point, an unidentified group from Mono Lake including a woman and baby also made its way up the eastern escarpment and over the crest—headed for Yosemite Valley.[4] In his 1864 travels with Frederick Law Olmsted, William Brewer noted that they encountered two other parties of tourists or miners, traveling through the mountains.[5]

With the Euro-American invasion, the Yosemite region was gradually settled and developed, by the use of various land laws, from the right of pre-emption to the famed Homestead Act of 1862. As early as 1857, Tom McGee, a Big Oak Flat merchant, apparently marked and cleared sections of the Mono Trail so his pack trains could supply a store he had established near Mono Diggings.[6] Not long thereafter, the first sheepmen began driving their flocks to the mountains meadows, trying to escape the drought of the low lands.

There was a growing parade of pioneers and pathfinders along the ancient Indian migration route. In 1865, Jeremiah Hodgdon moved into

Below: The Gobin's Hotel or ranch near Crane Flat was a stopping point along the Big Oak Flat Road throughout the late 1800s. With its nearby saloon it was something of a "last outpost" for those detouring to the Tioga wagon route. Photo courtesy of the Alice Milburn collection.

Following page: This mineral resources map for California published by John B. Trask in 1853, though ambitious, was primitive and inaccurate.

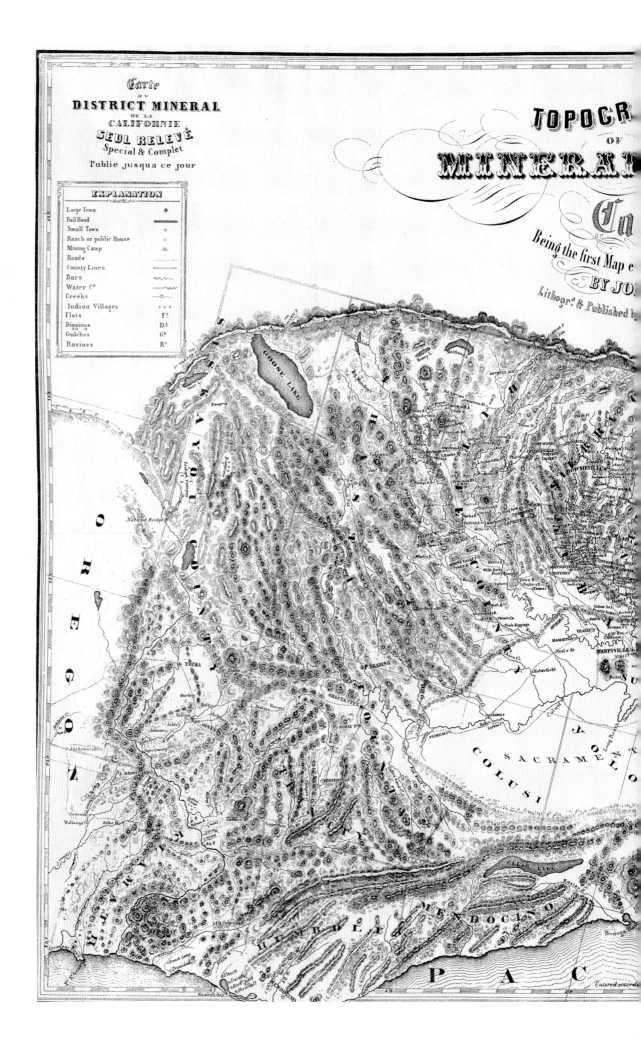

Carte
DU
DISTRICT MINERAL
DE LA
CALIFORNIE
SEUL RELEVÉ
Special & Complet
Publie jusqua ce jour

EXPLANATION

Large Town	⊛
Rail Road	▬▬▬
Small Town	⊙
Ranch or public House	○
Mining Camp	⚒
Roads	▬▬▬
County Lines	▬▬▬
Bars	～～～
Water Cº	～～
Creeks	～～
Indian Villages	ʌ ʌ ʌ
Flats	Fˢ
Diggings	Dˢ
Gulches	Gʰ
Ravines	Rº

TOPOGR
OF
MINERAL
Cal
Being the first Map e
BY JO
Lithogʳ & Published b

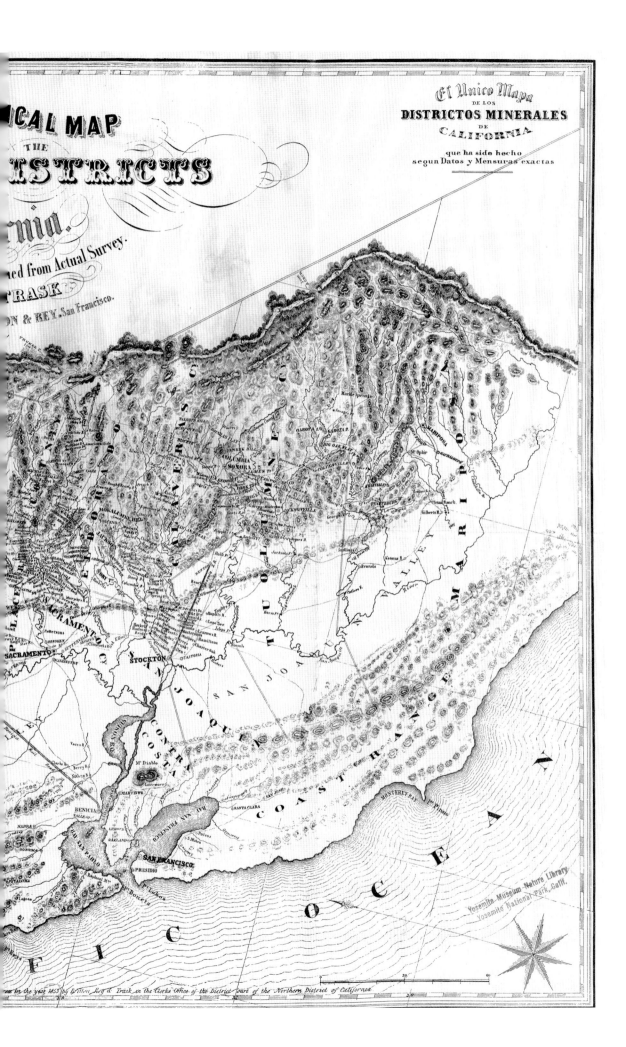

ICAL MAP

THE

ISTRICTS

mia.

ed from Actual Survey.

TRASK

N & KEY, San Francisco.

El Unico Mapa
DE LOS
DISTRICTOS MINERALES
DE
CALIFORNIA

que ha sido hecho
segun Datos y Mensuras exactas

PACIFIC OCEAN

In the year 1853 by Britton Rey & Trask in the Clerks Office of the District Court of the Northern District of California

Bodie, one of the major mining camps east of Yosemite, lured another round of prospectors and dreamers over the Sierra crest. Photo by W. W. Bryant.

a meadow that would one day bear his name. Five years later, Louis D. Gobin and his son began a sheep and cattle operation near Crane Flat and also supplied room and repast for early valley-bound travelers.

A handful of tourists also journeyed into the high country. Other way stations developed, including those at Garrote (Groveland), Coulterville, and Bower's Cave. These new establishments catered to the first travelers coming to the park by way of the Big Oak Flat and Coulterville toll roads, which had been completed in the early 1870s.

The quest for riches continued to lure the gold seekers to the high Sierra and the desert east of its crest. Around 1858, Leroy Vining took a renewed interest in the country he had unsuccessfully prospected earlier and moved back to the area near Mono Lake, making the arduous crossing by way of Bloody Canyon. Not far from the lakeshore, he established a small camp and settled down for the long haul. For the next few years, Vining was a one-man outpost on the frontier, doing whatever it took to survive.

Conflicting stories mark Vining's elusive trail. When Monoville (or Mono Diggings) became established, Vining took advantage of the new opportunity. Recognizing that the hard life of the frontier could be eased a bit by a stiff drink, Vining opened a makeshift saloon. He prospered, and subsequently the former Mariposan set up a small sawmill to supply building materials to the handful of newcomers who had migrated onto the high desert area.[7] In time, Vining married a Paiute woman and built a cabin along Rescue Creek at a site called Vinings Rancho on the early maps. Besides mixing drinks and milling lumber, he also ran a few cattle.

Vining became one of the stalwarts of the basin settlement, known to the locals as "Captain Vining." Around 1870, he died when his pistol slipped from its holster and discharged while he was hauling lumber from

Bodie to Aurora.[8] A half century would elapse before the outpost he settled would become known as Lee Vining—another of the place names on the emerging map of California, and the easternmost point on the trans-Sierra highway.

A few miles to the north, other events related to gold mining unfolded. The Mono Diggings[9] (later to be called Monoville) were developed about 1859, after miner Cord Norst found traces of gold near an abandoned Indian camp. As usual, the discovery touched off a short-lived mining boom.

One of those who heard of the strike was another hopeful from the Sierra's west side, George W. "Doc" Chase. A wayward dentist from Mariposa, he arrived on the scene not long after Leroy Vining, intent upon excavating gold rather than filling cavities. Chase tried his luck in the diggings for a couple of months without success, then decided to head back home. But instead of using Bloody Canyon and the Mono Pass trail, he journeyed by way of a higher but more direct footpath that ran toward the crest from Monoville.

Later to become known as Brown's Trail Pass, the rugged route was named for its founder, pioneer surveyor Lawrence A. Brown.[10] Little is known of the trail's precise route; documentation of its course was limited to a few early and incomplete maps. From Monoville, the trail reputedly ran up Mill Creek, went around to the south slope of Mount Warren, and continued west toward Tioga Peak. Next it led around the upper end of today's Ellery Lake, headed west along the shore of Tioga Lake, then climbed the final ridge to McLean's Pass.

As Chase went along the trail, he kept his eyes peeled for potential mine sites. Near the western end of Tioga Lake, Chase turned right and scrambled up the crest towards Gaylor Peak. He came upon what appeared to be a rich vein of ore that he felt warranted further exploring.[11] After

The historic Mono Pass trail led travelers through Bloody Canyon and its rocky terrain.

Top: Somewhere along the Gaylor Ridge, shown here, George Chase found ore he believed to be silver. He never was able to prove his claim.

Bottom: An aging window frame provides a glimpse of an abandoned building in Aurora, site of a silver lode that made Chase and others wealthy.

making a mental record of the location, Chase vowed to return when conditions allowed.

That opportunity arose a year later, in 1860, when he joined a group of Tuolumne County men who were headed to the mountains to look for a water supply for the their foothill diggings. The group consisted of Captain Allan S. Crocker of Crocker's Station, Judge Micajah M. McGehee of Big Oak Flat, Joshua E. Clayton, an expert miner, and Lawrence Brown, the aforementioned surveyor. Chase, of course, had an agenda that had nothing to do with finding water. After exploring the upper drainage of today's Lee Vining Creek, the group made camp near an unnamed high country lake (now Tioga Lake).

The following day, while the others rested in camp, Chase headed out for his vein, vowing that he would find "the biggest silver ledge ever discovered." Just west of the crest, slightly north of present-day Gaylor Peak, he relocated the promising ore. He continued his search until he found the vein about which he had dreamed. For the next few hours, Chase picked away at the mountainside, carefully selecting samples of ore and placing them in a small pouch. Confident he had found a lode with real potential, he flattened a tin can, scratched a crude message on its side, and placed it under a cairn of rocks; "The Sheepherder" claim had been established. With this accomplished, Chase returned to camp with his ore samples and high hopes.[12]

The next day the group separated. McGehee and Crocker headed back home. Brown, Clayton, and Chase proceeded to Monoville to assay the samples Chase had found. No sooner had they arrived at the assay office than Clayton was urged to analyze samples taken from a strike at Aurora in the Esmeralda Mining District just to the north. After a quick assay showed the presence of silver, the three men hastened to Aurora, where they were able to stake out some of the first claims on a rich silver lode.

The Aurora mines worked wonders and wealth for Chase, transforming him from a part-time dentist to a full-time mining investor.[13] The Sheepherder claim, never proven, faded into distant memory.

Hoping to escape the droughts of the plains, some livestock operators began moving their sheep into the lush Sierra mountain meadows. The livestock business in California, practiced since the days of the dons and the Spanish missions, faced enormous challenges in the 1860s. Shortly after California achieved statehood, the ranchers in the San Joaquin Valley

With drought conditions in the Sierra foothills, sheepherders drove their stock into the high meadows of the Yosemite area as a survival measure. Their presence in and treatment of the high country became controversial.

had to deal with very unpredictable weather and changing environmental conditions. In the spring of 1862, for example, the Central Valley was a huge inland sea, 400 miles long and 150 miles wide.

Only two years later, at the height of the 1864 drought, California's center resembled a dusty desert and was dotted with the carcasses of thousands of water-starved farm animals. The ranchers could either move their animals upslope or watch them die. The transit of sheep to the high country increased significantly during the Civil War, when the loss of Southern cotton raised the demand for wool. Thousands of animals were driven to the mountains for their life-sustaining meadow grass.[14]

Among the first European-American herders to visit the Yosemite high country were Fresno County stockmen Bob and E. T. Givens. As early as 1856, the two could see that their foothill ranch and the Central Valley's long, hot, and dry summers would not provide enough feed for their animals. From their home ranch in Morgan Canyon, the Givens drove their sheep up the San Joaquin River Canyon into Mariposa County and crossed Chiquito Pass, en route to Givens Lake. Then they would "follow the grass" to the higher meadows.

The herders were a hardy lot, leading lives of privation and isolation. They entered the Sierra from numerous locations, seeking out the grassy meadows nearest their foothill or valley ranches. Many of the herders were immigrant Basque, but their numbers also included Indians, Portuguese, Mexicans, and Chinese. Though the exact number of such herders is not known, Yosemite park historian James Snyder suggests that there were undoubtedly more than there are records for.

As the cattle and sheep business expanded, the competition for the meadows became fierce, and arguments became common. The herders claimed pre-emptive rights to the meadows that were open public lands. The sheepmen battled the cattlemen and other sheepmen, and those from the west side of the Sierra fought those from the east. In a few cases gunshots were exchanged. These were the so-called range or grass wars. "It was more about 'stealing grass' than anything else. But it was the only way the early stockmen could survive," one pioneer cattleman observed.[15]

The Givens brothers and the hard-pressed sheep-raisers who followed through the years left their mark on the mountains. The remnants of the Givens' high country corral are about a mile away from Tioga Pass. They left a trail of blazes—inscriptions carved into the bark of trees —as signposts to the unmapped high country. The names of herders are attached to many Yosemite mountain meadows, streams, and lakes.[16]

Other changes affected the Sierra as well. By 1851, a crude wagon route had been established over Sonora Pass, serving the pioneer farms and camps along the eastern Sierra.[17] A toll road over the pass was in service in 1862, over which were carried supplies for the Big Meadows area (later known as Bridgeport). Mono County came into being in 1864, as the march of civilization into the high mountain basin continued.

Concurrently, a growing number of landmarks acquired western names. For example, Brewer noted that Bloody Canyon earned its bad reputation

from the bloody cuts and bruises sustained by pack animals moving over the trail. At the bottom of the canyon, Sardine Lakes apparently were christened in 1860 when a pack string laden with sardines dumped much of the load into the waters there.

With increased population came greater investigation of the Sierra. In 1866, two young visitors from Philadelphia, Joseph Ferrell and Alfred Jessup, made the first known exploration of Tenaya Canyon, the big chasm above Mirror Lake then known as Lincoln Cañon, by white men—three years prior to John Muir's journey into the great glacial trench.

When Ferrell and Jessup set out, they stumbled on an old Indian trail leading up the hillside and into the glaciated gorge that loomed beyond. "It was a work of incredible difficulty to creep and clamber up the mountain side. In very many places we had to climb over the smooth rock for a great distance where the slightest slip of hand or foot would have precipitated one into a horrible abyss," they noted. Somehow the two managed to skirt the cascades above Glacier Valley. Fortunately, Ferrell and Jessup had had the foresight to bring along a rope, which they used repeatedly.

Overtaken by nightfall, the two mountaineers made a crude camp and settled down to spend the night in the open, warmed only by a small fire. Early the next morning, the pair pushed onward. Eventually they managed to reach the rim, where they located the main Mono Trail. They made their way back to the valley by way of Indian Canyon.[18]

John Muir's love for Yosemite and his interest in its glacial past brought still others to the high country. In 1872, Muir met William Keith, an emerging artist, and some of his Scottish kinsmen in the valley. After some discussion, he led the group to Tuolumne Meadows so that Keith could paint the vaunted Yosemite highlands. There, Muir took the party

Even before the Tioga wagon road was developed, John Murphy's Tenaya Lake cabin provided primitive accommodation for early trans-Sierra travelers. The cabin is long gone, but the nearby creek still bears Murphy's name.

on an exploration of Lyell Canyon. On reaching the point where the grandeur of Mount Lyell revealed itself, Keith ran wildly about, shouting and tossing his arms in the air "like a mad man," Muir observed.

Of the scene, Keith noted that "it was the grandest thing I saw." The artist and the author quickly reached agreement on the sublimity of the Yosemite scene. Over the ensuing years they would lend their artistic talents to capturing the wonders of the Sierra, while alerting the public about the need to preserve those wonders.

Entrepreneurs also made their way onto the high country trail. Among them was John Murphy, an early tourist guide and settler, who ventured up the old "'Injun' Trail" in the late 1870s. At an idyllic spot at the eastern end of the beautiful lake the Indians had known as Pyweack, Murphy established a homestead in 1878, hoping to graze his sheep there in summer. But after building a small cabin, Murphy realized that the great natural beauty of Tenaya Lake offered commercial possibilities. Observing the growing number of travelers bound for the high country, he and a partner began to provide spartan (if not primitive) accommodations during the summer season.

In 1881, Archie Leonard, an early Yosemite Valley packer and guide, began a packing operation between Yosemite Valley and the high country mines to the east. Along the way, some of his customers took lodging at Murphy's lakeside lodge.[19] During this period, Murphy carried a bucket of trout from the Tuolumne River and emptied it into the lake. His "coffee can" transplanted fishery thrived. In 1882, a reporter for a Bodie newspaper noted that the "lake is swarming with fish, some already two feet in length."[20]

In the following years, hundreds of travelers found their way to Murphy's mountain retreat. John Muir, Galen Clark, James Hutchings, and many other Yosemite pioneers stopped there, as did those who were to become involved with the Great Sierra Wagon Road. Others pitched their tents, rolled out their bedrolls, and enjoyed the scenery with no known objections from the owners who paid taxes on the property.[21]

The few Indians who continued to follow their ancestral ways were displaced, and their numbers dwindled. The trail of the first pathfinders among the high peaks of the Sierra had become the domain of the miners, herders, and tourists.

NOTES

1. Lafayette H. Bunnell, *Discovery of the Yosemite and the Indian War of 1851 Which Led to That Event* (Yosemite: Yosemite Association, 1990), 172.

2. Erwin G. Gudde, *California Place Names* (Berkeley: University of California Press, 1969), 175; Ralph R. Mendershausen, *Treasurers of the South Fork* (Fresno: Book Publishers, 1983), 34.

3. Former Yosemite park historian James Snyder speculates that Trask may have obtained some of his information from Leroy Vining or other miners, or from members of the Mariposa Battalion who had chased Tenaya and his tribe into the Yosemite high country in 1851.

4. Elizabeth Stone O'Neill, *Meadow in the Sky* (Fresno: Panorama West Books, 1984), 20.

5. Keith A. Trexler, *The Tioga Road—A History, 1883-1961* (Yosemite: Yosemite Natural History Association, 1980), 2. See the appendix for a reprint of this work.

6. Linda Wedel Greene, *Historic Resource Study: Yosemite*, vol. 3 (Washington, D.C.: U.S. Department of the Interior, National Park Service, 1987), lxiv; vol. 1, 244.

7. The first published mention of Vinings Rancho appeared on the Esmeralda and Mono mining map published by Britton & Co. in 1861. A copy of the map is in the map collection of the Bancroft Library, ref. 15.CsM55.

8. Lily Mathieu LaBraque, *Man From Mono* (Reno: Nevada Academic Press, 1984), 25.

9. Gudde, *California Place Names*, 208.

10. Susan Guhm, conversation with author regarding location of Brown's Trail Pass, Fresno, California, 24 April 1991.

11. Susan Guhm, "Doc and the Professor," *Yosemite* 51, no. 4 (fall 1989), 6.

12. Ibid., 6.

13. Ibid., 7.

14. Gene Rose, *Reflections of Shaver Lake* (Fresno: Panorama West Books, 1987), 18.

15. Jack Simpson, conversation with author regarding derivation of the name for Simpson Meadows, Fresno, California, 28 May 1988. Simpson is a third-generation Fresno County stockman.

16. Information developed by former Yosemite park historian James Snyder as part of his Yosemite Wilderness Surveys.

17. Text from state historical marker atop Sonora Pass.

18. J. N. LeConte, "Record of An Early Exploration of Tenaya Canyon," *Sierra Club Bulletin* X (January 1918), 276.

19. Greene, *Yosemite Historic Resources Study*, vol. 1, 206.

20. Trexler, *The Tioga Road*, 13.

21. Ibid.

CHAPTER 4

THE SILVER LINING
OF TIOGA PASS

For more than a decade Chase's tin can lay on the roof of the Sierra, rusting and forgotten. Brown's Trail Pass fell into disuse, while McLean's Pass remained a little-known landmark on the Sierran crest. The name "Tioga" had not yet been affixed to any of the features of the high country. But the dream of riches that precious metals might bring refused to die. Throughout the 1870s, reports in the West of gold and silver strikes spurred renewed exploration and excitement. In the larger Yosemite region, most of the mining action was confined to the Bodie and Aurora areas, the two mining camps located along the ill-defined California-Nevada border.

Despite continued use by an increasing number of herders and a declining number of Indians, the Mono Trail stood well away from the changes sweeping over California. But in 1874, a young herder from Sonora named William Brusky stumbled upon Chase's pick and shovel —and his flattened tin can of 1860. Though the crude claim marker was hardly readable, Brusky made out "Notice, we the undersigned. . ." and the 1860 date. He poked around the rock-strewn hillside as the adrenaline of gold fever infused his body.

Gathering up a few samples of ore he rushed back to his camp, where he related his discovery and displayed the ore to his father. The elder Brusky gave the specimens a cursory examination and pronounced them worthless. Over the next two summers, as his flocks grazed nearby, the undaunted younger Brusky pecked away at the mountain. He unearthed a promising vein in the summer of 1875.[1]

The following year, Brusky recorded his interests in the "Sheepherder Lode," which included the Tiptop, Lake, Sonora, and Summit claims. As the news of his finds filtered down the mountainside, it sparked a revival of interest in mining on the Sierra crest. Within a few weeks, a migration of miners, caught up in a frenzy that fed on itself, made claims all over the mountains.

The rush to the high country was led by various Sonora and Tuolumne

Opposite: The remains of the May Lundy Mine mark one of the few successful mining operations in the high country near Tioga Pass. Photo courtesy of the Fresno Bee.

45

County businessmen. Some of their interest stemmed from the success of mines in the Bodie and Mono Basin. Rumors overcame reason. Even residents of Yosemite Valley were swept up in the chase. Innkeepers Albert Snow and A. G. Black became investors in mining schemes,[2] and James M. Hutchings, the early Yosemite hotelier and entrepreneur, publicized the reports (and rumors) of gold and silver hot spots in typically embellished accounts.[3] The wheeler-dealers and the promoters had a field day, selling and trading claims and companies, with little ore ever reaching the surface or the assay office.

It was against this frantic background that mining gradually became established atop the crest, east of Yosemite. In October, 1878, the Tioga Mining District was established, marking the first time the Iroquois word had been used in the Yosemite area. The mining district provided a measure of legitimacy that attracted other hopeful prospectors. In short order, more than 350 mining claims were staked out within the district that became known as "Tioga Hill." The new district embraced a huge area that stretched from Tuolumne Meadows on the west to the foot of Bloody Canyon on the east, and extended four miles north and south of Brusky's claim.[4] Through the center of the district (supposedly) lay the "Great Silver Belt," a rich vein with high grade silver ore, that ran all the way from Mount Conness to Mono Pass. Within a year, the Summit, Lundy, and Fuller & Hayt mines had been established as working operations.

Remains of the Great Sierra Cabin on Tioga Hill.

In most cases, the early prospectors put hope before reason. Since the glory days of 1849, the miners had pursued their imagined bonanzas, roaming up and down the slopes of the Sierra, heads filled with fantasies of riches. From one end of the Sierra to the other, the hillsides were pockmarked with the shafts and tunnel waste of those who toiled for metallic-based wealth. The tales of great strikes were as big as the mountains. Gold and silver had a way of clouding men's minds and warping their judgments. The miners who searched Tioga Hill were no exceptions, and like so many others, their dreams of rich lodes and new strikes seldom materialized.

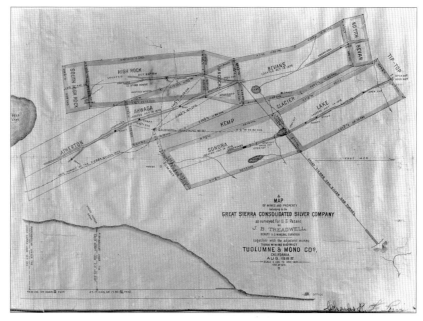

This map of the mines and property of the Great Sierra Consolidated Silver Company was prepared in 1882. The location of the map is described as the "main summit" of the Sierra Nevada Mountains.

Following reports of rich ores around Mono Diggings, the Homer and Jordan mining districts were established in early 1879. Across from the towering form of Mount Dana, a small mining camp emerged near today's Gaylor Lakes. Shortly thereafter, in 1880, the "city of Dana" was established, complete with its own post office. Over at Mono Pass, the Golden Crown and Ella Bloss Mines were developed alongside the historic trail.[5]

In 1881, Charles H. Forward, Franklin H. Watriss, and Wardon Wilson incorporated the Great Sierra Silver Company in the state of Illinois. Soon thereafter, in a complicated merger, it became the Great Sierra Consolidated Silver Company, bringing three nearby mines into one company run by a group of eastern and western promoters. In April, O. H. Brooks, the superintendent of the reorganized mine, went east to promote the new company to potential investors. Ambitious plans were laid to mine the "silver belt" vein.[6]

To reach the ore of the Sheepherder vein, the company came up with a new approach. Instead of using the tunnels that already had been started, it proposed to drill a new lateral tunnel from the eastern base of Tioga Hill. Such an approach would eliminate the need to remove the overburden (the surface materials covering the desired ore), while intercepting the vein more readily. Besides expediting the removal of ore and waste rock, the new lateral tunnel, it was hoped, would aid in the drainage of residual water, a common problem with many shaft or pit mines.

As work progressed, a small community took life at the head of the tunnel and became the company headquarters. Miners flocked to the area for work. A small sawmill was established, and cabins, stores, and a post office soon followed. In time, a saloon and other creature comforts were added. At first the high mountain mining camp was known as Bennett

The remains of the blower sit outside the Great Sierra Tunnel. The machine was used in conjunction with compressors and drills to burrow into the unyielding rock.

City, after the company president, Thomas Bennett, Jr. Later it was called Tioga, but eventually it took on the name Bennettville.[7]

Until the early 1880s, the only pack train access to Tioga Hill from the east side of the Sierra was limited to a route up Bloody Canyon and over Mono Pass, which was quite circuitous from Monoville. In 1881, a rough pack trail was built from Lake Canyon (just over the ridge and next to Lundy Canyon) to Tioga, but the longer Bloody Canyon remained the principal supply route. Other trails followed. By the 1880s, the mines in Lundy and Lake Canyons were thriving operations, and served as food and equipment supply bases for the Tioga mine. The rough trail from Lake Canyon apparently went up to Dore Pass to reach Bennettville, touching, perhaps, sections of Brown's Trail Pass.

While the mining company envisioned a community of 50,000 inhabitants on Tioga Hill, the remote and rugged location, reached only with difficulty over rough trails, hosted a population that was only a fraction of that figure.[8] Year-round operation of the mine got underway in the winter of 1881-82. Work on the proposed access tunnel began in February, 1882, with three shifts working around the clock. But the company had not foreseen the hardness of the high country rock. It soon became obvious that hand drilling was inadequate and that heavier machinery was needed.

A large steam engine, boiler, air compressor, drills, and other heavy equipment were ordered and shipped to nearby Lundy. Then began the

task of moving eight tons of machinery up the mountainside in one of the great epics of man and machine against mountain. Between Lundy and the mine were eight rugged miles, highlighted by 11,800-foot Dore Pass.

"The transportation of 16,000 lbs of machine across one of the highest and most rugged branches of the Sierra Nevada Mountains in mid-winter where no roads exist, over vast fields and huge embankments of yielding snow and in the face of furious windstorms laden with drifting snow, and the mercury dancing attendance on zero, is a task calculated to appall the sturdiest mountaineer; yet J. C. Kemp, manager of the Great Sierra Consolidated Silver Co. is now engaged in such an undertaking, and with every prospect of success at an early day—so complete has been the arrangement of details and so intelligently directed is every detail," the *Homer Mining Index* reported.[9]

Kemp's plan was to move the machinery over the frozen snow. On March 4, 1882, the cargo was transferred from large mule wagons at Lundy onto six large sleds. Two smaller sleds were loaded with bedding, food, cooking equipment, and other hardware to support the work crews. A dozen men, two mules, 4,500 feet of rope, and a series of block and tackles began the unfathomable over-the-summit journey. Wherever possible, rock outcroppings or trees were used as anchors for the pulleys. In their absence, large steel eyebolts were driven into the mountainside, and capstans or windlasses were also put to the task. Day after day the crews inched their loads up the precipitous, snow-covered mountains, hoping

Three men pose at the entrance to the Great Sierra Tunnel that was drilled into the side of Tioga Hill by the Great Sierra Consolidated Silver Company starting in 1882. Photo courtesy of the Alice Milburn collection.

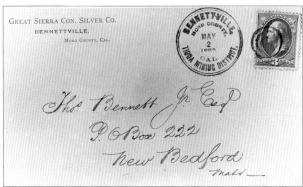

*Top: At its peak the 1880s Tioga mining
center of Bennettville boasted dozens of
buildings including a post office, and a
number of year-round residents. Photo
courtesy of the Alice Milburn collection.*

*Bottom: This letter mailed from Bennettville
bears the mining town's postmark.*

nothing would break or slip and send their precious
cargo plummeting into the deep canyon below.

The struggle wore on for nearly two weeks.
Winds and storms added to the problems inherent in
skidding the load up the mountainside. On the night
of March 15, after several days of heavy snows, a series
of avalanches thundered through the area. One such
avalanche hit the sleds carrying the mining equipment
and killed three men.[10] At Bennettville, a huge slide of
snow from Tioga Peak swept over the mining camp and
destroyed several buildings, including the main lodge,
temporarily trapping twenty-one men inside. Over the crest near the May
Lundy mine, another avalanche destroyed a building, leaving four dead.

No detailed record was kept of the route over which the machinery was
moved. Anyone who climbs the slopes of Lake Canyon and crosses Dore
Pass cannot help but feel tremendous admiration for J. C. Kemp and his
crew of movers. And once they managed to get the load up the mountainside, they faced the daunting task of easing it down the opposite slope.

Many stories have been passed down about the journey. Lee Symmons,
the late curator of the Mono County Museum, related that the crossing of
Saddlebag Lake was accompanied by sounds of cracking ice.[11] Neil Kelly, the
veteran operator of the Tioga Pass Resort, was told about numerous "roller
trees" that were used to move the sleds over the exposed or snow-free areas.

Day by day the giant sleds passed methodically across the snow-covered landscape. The climb to the top of Dore Pass was 4,500 feet, and the downhill trip to Bennettville involved approximately one mile of travel with a vertical drop of 1,100 feet. Finally, on May 6 after countless difficulties and several near disasters,[12] the needed equipment arrived at Bennettville, where it was quickly assembled and put to use.

Despite the added machinery and supplies, life in the emerging mining camp remained difficult. Travel to the high mines, particularly in winter, was fraught with danger and required unusual stamina and strength. Undoubtedly many persons perished after losing their way along the several variations of Brown's foot trail that were used to reach Bennettville.

In December 1881, for instance, H. B. Carpenter, a federal mineral surveyor, and Judge Harry P. Medlicott nearly died when caught on the slopes of Mount Warren by the first major storm of the season. Wet and frozen, they felt their way over the summit as hurricane winds came "breaking on the brow of the mountain, twisting and whirling in every direction and piling up snow in great ridges and mounds, so they could scarcely recognize the landmarks."[13]

Even before the ordeal of the heavy machinery move in 1882, the Great Sierra Consolidated Silver Company board of directors foresaw the need for a wagon road and approved its construction over the longer but comparatively gentle western slope. The new road would link the mine with Copperopolis on the Big Oak Flat Road. The projected cost for the road from Crane Flat to Bennettville was $17,000, but the mining company believed the road was a good investment because it would reduce freight costs and produce income from other users. Interestingly, at about the same time, a group composed predominantly of Great Sierra officials organized the California and Yosemite Short Line Railroad with the intention of building a rail line from Modesto to Mono Valley by way of Bennettville and Lee Vining Creek.

In the fall of 1882, the mining company approved funding for con-

Jerry Hodgdon, age 74, and his family pose in front of their cabin in Aspen Valley circa the 1930s. The original route of the Tioga Road passed by this structure, which was later moved to be part of the Pioneer Yosemite History Center in Wawona.

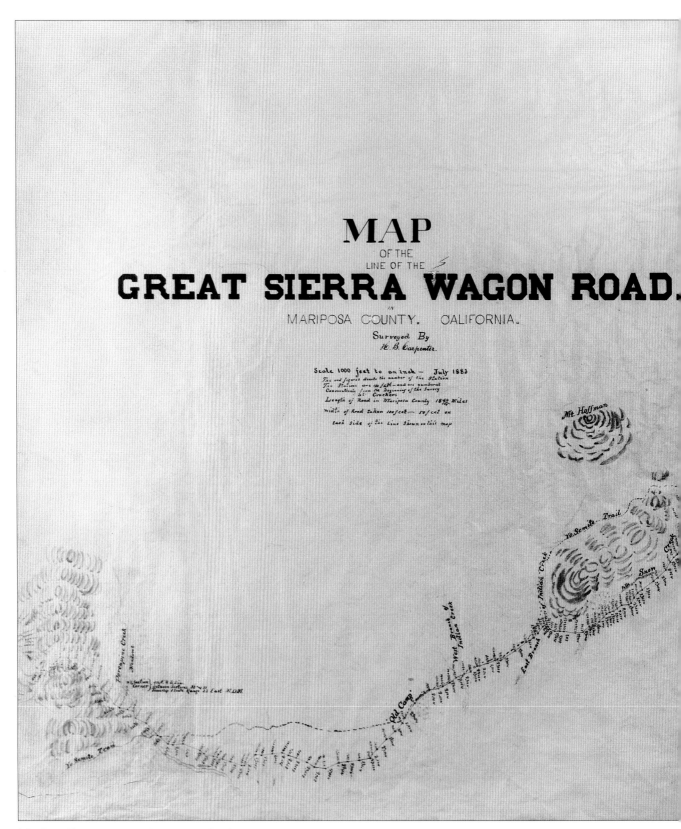

The Great Sierra Wagon Road was surveyed and roughly mapped by H. B. Carpenter in 1883.

struction of the wagon road. Charles N. Barney was named the engineer and William C. Priest his assistant.[14] To speed the road's completion, construction crews followed closely behind the surveyors. Besides determining the alignment for the wagon road, the surveyors were to select a route for the proposed railroad. The survey party managed to reach White Wolf before the winter weather forced suspension of work. Not far behind, the construction crews managed to dig their way to a point two miles east of Crocker's Station, an early landmark.

Work resumed in the spring of 1883 and proceeded at an amazing pace, particularly given the terrain involved. Unlike the present configuration of the Tioga Road, the wagon route went from Crocker's Station to the south fork of the Tuolumne River, then ascended to Aspen Valley. Next it climbed over the divide separating the south and middle forks of the Tuolumne River before turning toward White Wolf and on to McSwain Summit.

Eastward, the route tended to follow much the same route as the present road, crossing Yosemite Creek over a major bridge seven miles north of the rim of Yosemite Valley. The road continued to Porcupine Flat, traversed the headwaters of Snow Creek near Mount Hoffmann, and descended to Tenaya Lake. There it went on to Tenaya Summit and Tuolumne Meadows, then up along the Dana Fork of the Tuolumne River, bisecting Dana Meadows south of today's road, before reaching its terminus at Bennettville.

The survey crews reached Tioga Pass and the mining district in July, with the construction crews not far behind. Some 250 Chinese and other laborers, sweating and blistered and earning a wage of about $1.50 a day, pushed the road forward in segments using blasting powder, picks, shovels, and graders. In August, the *Homer Mining Index* reported that the "Great Sierra Wagon Road is rapidly approaching completion. Harry Medlicott's graders from this side have reached the upper end of Tuolumne Meadows, while Priest's pick and shovel brigade from the other side are on Rocky Canyon Creek, leaving a gap of little more than three miles, all of which is easy grading." On September 4, 1883, the entire fifty-six-mile stretch was finished, at the amazingly low cost of $61,095, and in just 130 days.[15]

The remains of the Great Sierra cabin above Upper Gaylor Lake.

Even by today's standards the construction of the Tioga wagon road was an extraordinary accomplishment. Its completion precipitated a large celebration in Sonora, a "big jollification" that attracted considerable attention. With a superior supply route to the mines, equipment could be moved by rail to Copperopolis and then on by wagon to Bennettville. While the privately-constructed road was never intended as a tourist's route, there were hopes that it could serve as a toll road for settlers and other travelers. The builders planned to recapture some of their costs by charging a use fee based on the size or number of the party.

The toll road history is unclear. While no record shows that any tolls were ever levied, they were posted. Charges were $5 for a freight team with two horses (the maximum fee), $1 for a horse and rider, and ten cents for a sheep or goat. Stories suggest that the tolls were so high they discouraged use and did not generate enough revenue to cover the wages of the toll collector. Whether tolls were collected or not, the new road did see limited use by miners, herdsmen, and a few recreational travelers.[16]

But the celebration and excitement over the mountain route were short lived. By early 1884, reports began filtering back that the mining company was in financial trouble. The promoters had not anticipated the hardness of the rock or the difficulty of supporting a remote mining operation at an elevation of 10,000 feet. Even with the drilling machinery, the lateral access tunnel had been pushed only 1,700 feet into the mountainside—without producing one ounce of millable ore.[17]

The Great Sierra Consolidated Silver Company suspended mining operations in July, 1884, and Bennettville withered, like so many other mining camps.

To complicate matters, Eastern stockholders felt western investors weren't meeting their financial commitments or paying their assessments. Some of the smaller western stockholders believed they were being squeezed out and refused to advance any more money. When on July 3, 1884, the Great Sierra Consolidated Silver Company's financial position worsened, the executive committee suspended operations.

The big money of the company, concentrated in Thomas Bennett and William and Rhodolphus Swift, the latter owners and operators of a fleet of whaling ships and forefathers of the giant meat packing company, felt the mine could resume operations if the company reorganized. Unfortunately, the situation deteriorated even more. With the cessation of operations, Bennettville began to empty, as the miners drifted away to look for employment elsewhere. The damage was irreversible; Bennettville withered, like so many other mining camps.

In an effort to learn the true value of their holdings in 1885, the eastern stockholders sent William Swift and an English mining engineer to Bennettville to make an on-site inspection. The engineer placed a value of $12 million on the company's assets, which the stockholders then assigned to Swift as trustee. In a strange turnabout, in 1887 Swift sued the Great Sierra Consolidated Mining Company and obtained a judgment for more than $277,000.[18]

While work on the mine tunnel was resumed for a brief period in the late 1880s, a report by the state mineralogist came as the final blow. It noted that while the ores of the Great Sierra, Sheepherder, and Golden Crown Mines of the Tioga Mining District were relatively good (averaging $25 a ton for both gold and silver), the remote location, high freight rates, harsh weather, and other problems made mining impractical. The state report also vindicated Brusky, albeit belatedly: he had committed suicide in 1882, after rumors began to circulate that he had "salted" his claim, that is, added enriched ore to bolster the value of the mine.[19]

The abandoned mill of the May Lundy Mine in Lake Canyon was perched at 11,000 feet. Workers had to climb 4,500 feet up Mill Creek to reach the mine.

Sierran winters at inhospitable places like Bennettville and Lundy. It is hard to imagine the hardships and privation the Tioga miners withstood. For six months of the year, the only access to Lundy or Monoville to obtain food and supplies was by foot or skis.[20]

From Lundy Pass south to the Minarets and Mammoth Lakes, there was a great deal of mining exploration and activity in the late 1880s. Again, traces of gold, silver, zinc, lead, tungsten, and other elements were mined and assayed. In most instances the available concentration could not justify commercial production.[21] Of all the mines established, only one, the May Lundy, located ten miles northeast of Tioga, actually produced any great wealth.

The Lundy Canyon trail had been developed in the mid-1860s, when another early pioneer, William O. Lundy, came into the high canyon northwest of Mono Lake. Initially, he established a timber claim and provided lumber for the mines at Bodie.[22] When miners from Bodie began prospecting around Mono Lake in the summer of 1879, Lundy and others extended the search into what would become Lundy Canyon.

Numerous claims were established in Lundy, but the most promising ones soon organized into what evolved as the Wasson Mining District. Out of the district, two principal mining companies emerged. The Homer Mill and Mining Company worked in upper Lundy Canyon, where the town of Wasson emerged; the May Lundy Mine was perched high on the slopes of Lake Canyon, above the community of Lundy.[23]

The May Lundy mine occupied an isolated location at 11,000 feet on the east-facing slope of Mount Scowden. To reach the mine required a long, arduous climb of 4,500 feet up Mill Creek. Despite this remoteness, when the mine was productive, the canyon community boasted its own post office, a large hotel, several boarding houses, and dozens of shops and businesses. It also had its own newspaper, the *Homer Mining Index*, and, anchoring the mining community, seven saloons.

In 1883, there was speculation that the wagon road from Bennettville would be extended at some future date to Lake Canyon and down to Lundy.[24] "Early next spring, connection will be made between the May Lundy and the Great Sierra Wagon roads. This will give Mono County another outlet, a short-cut through Lundy and Tioga to the railroad, cheaper fares and freight, and at once open up one of the richest . . . mineral belts in the state. With a well-stocked stage-line on the road, passengers from Bodie could be landed in San Francisco in twenty-four hours, and at little more than half the cost of the present mode of travel. Freight would also come at about half the time now required."[25]

But it was not to be. In less than a year, mining operations had begun to shut down. While it operated, the May Lundy made money, producing over $3 million in silver. In many respects, the success of the May Lundy sustained the mining fever and much of the high country travel in the area. But as fortunes turned, the miners left their high work places, leaving their faded dreams of gold and silver.

With the closure of the mines, the Great Sierra Wagon Road began to fall into disrepair. As the miners vacated the high country, the notion of a railroad across McLean Pass were abandoned also. For most of those involved—from the lowly miners to the monied investors—the high mountain mines were simply monuments to the folly that gold fever engendered. Today, only a couple of battered buildings, some rusting machinery, and an old ore pile stand as fading reminders of those who toiled for riches atop the Sierra at Bennettville.

NOTES

1. Linda Wedel Greene, *Historic Resource Study: Yosemite*, vol. 1 (Washington, D.C.: U.S. Department of the Interior, National Park Service, 1987), 245. While Brusky unearthed the ore in 1875, it wasn't until two years later that an assayer found the sample to contain considerable silver.

2. Ibid.

3. Elizabeth Stone O'Neill, *Meadow in the Sky* (Fresno: Panorama West Books, 1984), 12.

4. Carl P. Russell, "Early Mining East of Yosemite," *Sierra Club Bulletin* XIII no. 1 (February 1927), 40-53.

5. Greene, *Yosemite Historic Resource Survey*, vol. 2, 946.

6. Thomas C. Fletcher, *Paiutes, Prospectors, Pioneers* (Lee Vining, Calif.: Artemisia Press, 1987), 66-7.

7. Greene, *Yosemite Historic Resource Study*, vol. 1, 247.

8. Fletcher, *Paiutes, Prospectors, Pioneers*, 68.

9. *Homer Mining Index*, June 1883; and Keith A. Trexler, *The Tioga Road—A History, 1883–1961* (Yosemite: Yosemite Natural History Association, 1980), 3.

10. Douglass Hubbard, *Ghost Mines of Yosemite* (Fredericksburg, Texas: Awani Press, 1958), 15.

11. Lee Symmons, interview with author, Bridgeport, California, 1974.

12. Trexler, *The Tioga Road*, 4.

13. Hubbard, *Ghost Mines*, 17.

14. Trexler, *The Tioga Road*, 7; Greene, *Yosemite Historic Resource Study*, vol. 1, 250; Erwin G. Gudde, *California Place Names* (Berkeley: University of California Press, 1964), 257.

15. Greene, *Yosemite Historic Resource Study*, vol. 1, 251.

16. Nathaniel Ellery, "Status Report on the Mono Lake Road," in *Report of the State Engineer, 1907-1910* (Sacramento: California State Printing Office, 1910), 178.

17. Greene, *Yosemite Historic Resource Study*, vol. 1, 256.

18. Ibid., 257.

19. Joseph Garrard, *The Report of the Acting Superintendent of Yosemite National Park, 1903* (Washington, D.C.: U.S. Government Printing Office, 1904), 12.

20. Lee Symmons, interview with author, Bridgeport, California, 24 August 1978. Several pairs of early skis can still be seen at the Mono County Museum at Bridgeport.

21. *Minarets, California, Studies Related to Wilderness Areas*, U.S. Geological Survey Bulletin 1516-A-D (Washington, D.C.: U.S. Geological Survey and Bureau of Mines, 1982), 102-107.

22. Gudde, *California Place Names*, 186.

23. Fletcher, *Paiutes, Prospectors, Pioneers*, 59, 60.

24. Ibid., 21.

25. *Homer Mining Index*, 3 November 1883.

CHAPTER 5

THE MONO, MILITARY, AND MUTTON TRAIL

One of America's foremost historians, Frederick Jackson Turner, observed that the development of the American West followed a sequence of pioneers. Into the land of the Indians came the first white explorers. They were followed by a series of exploiters and entrepreneurs pursuing their dreams and aspirations.

In the case of Yosemite, the cast included mountain men, soldiers, miners, market hunters, sheepmen, and loggers. New pioneers arrived via the old Mono Trail, drawn by the wondrous tales of Yosemite. Many of them would leave their marks on the American conservation and preservation movement.

Turner concluded that by 1890 the western frontier had been tamed. The continent had been crossed. There was no more open land; the door of the frontier had been closed.[1] Up until this time, Congress had sought to encourage western growth and development with a series of generous land acts that passed large parcels of public land into private ownership. The 1862 Homestead Act, the 1872 Mining Act, and the Timber and Stone Act of 1876 had opened the doors of both opportunity and abuse. Many pioneers felt that the natural resources of the west were endless. The trees, minerals, and grazing lands were just waiting to be utilized. The mind set of the times was based on "manifest destiny," a concept originated in the early 1800s that envisioned an unending cycle of growth and development spreading across the continent.

As the "last stop," California, with its great geographic diversity and abundant natural resources, was visited with many abuses. The various land acts were regularly subverted and circumvented. Land was acquired fraudulently, often through an extreme interpretation of the Swamp and Overflow Act. That measure, intended to encourage the drainage and productive use of swamplands, was used in the claiming of numerous mountain meadows. By placing a rowboat on a wagon and then hauling it across a meadow, a claimant could swear that he or she had traversed the area by boat, thereby gaining ownership of "the swamp." The high country

Opposite: Several African-American infantry soldiers of the U.S. Army, known as buffalo soldiers, are shown in Yosemite in 1899. Buffalo soldiers and other U.S. Army cavalry patrolled the park's high country from 1891 until 1914. Photo by Celia Crocker Thompson.

Tuolumne Meadows sheep grazing became a pivotal issue in the campaign that led to the 1890 designation of Yosemite National Park.

of Yosemite did not escape the siege; hundreds of timber, mining, and land claims were filed in the area.

Livestock and ranching activities also contributed to the mistreatment of the land. Since the days of the Spanish missions, livestock had grazed practically anywhere they chose. Even after statehood, "no fence laws" provided ranchers additional (and destructive) privileges, allowing their animals to roam free. By the late 1880s, it was obvious that the damage done by livestock was becoming severe.

Though John Muir had once worked for Snelling sheep rancher Pat Delaney, the wandering Scotsman became troubled by the harm inflicted on the mountains by the "hooved locust [*sic*]" and the herder's fires. In Muir's writings and speeches, he called attention to the degradation of the Sierran high country occasioned by this grazing.

Robert Underwood Johnson of Century Magazine *helped lead the crusade for park protection.*

In the summer of 1889, Muir, joined by Robert Underwood Johnson, an associate editor of *Century Magazine*, journeyed to Toulumne Meadows. There they beheld the fouled Tuolumne River and a devastated landscape left behind by the "meadow mowers." It was a painful sight for Muir. "Incredible numbers of sheep are driven into the mountains every year, many more than there is food for. Not only are the moisture-absorbing grasses and flowers devoured. . . but the bushes are stripped bare. . . as if devoured by locust," he lamented.[2] Johnson was similarly appalled. Around their campfire, the two men began to formulate a plan to protect Yosemite. What they envisioned was a federal preserve similar to Yellowstone National Park, established by Congress a few years earlier.

Their strategy was to alert the public to the perils facing the Yosemite high country. Muir proposed writing a series of articles that would describe the damage and the need for protection; Johnson agreed to print them in his widely-circulated magazine. Muir returned home and began to pen some of his most impassioned and eloquent prose. "But no temple made with hands can compare with Yosemite. Every rock in its walls seems to glow with life."[3] The two articles that resulted, "Features of the Proposed

National Park" and "The Treasures of Yosemite," appeared in *Century Magazine* the summer of 1890, and the crusade was on.

Muir and Johnson gained support for protection of the Sierra from other forces. South of Yosemite, Visalia newspaper editor George Stewart called for the safekeeping of the giant sequoias in the Kaweah River drainage, emphasizing the threat their diminution would pose to the watershed and, more importantly, to San Joaquin Valley agriculture.[4]

With growing public awareness of the need to care for these natural resources came increased political pressure. Johnson began to work the Congress, seeking support and legislation for a Yosemite National Park. Muir believed the proposed park boundaries should include the headwaters contained within all the mountains surrounding Yosemite Valley. In time, Johnson's and Muir's efforts gained the support of a long list of publications and politicians, including California Governor Robert W. Waterman and bureaucrats in the Department of the Interior.

In March, 1890, Rep. William Vandever of California's Sixth Congressional District introduced a bill based largely on Johnson's and Muir's recommendations. It called for the creation of a national park surrounding the existing state grant, which included Yosemite Valley and the Mariposa Grove of Big Trees. The bill passed the House without debate and was moved to the Senate, where it encountered only token opposition. On October 1, 1890, five days after Congress had approved the creation of Sequoia National Park, "reserved forest lands" to be known as Yosemite National Park Reserve were also established. Both bills received quick presidential approval.

So the campaign hatched around a Tuolumne Meadows campfire proved to be a success. John Muir went on to gain literary and conservation fame, becoming known by many as the "Father of the National Parks." Robert Underwood Johnson stepped back into the folds of obscurity, largely unrecognized for his role in promoting the park and the conservation movement. While Muir's compelling words gave the preservation movement much of its momentum, it is doubtful that the Yosemite legislation would have survived without Johnson's influence, both at the *Century Magazine* and in Congress. Maymie Kimes, a recognized Muir scholar, once observed that although Muir had presented "the message," Johnson had done "the dirty work, getting the bill through Congress."[5]

Because national parks were new to the government, there were not existing employees to manage and protect them. At Yellowstone, Congress had assigned the U.S. Cavalry this job.[6] Citing this precedent, Interior Secretary John W. Noble asked Secretary of War Redfield Proctor to send cavalry troops to patrol the new California parks as well. When Proctor procrastinated, Noble went directly to President Benjamin Harrison, who produced a more immediate response.

On May 19, 1891, the U.S. Cavalry came onto the Yosemite scene, when "I" Troop of the Fourth Cavalry rode into the park from the San Francisco Presidio. Led by Captain A. E. Wood, the troopers were directed to protect the park, principally from trespassing stockmen. With a base

Left: Captain A. E. Wood was the first military commander in Yosemite, coming to the park with the U.S. Cavalry in 1891 and serving as acting park superintendent.

Right: The U.S. Army troopers patrolled the Tioga Road for twenty-five years.

camp established at Wawona, the cavalrymen made their first inspection of the Yosemite high country, where Wood saw herder-related problems first hand. En route, he also observed the poor condition of the Great Sierra Wagon Road. The captain reported that the road was "a good mounted trail, and as such, is of much importance,"[7] although it needed major repairs to sections damaged by washouts, slides, and downed trees.

Wood quickly learned the political realities of his job, finding himself without funds to repair the road or the legal muscle to keep the herders out of the park. While the activities of miners, hunters, and loggers were incompatible with the purposes of the new park reserve, their impact was insignificant compared to that of the herders. At first, Wood tried to discourage illegal grazing by sending written notices to neighboring sheep and cattlemen, warning them to keep their animals out of the park. Then he worked to convince the herders that he had the legal authority to arrest them, but this strategy failed after a federal attorney served notice that he would not prosecute any such cases. The captain discovered, too, that the herders were a wily lot and intimately familiar with the mountains. Furthermore, they felt they had an inalienable right to the lush meadow grasses.[8] When caught inside the park, the offending herders would plead ignorance or innocence (often in their native Spanish, Portuguese, or Basque), then keep on doing what they had been doing for years.

When the cavalry returned for their summer patrols in the summer of 1892, Wood tried another approach that had proven successful at Yellowstone. Under that system, troopers finding a trespassing flock would escort the offending herder to the nearest boundary, then drive his sheep to the opposite side of the park, scattering the bands and creating havoc for the herder. Faced with this prospect and its attendant loss of animals, the sheepmen began taking their flocks elsewhere.

Over the years the cavalry came to Yosemite either by a long horseback ride from the Presidio or by train from Oakland to Madera. On horseback, the units entered the San Joaquin Valley by way of Pacheco Pass. Near Madera they would split into two groups: one company headed for Sequoia National Park and the other to Yosemite and its base in Wawona that became known as Camp A. E. Wood. From that location the Yosemite contingent made extensive patrols to the distant boundaries of the 932,00-acre park, often staying out as long as a month. For many of those patrols, the Tioga wagon road was their main route.

During the spring of 1894, following the unexpected death of Wood from natural causes, Capt. G. H. G. Gale and "C" Troop of the Fourth Cavalry journeyed to the park from the Presidio of San Francisco. As part of his command, Gale oversaw the first thorough survey made of the canyons north of the Tuolumne River. Besides chasing the herders from the park, the troopers also brought the first semblance of law and order to the high country.

The following year, Company "K" of the Fourth Cavalry, which had served at Sequoia National Park the previous summer, was posted to Yosemite. Led by Captain Alexander Rodgers and assisted by Lieutenants McClure, Smedberg, and Benson, the cavalry resumed the pursuit of the herders and their flocks.[9] Rodgers urged harsher penalties for the persistent herders. "They band together and hire men who act as scouts, and from commanding points, watch trails. When the troops are seen, they give warning and the sheep, which are just inside the line, are driven out. With the small force I have, it is very difficult to keep out the sheep," he wrote in his official report.[10]

Tuolumne Meadows, the largest meadow system in the park (and a favorite for some of the early herders), became one of the "targeted

In this re-enactment in 1987, park interpreter Tom Smith portrays the role of a U.S. Army cavalryman assigned to protect Yosemite. Before the National Park Service was established, federal troops patrolled the park. Photo by author.

areas." On his August patrol, McClure took twelve mounted soldiers and five mules carrying provisions into the upper Tuolumne River drainage near today's Young Lakes. Near Mount Conness, he encountered several herders. Although some of the interlopers managed to get away, his soldiers arrested four "prisoners," who were marched back to Wawona.[11]

McClure returned to the same area a week later, and finding two flocks of sheep, began pursuit of their custodians. "The herders fled up into the rocks, and we were unable to capture them; so I had one or two shots fired to frighten them. I do not think they have stopped running yet."[12] He noted that there was plenty of fresh mutton in camp during the next few days.

Lt. McClure and his troops climbed through Lundy Canyon in 1894 and reached the top of Mount Warren.

During its 1894 patrols, McClure's unit came through deserted Lundy Canyon. "This trail was that from Lundy to Tioga, and it passes over the very summit of Mount Warren, at altitude of 12,000 feet." While he pursued sheepherders, McClure made the first maps of the upper Tuolumne drainage, gradually figuring out the maze of canyons and peaks. On a subsequent foray, his troopers captured two herders, who, in exchange for their release, showed McClure the way through the labyrinthine ridges between Matterhorn Canyon and Return Creek. He discreetly designated the route "McClure Pass."[13]

The cavalry made circular patrols through the park and established a number of patrol stations in the backcountry. Because they relied on the Great Sierra Wagon Road for access to the northern section of the park, the soldiers organized a road repair party in 1895. While some of the troopers questioned the legality of such repairs, noting that government resources were being expended on what was essentially "a private road," the work went forward.

As the patrols swept ever wider, sheep grazing conflicts intensified, particularly due to increasing competition from other stockmen. Normally, the mounted patrols ran from late June to early September, the so-called grazing season. Then it was back to the Presidio until the next year.

As the 1890s wore on, the competition among the ranchers for stock-sustaining meadow grass reached a peak. South of Yosemite, range wars erupted as sheep- and cattlemen battled for control of the mountain meadows. The killing of herders at Graveyard and Blayney Meadows underscored the ferocity of the conflicts, also know as the "grass wars." Along the San Joaquin River, at Miller's Crossing, the enigmatic land and cattle baron Henry Miller built a bridge that allowed his flocks to cross the river. To ensure his grazing rights, Miller put iron gates on the bridge and installed armed guards as well, forcing other sheepmen to look elsewhere for river crossings.

The sheep interests did not give up the Yosemite grasslands without a struggle. Many of the Basque ranchers, who had settled in the Owens Valley and the Mono Lake Basin after the 1860s, felt they had proprietary rights to their "backyard range." They argued that their early use of the mountain meadows predated the creation of the park. A handful of sheep-men threatened armed resistance, while others reportedly tried to bribe some of the soldiers with whiskey, as their need for feed grew desperate.[14]

In her book *The Flock*, Mary Austin—who hailed from the Owens Valley community of Independence—took a sympathetic view when she wrote about a sheepherder known as Jacques. "What shall you do now Jacques, now that the Yosemite Park Reserve has been closed off to grazing?" she asked. "I shall feed my sheep. I shall feed them in the meadow under the dome, in the pleasant meadow where my camp is, where I have fed them for fifteen years," the herder replied. Austin pointed out that the sheepmen were not beyond an occasional bribe or bottle. "Five gallons of whiskey," said Jacques. "I pay to get in and take my own chance of being found and forced out. We take off the bells and are careful of the fires. Last year I was in and the year before, but this summer some fools going about with a camera found me and I was made to travel," the herder's story continued.[15] Apparently, the herder reasoned that five gallons of whiskey was a cheap price for two months of feed.

Along the eastern edge of the park the herders grazed their animals right up to the boundary line, then moved on into the park whenever they felt it was safe. Warren and Lee Vining Canyons remained prime sheep grazing and staging areas, even after the Mono and Inyo National Forests were set aside in 1908.

Following several drought years in the late 1890s, the stockmen fought unsuccessfully to have the ban on grazing rescinded in Yosemite, Sequoia, and General Grant Parks. They contended that the pasture on the adjacent forests was completely allocated and that forcing the sheep from the parks would be the same as starving the animals.

"Thousands of Sheep Will Starve," "Sheep Ejected from Parks," and "Orders Ignored—Sheep Men Will Stay in the Yosemite" trumpeted the headlines of the *Fresno Morning Republican* as it followed the sheep controversy.[16]

To support the cavalry, the government hired a special task force to remove the sheep from the Sierran parks. In June of 1898, special agent J. W. Zevely of the Department of the Interior was authorized to hire ten assistants to expel the flocks from the parks. One agent estimated there were 75,000 sheep in Yosemite. Another figured that 150,000 sheep had been driven from the park back over the Sierra into Inyo and Mono Counties.[17]

"There is a general disposition among the sheepmen to ignore the order, and a prominent wool grower, who did not care to have his name published, remarked yesterday that it would take the herdsmen all summer to get the flock out of the reservation. If the government officers are inclined to force them to move more rapidly, he said, the sheep will be left to roam in the hills and the owners will come down into the valley and wait until the government gets tired of caring for the flocks."[18]

In 1987, a park crew removed and saved for preservation the trunk of a dead tree containing a "blaze" left by cavalry troopers in the 1890s. Many such carvings by the early sheepherders also have been located in the high country. The park service has sought to protect such historic reminders of early park users and visitors. Photo by author.

Despite the cavalry's diligence, herders with their sheep and dogs regularly slipped into Yosemite's high meadows to take advantage of the plentiful grazing.

When the cavalry was sent off in 1898 to Cuba during the Spanish-American War, the sheepmen stormed back into the park. "The military being drawn off for a business better suited to their degree, and the Park left to insufficient wardens, they surged into it from all quarters. They snatched what they could, and when routed went a flock-length out of sight and returned to the forbidden pastures by a secret way."[19] As the situation continued to deteriorate, the First Utah Volunteer Cavalry was summoned to the park to help the two over-worked civilian wardens. At the end of the season, Capt. Joseph E. Caine reported that his troops had sent away an unbelievable 189,550 sheep, 1,000 head of cattle, and 350 horses, and captured 27 herders (besides putting out more than a dozen fires the intruders had started).[20]

It was during this period that the park obtained funds to hire Archie Leonard and Charles Leidig as the first civilian rangers in Yosemite. The two men had been around the area for years, Leonard as a packer and guide and Leidig as the son of an early Yosemite innkeeper. As the first non-military "park rangers," they were assigned to patrol the park during the winter months when the cavalry was absent. With their appointment, a measure of year-round protection had come to Yosemite.[21] At the conclusion of the war, the regular cavalry returned and gradually regained control of the park.

Despite the army's diligence, however, the sheep and cattlemen slipped into the mountain meadows whenever they could. In 1902, the adjoining Sierra Forest Reserve established grazing allotments—permits that authorized stockmen to graze a specified number of animals on a designated area within the reserve during the summer months. The allotments represented a significant step in the government's evolving efforts to gain control of the public lands. Of course, the animals couldn't read the early maps, and often wandered into the adjacent park.

A half-dozen permanent rangers were hired to patrol the huge reserve, and frequently moved into and out of the park as they made their patrols. One of them, Gene Tully, noted that removing trespassing sheepmen was only part of the often difficult and dangerous job. "It was a hard, lonely, and sometimes dangerous life. Sudden illness, a fall, weather, slides and the threatened vengeance of a resentful stockman made early rangers always watchful," said Tully.[22]

As the "roving ranger" in charge of grazing, Tully used the Tioga wagon road. He would leave North Fork and ride toward Hites Cove, crossing the Merced River to reach Lake Eleanor and the land now in the Stanislaus National Forest. After patrolling this northern territory, he would ride the Tioga wagon road, cross Mono Pass, and descend through Bloody Canyon, which lay within the eastern district of the reserve. Next he would wind his way down the eastern slope of the Sierra, checking the high meadows for trespassing sheep. After venturing well south of Mount Whitney, Tully would turn north and begin his long trip home by way of Kings Canyon and the San Joaquin River. After six weeks and 600 miles in the saddle, he would arrive home in North Fork.[23]

The soldiers brought law and order (as well as a source of funding) to the embryonic but fragmented collection of national parks. Even with their abbreviated summer stay in Yosemite, the cavalry eliminated most illegal grazing by the end of the century, while greatly decreasing poaching and market hunting. Usually, the military's stay in the park coincided with the visitor, grazing, and fire seasons—times when help was most needed. The army also provided operating monies to cover supplies, trail-building materials, etc., with substantial summer expenditures (a sum of $7,742 at Yosemite in 1897, for example).

The soldiers that arrived in 1896, the "B" Troop of the Fourth Cavalry, were under the command of Lieutenant Colonel S. B. M. Young. He not only kept a keen eye on the herders, but established the first entrance stations to the park. In an attempt to control poaching, Young ordered that visitors' firearms be impounded upon their entrance to the park. His expanded list of park regulations reflected a degree of chivalry: pistols were permitted only when the man carrying one was accompanied by a woman! Young's gun control efforts were wide-ranging. Some of his own soldiers were caught poaching, and they, too, had their guns impounded. By summer's end, Young's men had confiscated over 200 firearms, and the military had established another measure of control within the park.[24]

Other national trends in land use would touch the Tioga country.

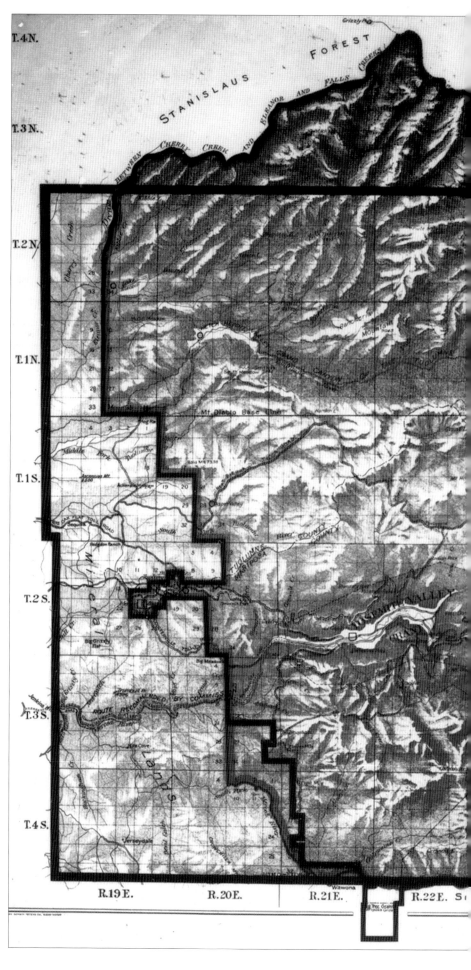

YOSEMITE'S TIOGA COUNTRY

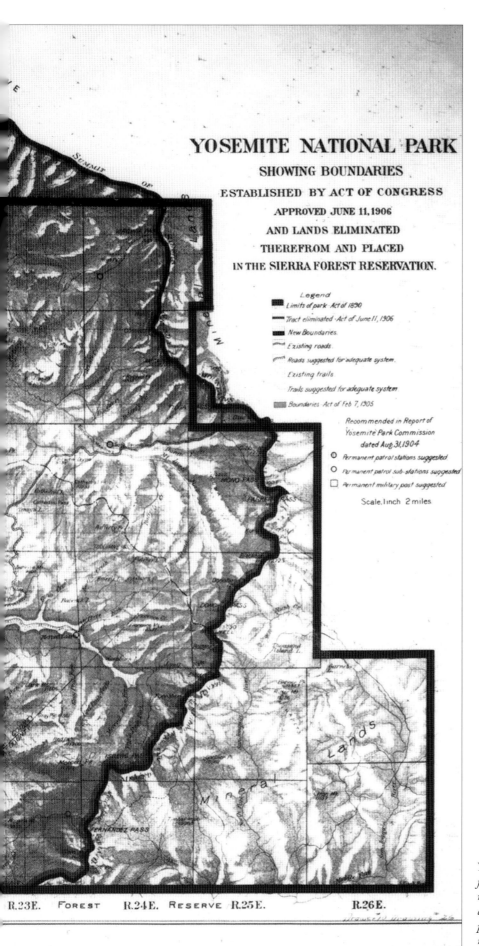

YOSEMITE NATIONAL PARK

SHOWING BOUNDARIES

ESTABLISHED BY ACT OF CONGRESS

APPROVED JUNE 11, 1906

AND LANDS ELIMINATED

THEREFROM AND PLACED

IN THE SIERRA FOREST RESERVATION.

Legend

Limits of park · Act of 1890

Tract eliminated · Act of June 11, 1906

New Boundaries.

Existing roads.

Roads suggested for adequate system.

Existing trails

Trails suggested for adequate system

Boundaries · Act of Feb 7, 1905

Recommended in Report of
Yosemite Park Commission
dated Aug. 31, 1904

⊕ Permanent patrol stations suggested

○ Permanent patrol sub-stations suggested

☐ Permanent military post suggested

Scale, 1 inch 2 miles

Yosemite's boundaries have been modified frequently, with changes including the 1905 removal of the Minarets, Devils Postpile, and considerable acreage to the west of the park, and the 1906 recession of the state-managed Yosemite Valley and the Mariposa Grove of Big Trees.

Colonel Harry C. Benson, who served as acting superintendent in Yosemite from 1905-08, was known for his devotion to duty and the number of trails he developed in the park's backcountry.

Following the creation of Yosemite in 1890, President Harrison began to designate additional reserves to provide limited protection to the nation's rangelands and timberlands. The Yellowstone Timberland Reserve became the first, in 1891.[25] On February 14, 1893, the Sierra Forest Reserve was created as the sixth and largest reserve in the nation. At approximately six million acres, it surrounded most of Yosemite and included much of today's John Muir and Ansel Adams Wilderness Areas and lands now within the neighboring Inyo, Stanislaus, Sequoia, and Sierra National Forests and Kings Canyon National Park.[26]

While Congress had created Yosemite National Park, the new forest reserves were established by presidential proclamation, to be administered by the General Land Office of the Department of Interior. Initially, the distinction between park reserves and forest reserves was blurred, as both were administered by the Department of the Interior. To clarify the distinction between these public land types, the U.S. Forest Service was established and placed under the Department of Agriculture, but not until 1905. With responsibility for the forest reserves, the new agency was charged with utilitarian conservation, permitting authorized but regulated uses of public lands, including the first grazing allotments.

To help demarcate the line between park and forest, the troopers assigned to Yosemite posted the boundary of the neighboring Sierra forest in 1894, but then returned to their park patrols. The few seasonal rangers hired by 1898 often crossed the park to get to the eastern slope of the reserve.[27] It was not until the end of the decade that the first seasonal patroller (later to be called "ranger") was hired for the Sierra Forest Reserve.

The demand for the services of the cavalry caused the government to realize that the parks could not exist without some continuing presence to provide direction and control. As the first contingent to "range" the parks, the cavalry furnished a model for a permanent ranger force employing the military-style chain of command.

When the cavalry finally left the park, it left behind a long trail of accomplishments. Besides controlling illegal grazing, the mounted soldiers eliminated much of the poaching that had once been prevalent. In their travels, the troopers came to know the park as well as anyone. Along with the U.S. Geological Survey and the Sierra Club, they developed some of the first maps and located and built some of the first trails.

The troopers also repaired the Tioga wagon road, but the route seemed to require annual work, which was never enough. One cavalry report noted that campers en route to Tuolumne Meadows were often forced to make their own repairs so they could proceed to their destination. "Impassable" and "unusable" became the most common adjectives used to describe the not-so-old road. "The Tioga Road should either be repaired by the company owning it or taken possession of by the government. Nearly all, if not all, of the bridges on the road are down, and a loaded wagon in some instances has to pass over public lands for a considerable distance to get to the road and the bridge sites. The owners make only a pretense of repairing it to prevent their charter from being revoked," wrote Joseph Garrard, the acting superintendent in 1903.[28]

Of the military's presence in the park, John Muir had positive impressions. "On this ramble I was careful to note the results of the four years of protection the region had enjoyed under the care of the Federal Government, and I found them altogether delightful and encouraging. . . The flowers and grasses are back again in the places as if they had never been away, and every tree in the park is waving its arms for joy. . . Blessings on Uncle Sam's blue coat," he exclaimed.[29]

When the early mountaineers went "tramping" through the high country, they often encountered the cavalry patrols. Sometimes the cavalry came up with "leg of mutton" for the campers. At other times the exchange was reversed, as in 1905, when Colonel Benson rode into Tuolumne Meadows looking for a cup of tea. Drawn by the smoke of Sierra Club member Harold C. Bradley's campfire, Benson made a brief stop, declining an invitation for dinner. Benson explained that he could not spend the night; he was on his way back to the cavalry's Wawona outpost, thirty-five rough miles away. "He could cover the park in a day," Bradley wrote, attesting to the character and vigor of the cavalry's leadership.[30]

In the early twentieth century, significant administrative changes affected Yosemite and the Sierra Forest Reserve. Yielding to pressures

Gabriel Souvulewski began work in Yosemite with the U.S. Cavalry, and with the conversion to a non-military administration stayed on, becoming the first civilian supervisor of Yosemite.

from the mining industry and other promoters, Congress, in 1905, transferred the majestic Minarets and Devils Postpile areas, previously included in Yosemite, to the forest reserve, so that grazing, mining, and some limited logging would be permissible. As noted above, around the same time, the reserve system was re-organized under the U.S. Forest Service, and ultimately the Department of Agriculture and its chief forester Gifford Pinchot.

Yosemite's first civilian rangers, hired after the departure of the U.S. Army troops, are shown on horseback in 1915. Photo by George Fiske.

In 1906, state-managed Yosemite Valley was re-ceded to federal control, and the cavalry moved its headquarters from Wawona into Yosemite Valley. Two years later, the Sierra Forest Reserve, which had grown to over 6.6 million acres, was separated into the Inyo, Mono, Sequoia, and Sierra National Forests. The Stanislaus Forest Reserve was created in 1902, and enlarged by boundary adjustments after 1908. The Mono National Forest, with its original headquarters in Lee Vining Canyon, was eventually split up and shared between the Toiyabe and Inyo National Forests.

Finally, Congress created the National Park Service in 1916, formally ending the cavalry's involvement in the park. The army's contributions to the organizational blueprint of the service were extensive. The mounted soldiers had set the foundation for the creation of a professional park staff, molded along military lines and committed to the protection of the new parklands. The names of Yosemite's lakes, peaks, meadows, and waters memorialize the work of the troopers. Across the high country of the park, places like Rodgers Peak, Young Lakes, Benson Lake, and Forsyth Peak bear witness to the military men who rode the Tioga trail.

When the National Park Service took formal control of Yosemite, several of the soldiers, enamored by the charms of Yosemite, switched employment to the nascent park agency. One such soldier, Gabriel Sovulewski, a native of Poland, worked in the park as a private with Company "K," and later became one of the first park administrators.

Almost every spring during his many years in the park, Sovulewski would follow the old trans-Sierra route to oversee the snow removal efforts. As he gazed out over the mountains and meadows, his thoughts drifted back to the days when his cavalry unit had patrolled the park. Yosemite had changed his life—and the lives of countless others.

NOTES

1. Ed Marston, *Reopening the Western Frontier* (Washington, D.C. and Covelo, Calif.: Island Press, 1989), 3-4.

2. *San Francisco Daily Evening Bulletin,* 29 June 1889, 1; William F. Kimes and Maymie B. Kimes, *John Muir—A Reading Bibliography* (Fresno, CA: Panorama West Publishing, 1986), 49.

3. Kimes, *John Muir—A Reading Bibliography,* 49.

4. Lary M. Dilsaver and William C. Tweed, *Challenge of the Big Trees* (Three Rivers, Calif.: Sequoia Natural History Association, 1990), 66.

5. Maymie Kimes, telephone interview by author, 4 April 1992.

6. *Congressional Record,* Vol. 14 (23 February 1883): 3193. Representative McCook sought an amendment to a bill authorizing the U.S. Army to patrol Yellowstone National Park.

7. A. E. Wood, *Report of the Acting Superintendent, Yosemite National Park* [1891](Washington, D.C.: U.S. Government Printing Office, 1891), 7. Copy in Yosemite Research Library.

8. James Snyder, interview by author, Yosemite National Park, 1996.

9. Erwin G. Gudde, *California Place Names* (Berkeley: University of California Press, 1969), 26.

10. Alexander Rodgers, *Report to Interior Secretary John W. Noble,* 22 August 1895 (Washington, D.C.: U.S. Government Printing Office, 1895). Copy in Yosemite Research Library.

11. Elizabeth Stone O'Neill, *Meadow in the Sky* (Fresno: Panorama West Publishing, 1984), 56.

12. N. F. McClure, "Explorations of the Cañons North of the Tuolumne River," *Sierra Club Bulletin* I, no. 3 (January 1895): 170.

13. Ibid., 165–173.

14. Mary Austin, *The Flock* (New York, Boston and London: Houghton-Mifflin, 1906), 192.

15. Ibid., 191.

16. *Fresno Morning Republican,* 7 July 1898, 28 July 1898, and 3 March 1899.

17. *Fresno Morning Republican,* 21 June 1898.

18. *Fresno Morning Republican,* 7 July 1898, 3.

19. Austin, *The Flock,* 194.

20. Joseph E. Caine, *Acting Superintendent Yosemite National Park, Report for 1898* (Washington, D.C.: U.S. Government Printing Office, 1899), 1055. Copy in Yosemite Research Library. Former park historian James Snyder believes these figures are questionable because the cavalry did not have the resources to make such counts.

21. O'Neill, *Meadow in the Sky,* 58.

22. Gene Rose, *Reflections of Shaver Lake* (Fresno: Panorama West Books, 1987), 107.

23. Gene Tully, personal letters and papers, transcribed by John Lewis, 480-485. Special Collection, Madden Library, California State University Fresno, John Lewis Collection. Gene Tully was one of the first rangers on the Sierra Forest Reserve. From 1903 until 1914, he was in charge of grazing on the forest; he is credited with helping remove trespassing sheep from Yosemite. "Tully's Hole" on the John Muir Trail, a location where Tully used to graze his pack animals, is named in his memory.

24. S. B. M. Young, *Report to Interior Secretary David R. Francis, 15 August 1896* (Washington, D.C.: U.S. Government Printing Office, 1896). Copy in Yosemite Research Library.

25. U.S. Department of Agriculture, Forest Service, *Highlights in the History of Forest Conservation,* AIB-83 (Washington, D.C.: U.S. Government Printing Office, 1976), 15.

26. Gene Rose, *Reflections of Shaver Lake,* 106.

27. Ibid., 107.

28. Joseph Garrard, *Report of the Acting Superintendent Yosemite National Park in California for 1903,* vol. 1 (Washington D.C.: U.S. Government Printing Office, 1903), 6.

29. Kimes, *John Muir—A Reading Bibliography,* 58.

30. Harold C. Bradley, "Colonel Benson – Rover," *Sierra Club Bulletin* XXXIV, no. 6 (January 1949): 15-16.

CHAPTER 6

THE MOUNTAIN TRAMPERS AND THEIR TRAILS

With his explorations of the peaks and glaciers of Yosemite, John Muir loosed an avalanche of interest in the mountains of California. Of those he introduced to the Sierra, few were affected so deeply as Dr. Joseph L. LeConte, a professor of geology at the University of California. In the summer of 1870, shortly after his appointment to the fledgling university in Berkeley, LeConte led a group of nine college students to Yosemite Valley, where they had a chance encounter with Muir. After some brief introductions, Muir agreed to lead the professor's group along the route of the Mono Trail across the Sierra to Mono Lake. It was the start of an adventurous outing and a lengthy and lasting friendship between the two men (an association later continued by the geologist's son, Joseph N. LeConte).

Its first night out, LeConte's party camped at a small meadow above the landmark known as the Three Brothers on the north rim of Yosemite Valley. The following morning Muir lead them east, where they came upon an empty herder's camp. A large pot of mutton stew was simmering, and without a moment's thought, Muir invited the university party to partake, knowing the herder would not object; there was always more mutton to be had. When the herder showed up, he was as hospitable as Muir had suggested—much to the satisfaction of everyone's appetite.

The group then moved on toward Tenaya Lake, carefully picking its way over the faint Indian trail. "The trail is very blind, in most places detectable only by the blazing of trees and very rough," LeConte observed.[1] After setting up camp and partaking of dinner, Muir and LeConte strolled along the shore of the lake after dinner, reveling in the glories of a Sierra sunset.[2] "It was full moon. I never saw a more delightful scene," LeConte waxed enthusiastically at the high country setting.[3] A trained geologist, he reported seeing "the polishing and scouring of ancient glaciers," an observation that would later bear on the debate over Yosemite's geologic origins.[4]

Opposite: John Baptiste Lembert settled in Tuolumne Meadows around 1882. He built a small cabin there directly over one of the soda springs.

For many summers following his first visit in 1870, Joseph L. LeConte (on horseback) traveled to Yosemite, often in the company of his family.

The next day the newcomers followed Muir to Tuolumne Meadows. LeConte wrote that there were thousands of sheep in the area and that his group expected "to live off mutton" until they crossed the mountains. As for Tuolumne Meadows, the professor described it as a "beautiful grassy plain of great extent, thickly enameled with flowers, and surrounded with the most magnificent scenery."[5] The group soon experienced some typical high country weather—an afternoon thunderstorm. "The storm did not last more than an hour. After it, the sun came out and flooded all the landscape with liquid gold. I sat alone at some distance from the camp and watched the successive changes of the scene. . . Oh how exquisite," LeConte wrote.[6]

He estimated that there were between twelve and fifteen thousand sheep in the area, devouring the meadows. Accordingly, the mountaineers were well fed. "The sheep we bought yesterday is entirely eaten up in one day. We bought another here—a fine, large, fat one. In an hour it was butchered, quartered and a portion on the fire cooking."[7] For the next several days his group roamed over much of the surrounding territory. At times, LeConte lectured and studied the natural history of the area, while Muir related his experiences and observations, adding to the students' appreciation of the mountains.

After nearly a week, the university group moved its camp to the base of Mount Dana, where the students climbed and explored the peaks and ponds along the crest. Next, the group turned toward Mono Pass and proceeded down Bloody Canyon. There, along the historic Native American migration route, LeConte's group encountered Indian parties, with some individuals begging tobacco.

At Mono Lake, Muir, after many fond farewells, left the party. Turning to the north, LeConte and his students traveled up the east side of the Sierra to Lake Tahoe and finally back to the Bay Area. The five-week high country outing was a success and a major turning point in LeConte's life, cementing his relationship with Muir and with the mountains. Two years later, in 1872, the professor and Muir were back in the high country, where the latter was refining his glacier hypothesis—one that LeConte would corroborate and present to the academic and scientific communities.

In 1875, while pursuing both research and recreation, LeConte again returned to the Sierra, this time with his family along. After gathering in Yosemite Valley, they moved up to Tuolumne Meadows. John Muir also was in the area at the time introducing Scottish painter William Keith to the grandeur of this special mountain world.[8] LeConte and his family made their return via Mono Lake and the east side. Again and again through the 1880s, LeConte came back to the high country, often joined by his wife, who was similarly touched by the magic of the Sierra Nevada. In 1889, LeConte spent most of the summer with his son, "Little Joe," hiking among the peaks and spires of the Yosemite high country.

As LeConte's glowing accounts of the mountains were disseminated, a growing circle of students and scholars from Berkeley and around the Bay Area began to visit the high country. After the route of the Great Sierra Wagon Road was established in 1883, LeConte and some of his followers used the road to reach what was to become their favorite camping spot, the Soda Springs of Tuolumne Meadows.

In the late summer of 1890, J. N. "Little Joe" LeConte and three young Berkeley friends visited Soda Springs at the conclusion of a sixty-seven-day "grand tour" of the High Sierra.[9] They had hiked over 650 miles through the southern Sierra, then moved up the east side, re-supplied themselves, and headed up Bloody Canyon toward Mono Pass. Atop the pass the party was deluged by the worst thunder and hail storms the young Leconte had seen in the Sierra. Tired and wet, the group slogged on to Tuolumne Meadows. "We tramped dejected down the old Tioga Road, walking through creeks without the least hesitation," LeConte wrote.[10]

In Tuolumne Meadows they stayed at the cabin of John Baptiste Lembert. A New Yorker by birth, Lembert filed a homestead claim at Tuolumne Meadows around 1885, and built a small cabin and barn near Soda Springs, complete with angora goats. Lembert managed to make

Besides exploring the Sierra, "Little Joe" LeConte followed John Muir as Sierra Club president, filling the job from 1915-1917.

The rustic homestead cabin of John Baptiste Lembert (third from right) was built near Soda Springs on the edge of Tuolumne Meadows.

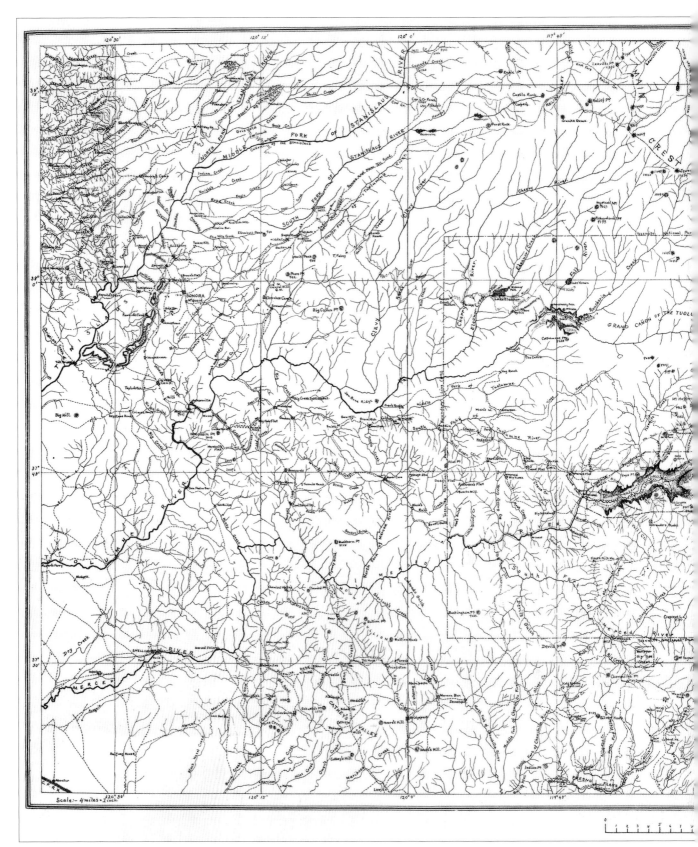

*Joseph N. LeConte prepared this map on behalf
of the Sierra Club in 1893. It was the product of
hundreds of miles of travel in the Sierra.*

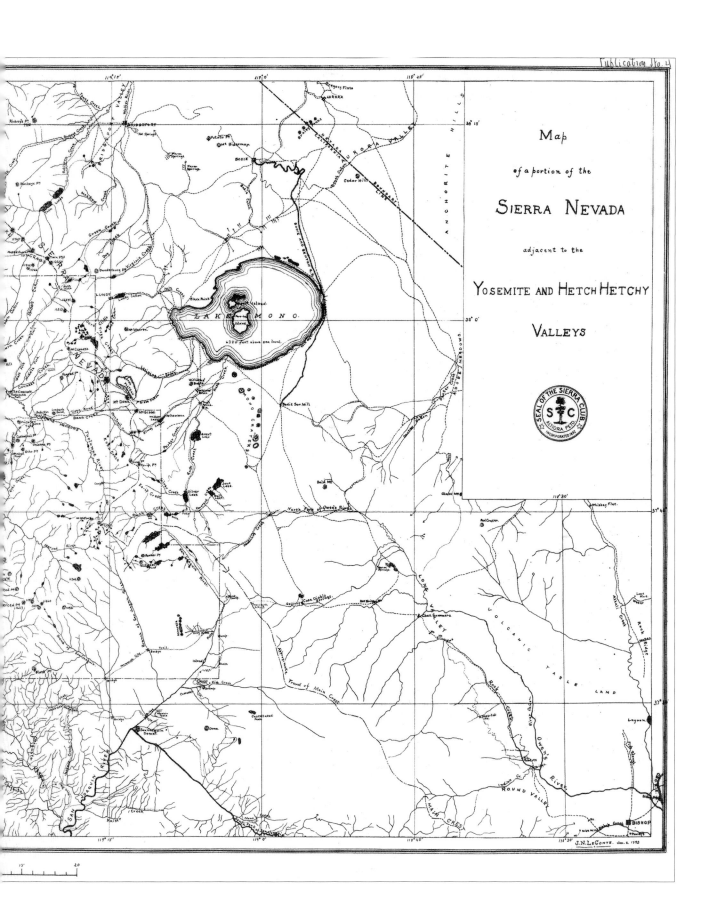

Map

of a portion of the

SIERRA NEVADA

adjacent to the

YOSEMITE AND HETCH HETCHY

VALLEYS

J. N. LeConte. Jan. 6, 1893

In its heyday, around the turn of the last century, Crocker's Station, the main stage coach stop along the Big Oak Flat Road to Yosemite, was home to nearly two hundred residents.

ends meet by selling the effervescent spring water to Yosemite Valley residents and tourists. He became a friend to many of those who passed through the mountains, his small cabin and barn serving as landmarks along the wagon road.[11]

Lembert became acquainted with many of the high country herders, and through them gained a vast knowledge of the routes and trails radiating out of the meadow. Consequently he was sought out for directions by many of those traveling the high mountains. Lembert's role in the history of the Yosemite high country is memorialized in Lembert Dome, the large granitic block that rises at the eastern end of Tuolumne Meadows and overlooks the Tioga Road.

With the completion of the wagon road, H. R. Crocker developed a stage stop on the western end of the route near its junction with the Big Oak Flat Road. As his business prospered, it became known as Crocker's Sierra Resort, offering board and room to stage travelers bound for Yosemite. Over the years the resort evolved into a mountain community of nearly two dozen cabins and stores. From the Bay Area, the approach to Yosemite through Coulterville and Crocker's Station (as it was later called) was much shorter than the one used by LeConte on his first trip, through Mariposa and Wawona; it was also more direct than the railroad route farther to the south through Berenda and Raymond.

But as the wagon road's reputation became known to the high country travelers, its condition began to deteriorate. The lack of maintenance following the failure of the mining company and several rough winters left downed trees, slides, and washouts blocking the way. "The road is very rough in places, but is not impassable," observed one of the early travelers. It was suggested that a light wagon, better able to take the bumps and boulders, might be more suitable for traveling the road.[12]

During the visit of J. N. LeConte's group in 1890, members of the party climbed Mount Conness, where they encountered a government survey party that had arrived a few days before.[13]

The nine-person team from the U.S. Coast and Geodetic Survey, under the direction of Professor George Davidson of the University of California, had been sent afield to improve the accuracy of existing maps. To that end, they planned to take triangulation measurements from the summits of Mount Conness and other Sierran peaks, where teams of "heliotropers" would flash large signal mirrors to the home station atop Mount Diablo, east of Oakland.

The task proved to be a formidable one for the surveyors.[14] The heavy winter of 1889-90 had blanketed the high country and its wagon route with unusually deep snows. When an advance survey party arrived at Crocker's Station in May, it found eight feet of snow blocking the wagon road. A subsequent check of Bloody Canyon showed that the east slope approach to Tuolumne Meadows would be "impracticable before the end of August, if then."[15]

The survey party gathered at Crocker's in early July and finally began to move up the wagon route. Although it had not been maintained for only three years, the road was in poor condition. Deep snow and fallen trees clogged sections of the road, making progress difficult. "The four-horse teams, which had hauled 4,000 pounds each from Oakdale, now found it hard work to pull 1,500 pounds over the leveled snow or the brushed mud ruts. Bridges and culverts were found carried away and had to be rebuilt," Davidson observed.[16]

At Yosemite Creek, the survey members found the main trusses of the bridge broken, which halted their progress. Davidson's crews went to work, establishing a camp and then rebuilding the bridge in less than two days. An estimated 20,000 sheep and their herders also awaited removal of the obstacle. When the party reached Tuolumne Meadows it encountered more problems. "The fords were unfordable, and assistant Gilbert improvised a raft for ferriage of the men, animals, provisions, camp equipment and instruments" across the stream that was swollen with run-off from the melting snows.[17] Finding the trail to Mount Conness also impassable due to snow and downed trees, the party, with the permission of John Lembert, established a temporary camp in Tuolumne Meadows.

Again, work parties were dispatched, and with "great labor opened the trail to a previously established 'heliotropers' camp about 1,800 feet below the summit of Conness." For the next twenty days, Davidson's crew struggled to establish a footpath from the base camp to the summit. They then carried lumber and concrete to the top of the peak, where they built

During July and August of 1890, Professor George Davidson of the United States Coast and Geodetic Survey, together with his assistants, occupied the summit of Mount Conness for the purpose of closing a link in the main triangulation which connected with the transcontinental surveys.

a small observatory perched on the sheer lip of the mountain. Finally, suspending the "great Theodolite" on a special carrier, four men muscled the nearly 200-pound encased instrument up to the observatory.

With all necessary devices in place, the measurements began in earnest. Thunderstorms often slowed the work, but gradually the baseline figures and other needed readings were recorded. "Every moment of the month of August and a week in September was utilized for observing, and more than 2,500 observations were made."[18] Davidson noted that the unrivaled visibility from the summit enabled readings to be made at any time of the day. When the survey left its mountain top outpost, it had completed one of the most ambitious and exacting surveys ever made in the West.[19]

The small observatory perched by the Davidson party on Mount Conness required enormous effort, both in transportation of materials and in construction.

Another early route to Yosemite was up the east side of the Sierra by way of Monoville, the largest settlement south of Lake Tahoe at the time. In 1887, a Carson City newspaper suggested that the typical "eastern tenderfoot or tramp" could easily reach Yosemite Valley by way of Carson City "without a very protracted siege of hunger." All the traveler had to do was cross the 12,000-foot crest of the Sierra between Lundy Canyon and Tioga Pass (on foot), and then hike on to the valley. "After emerging from Lake Canyon, a lateral moraine at right angles south of Mill Creek Canyon, Mount Warren Divide is crossed at an altitude of nearly 13,000 feet [*sic*], almost even with the summit of mount Dana, which lies directly opposite. . . From here it is all down hill along the shores of beautiful Tenaya Lake . . . and only a few miles further on, and Yosemite, that wonderful gash in the crust of the earth yawns before the tourist, 2000 feet below him. This 'real route to Yosemite' provides game and fish, all the way, the loveliest spots for camping if one wishes to go by easy stages."[20]

During the late 1800s after the Lundy and Tioga Mines failed, the Mono Lake Basin slumbered in the shadow of the Sierra, waiting for its day in the sun. The maps of that period make no mention of a Lee Vining settlement, only "Rancho Vining."[21] For many years, most activity in the area occurred at Mono Diggings, Lundy Canyon, and Hammond's general store (all north of the present Lee Vining). Most of the original Euro-American settlers were miners and merchants, whose greatest "strikes" were dug from the pockets of wealthy eastern investors.

As their fortunes faded, many of the miners turned to farming and ranching. Those who had cut timbers for mine shafts now milled lumber for ranches and corrals. In 1878, the Porter sawmill began operation in Lee Vining Canyon at a site about two miles west of Lee Vining's original mill.[22] Over time, farm houses and barns began to dot the vast high country basin. Living conditions were as remote and harsh as the location itself. Reflecting the severity of the situation, a small settlement known only as Poverty Flats sprang up along the western shore of Mono Lake, then disappeared into wastelands.

The main north-south route on the east side of the Sierra Nevada lay to the east of Mono Lake, where the Esmeralda Toll Road was replaced by the Bodie Railway and Lumber Co. Rail Road in 1881. A few years later, another toll road was established between Monoville and Mammoth City, some forty miles to the south. Running along the west side of the lake, the route was set well above today's modern north-south highway.[23] Even the creation of Yosemite National Park in 1890 sparked little interest or development in the Mono Lake region. In most respects, the basin remained a remote wilderness, with a few barns, ranch houses, and abandoned mines the only human marks on the landscape.

Meanwhile, several persons who had hiked with Muir and LeConte conceived the idea of an organization to advance the efforts of those early Sierra trailblazers. At Berkeley, the center of "Sierra tramping," students and faculty had discussed the idea of forming such a club or association for some time, and professor J. H. Senger became a driving force for the movement.[24] Several names for the proposed organization were suggested. Muir volunteered "Alpine Club" and committed his support to the proposed organization.[25]

Eventually a student suggestion found favor, and with the help of a large number of mountain enthusiasts (inspired in no small way by LeConte's initial excursion trip along the old Mono Trail), the Sierra Club came into existence on June 4, 1892. "The one thing which finally brought the matter to a head was the creation of Yosemite, Sequoia, and General Grant national parks in October of 1890," LeConte's son wrote years later.[26] A charter and bylaws were drafted. Although the senior LeConte was in Europe at the time, he was recognized for his pioneering efforts and designated as one of the organization's charter members. Muir was elected the club's first president and served until his death twenty-two years later.

One Sierra Club member who was influential in the development of trails in the organization's namesake mountains was Theodore S. Solomons of San Francisco. As a troubled teenager, Solomons had been sent to his uncle's Fresno ranch for some on-the-farm therapy (otherwise known as manual labor). There, while tending cattle, he was stunned by the beauty of the distant, snowcapped Sierra to the east. Solomons vowed that someday he would visit that mountain world. After graduating from high school, Solomons acted on that vow, visiting Lake Tahoe, where he began to develop his hiking and survival skills.

In May 1892, Solomons, accompanied by Sierra Club members Little Joe LeConte and Sidney Peixotto, traveled to Tuolumne Meadows and began to prospect a route to the south. Most of the Sierra high country was as yet unexplored and unknown—a terra incognita—familiar only to a few miners, mountaineers, and herders. While LeConte, Lembert, and other trailblazers had sought a trans-Sierra crossing, Solomons and his companions hoped to find a route that would allow them to travel the

Theodore S. Solomons used the Tioga wagon road to launch his quest for a Sierra crest trail connecting Yosemite and Kings Canyon. Photo from the Shirley Sargent collection.

These tandem cyclists, shown posing in Yosemite Valley, followed later in the tire tracks of W. B. Holland of Fresno, who crossed the Sierra Nevada via Tioga Pass on his bicycle in 1894.

entire length of the range from Yosemite to Kings Canyon, somewhere along its crest. After a few weeks, LeConte[27] and Peixotto returned to their respective homes, leaving Solomons to trek alone.

Accompanied only by his mule, Solomons picked his way through the maze of canyons and ridges of the sprawling upper San Joaquin River basin. There was no word from the explorer for nearly a month, and as autumn weather approached, his Bay Area friends began to worry about his safety. Slowed by his inability to find a crossing of the San Joaquin River (apparently he used Sheeps Crossing), Solomons didn't appear in Wawona until September 10, 1892, having completed something of a circle of Yosemite. There he met Galen Clark, who informed Solomons that a search party was about to begin looking for his body, fearing that the hiker had been killed by a bear.[28]

Not every high country traveler journeyed on foot or horseback. On August 28, 1894, the *Fresno Morning Republican* reported that W. B. Holland had returned from a 782-mile cycling trip that included the first-ever crossing of the Sierra by bicycle. Without direct reference to the Tioga Road, the article details a loop trip from Fresno west to Monterey, then east to Placerville and Carson City, south to Mono County, and back through Yosemite to Fresno.

"The difficult part of the trip began in Mono Co. He made up his mind to do what no one else had ever done and what no one else would be apt to attempt, and he mounted his wheel and headed west across the Mono desert toward the base of the Sierra Nevada. He soon passed beyond all roads and only a narrow trail traveled by miners and sheepherders led up the mountains.

"This distance was nine miles to the summit, and the mountains rose in that distance 9,000 feet. It was a big undertaking to walk and push the wheel up the rough trail, but a Chinese sheepherder came along at that time, and for a consideration, he strapped the bicycle on the back of a mule and packed it up that nine steep miles. From the

Opposite: Theodore S. Solomons, often called the father of the John Muir Trail, surveys the Evolution Basin country near Kings Canyon, circa 1915. Photo courtesy of the Shirley Sargent collection.

In 1895, Solomons (right) and his traveling partner Ernest C. Bonner established a route from Yosemite to Kings Canyon that foreshadowed the creation of the John Muir Trail. Photo courtesy of the Shirley Sargent collection.

top of the mountain the general grade of the trail was downhill to Yosemite, and Mr. Holland pushed his wheel and made the distance in a couple of days."

The article related a chance meeting with an old hermit who lived in a meadow on the western slope of the pass—but failed to identify the "very strange person" and finely educated man as, undoubtedly, John Lembert, the pioneer settler of Tuolumne Meadows.

The report of Holland's epic bicycle ride noted that the greatest distance he pedaled in one day was about one hundred miles—but "the nine miles were harder than the 100 miles." It also mentioned that the "Indians in Mono County fled like deer" when they first caught sight of Holland's bicycle.

Theodore Solomons next returned to the Sierra in the summer of 1894, when he resumed his trek of two years earlier. He was accompanied by another Sierra Club friend, Leigh Bierce, also of San Francisco. In preparation for their trip, the two had talked with Muir and secured his advice on the mountains south of Yosemite. The pair left Tuolumne Meadows around the first of September and stumbled through the uncharted wilderness of the park around the Minarets. Gradually they pushed their way around Silver Divide into Vermilion Valley, on the Mono Creek tributary of the South Fork of the San Joaquin River. The end of the month found them in the Bear Creek country, as the days began to shorten and get colder.

They awoke on the morning of September 30 to find that nearly four feet of snow had fallen during the night. "We were on top of the Sierra, some 75 miles of nearly waist-deep snow between us and the nearest settlement," Solomons related.[29] The two men abandoned their equipment and shot their remaining mule so he would not suffer, then headed for Fresno. After three days of struggling through the snow, they happened upon a herder who revived them with a steaming leg of mutton. On October 8, the two men staggered into Fresno, far from their planned destination, but alive and undaunted.[30]

In June of the following summer, Solomons set off for the Bear Creek country with yet another partner, Ernest C. Bonner. By mid-July they had made their way to the South Fork of the San Joaquin River and a high mountain bowl Solomons named Evolution Basin. The two spent several days in this wonderland of mountains and meadows, making first ascents and naming the crown of six towering peaks after famed evolutionists and scholars Charles Darwin, Thomas Huxley, Herbert Spencer, Alfred Wallace, Ernst Haeckel, and John Fiske.

Solomons and Bonner continued into the Kings River drainage and became faced with some of the most rugged terrain they had yet encountered. After multiple demanding climbs and descents, they arrived in Kings Canyon on July 28, 1895. "I had now completed a kind of reconnaissance of the unexplored High Sierra. It fell short by perhaps 95 percent of the original preposterous scheme of a complete exploration, but I had at least followed down the range from Yosemite to the Kings River Canyon, and that is what I had made up my mind to do."[31] Solomons had proven that a crest line trail was possible, and his efforts foreshadowed the John Muir Trail that eventually would run from Yosemite Valley to Mount Whitney.

Notes

1. Joseph L. LeConte, *Journal of Ramblings through the High Sierras of California* (Yosemite: Yosemite Association, 1994), 53.

2. Joseph LeConte and William Dallam Armes, *The Autobiography of Joseph LeConte* (New York: D. Appleton and Co., 1903), 16-21.

3. LeConte, *Journal of Ramblings*, 54.

4. Ibid.

5. Ibid., 56.

6. Ibid., 58.

7. Ibid.

8. William F. Kimes and Maymie B. Kimes, *John Muir—A Reading Bibliography* (Fresno: Panorama West Books, 1986), 13 (item 46).

9. Joseph N. LeConte, "My First Summer in the Kings River Sierra," *Sierra Club Bulletin* XXVI, no. 1 (February 1941): 9-14. This is an account of LeConte's 1890 trip with Hubert P. Dyer, Cornelius Lakeman, and Fred S. Phelby.

10. Ibid.

11. Linda Wedel Greene, *Historic Resource Study: Yosemite*, vol. 1 (Washington, D.C.: U.S. Department of the Interior, National Park Service, 1987), 201.

12. Keith A. Trexler, *The Tioga Road—A History, 1883–1961* (Yosemite: Yosemite Natural History Association, 1980), 7.

13. George Davidson, "The Occupation of Mount Conness," *The Overland Monthly* 15 (February 1892): 114-125.

14. Ibid.

15. Ibid.

16. Ibid.

17. Ibid.

18. Ibid.

19. Ibid.

20. "How to Go to Yosemite Valley," *Carson Daily Index*, 28 May 1887; reprinted in *Yosemite* 52, no. 3 (summer 1990): 9.

21. Clayton's 1861 Map of Esmeralda and Mono, 1861; Bancroft Library, University of California, ref.15.CsM55.

22. Thomas C. Fletcher, *Paiute, Prospector, Pioneer* (Lee Vining, Calif.: Artemisia Press, 1987), 72.

23. Ibid., 53.

24. Joseph N. LeConte, "The Sierra Club," *Sierra Club Bulletin* X, no. 2 (January 1917): 135-145.

25. Ibid., 135-142.

26. Ibid., ix.

27. Theodore S. Solomons, "The Beginnings of the John Muir Trail," *Sierra Club Bulletin* XXV, no. 1 (February 1940): 28-31.

28. Ibid., 30.

29. Ibid.

30. Hal Roth, *Pathway in the Sky* (Berkeley: Howell-North Books, 1965), 32.

31. Shirley Sargent, *Solomons of the Sierra* (Yosemite: Flying Spur Press, 1989), 40.

CHAPTER 7

THE SIERRA CLUB AMONG THE MOUNTAINS

The Sierra Club's purpose was "to explore, enjoy and render accessible the mountains of the Pacific Coast . . . and preserve the forest and other natural features of the Sierra Nevada."[1] Because its roster included a group of mountaineers, scientists, and laypeople who wanted to preserve and protect the Sierra Nevada while enjoying and learning about it, it's not surprising that group expeditions were proposed as a club activity.

One member (who became a frequent outing participant), Lincoln Hutchinson, developed a list of sixteen possible "wagon trips" that could be made to the area between Lake Tahoe and the southern Sierra. At the top of his list stood Tioga Pass, which Hutchinson described as "probably the finest of the wagon-trips . . . the road is very rough in places but not impassable." He noted that the route offered wonderful side trips to such places as Hetch Hetchy, Mount Conness, and Mount Lyell, but warned that "the horses should be strong animals, built for endurance rather that speed" and urged a leisurely pace.[2] "Be content to travel slowly," he advised, knowing that the crumbling wagon road allowed little choice.

In July 1900, his brother J. S. Hutchinson and a group of Sierra Club friends decided to visit the area around Mount Dana. In describing the wagon road they used as their trail, Hutchinson remarked on its condition. "[S]everal times we had kept company with this road in its ups and downs, turning and twisting, from Crocker's to the Meadows, and had often wished to see the location of the old Tioga Mine, which had led men, eighteen years ago to expend $62,000 in building this substantial road through a rough and rugged country. For a mile or two after our start we kept on the level; then the road was forced by the stream to take to the side of the mountain, and it soon became exceedingly narrow, but not in the least dangerous. In places it was rough, but still no great care was needed in driving our spring wagon over it.

"About a mile up the grade we met a small band of Indians on horses—about eight in all . . . probably crossing the mountains from the Mono Plain. They seemed surprised at the sight of us with our wagon. Attempts

Opposite: The Sierra Club's Parsons Lodge (built in 1915) has long been a meeting place for members and park visitors in Tuolumne Meadows. The lodge, shown here in 1939, became property of the National Park Service in 1973.

J. S. Hutchinson and his Sierra Club group visited the remains of the Tioga Mine in 1900. The old stable building, shown here, still stands.

to carry on a conversation with them were almost futile, for their English vocabulary was exceedingly small, and our Indian vocabulary still smaller."[3]

In broken English, one Indian warned the travelers that the road above was "no good," the proof of which Hutchinson's party soon established. On a steep hillside above a rushing creek, the road had washed away, forcing the group to make emergency repairs before they could proceed. Unhitching the horses and roping up the wagon, the group managed to move the wagon around the washout and up the road. A short distance beyond they came upon a large downed tree blocking their way. Camping that night in a small meadow west of Mount Dana, the party moved on the next morning to explore the remains of the Tioga Mine.

The abandoned mine was an eerie sight, rapidly becoming a ghost town. Hutchinson observed: "The buildings of the mining settlement consist of an assay office, blacksmith shop, storehouse, boarding houses, workshops and cabins of various sorts, all in fairly good state of preservation considering the length of time they have been neglected. The foundations of many are somewhat askew, and the roofs of others are crushed by winter snows. The whole settlement has the appearance of having been deserted without a moment's notice, as though the population, fearful of some great cataclysm, had suddenly fled as for a burning Vesuvius."[4]

Hutchinson's group spent three more days roaming along the crest before heading home. The members were satisfied with what they saw, according to their leader. "The trip to Saddlebag Lake and Mt. Dana can be recommended because of the beautiful and varied views obtained on each, and also because of the ease with which the trips can be taken. . . We all returned to the Meadows, well pleased with the few days which we had spent about the mountains, he reported.[5]

When the nine-year-old Sierra Club decided to hold its first "official" high country outing in 1901, its members used the old Mono Trail as well as the abandoned Tioga wagon road to reach the site of their encampment, Tuolumne Meadows. After gathering in Yosemite Valley, where the

experience was marred by the sudden death of professor Joseph LeConte, the ninety-six adventurers headed up the Yosemite Falls Trail and into the park's high country. A supply train had left Merced a week earlier, but it was delayed by downed trees, lingering snow, broken bridges, and other obstructions. The main hiking group eventually rendezvoused with the supply wagons at Porcupine Flat, where outing members held their "first truly Sierra Club pow-wow" around a glorious campfire.[6]

"From Porcupine Flat to the permanent camping place, the trip was made interesting by obstacles to be surmounted, and it was a sight to see dignified college professors, wily limbs of the law, deft doctors and reverend clergy men join gleefully in rolling rocks, lifting logs and shoveling snow to make way for the commissary, while the road-makers sent out by the owners of the Tioga Road used dynamite, where blasting was necessary, and moved more serious obstacles with their teams."[7]

Along the route, the campers stopped at Tenaya Lake, where they spent another night. Gradually, the privately-owned road was cleared and the camping gear and supplies moved up the mountainside. When the group reached Tuolumne Meadows, it set up base camp on the south side of the Tuolumne River opposite Lembert Dome. There at "Camp Muir," the campers pitched their tents and laid out bedrolls, pinning together blankets that served as their sleeping bags. Meanwhile, a pair of professional cooks set up a permanent kitchen, and began the task of feeding the ever-hungry hikers.

This initial high country outing included several individuals who would

The Sierra Club's first outing at Tuolumne Meadows in 1901 gave the young organization motivation and mission. Among those present were John Muir, William Colby, and Edward Parsons. Photo courtesy of James Snyder.

guide the destiny of the club for many years. Club president John Muir was there, along with William E. Colby, club secretary and chairman of the outing committee, and newcomer Edward T. Parsons, who acted as Colby's assistant. A native of New York, Parsons had found success in the business world and pleasure among the peaks of North America. He had gained experience as a mountaineer with the Appalachian Mountain Club, the Mountaineers of Washington, and the Mazama Club of Oregon.

Colby and Parsons put together an ambitious schedule of hikes and field trips, some involving treks of up to twenty miles. On the first major hike, forty-nine members of the group, relying on the wagon road for a trail, hiked from Tuolumne Meadows to the base of Mount Dana, then scrambled to the 13,000-foot summit. "The climb of Dana was a tedious one," Parsons observed, "but the thrill of conquest and the fascinating features of mountain scenery amply repaid the trampers." Parsons also paid solicitous tribute to the "vigor and endurance of the Berkeley girls, not one of whom were a drag on the progress of the excursion."[8]

Two days later, twenty-six trampers set out on the outing's most strenuous trip—an overnight hike to 13,120-foot Mount Lyell, Yosemite's highest peak. After establishing a base camp in Lyell Canyon, the mountaineers headed upwards the following morning. "Snow was soon encountered and some steep snow-climbs enjoyed. Good progress was made up on to the Lyell Glacier, and along the snowfields that extended several miles up the broken rocky pinnacle at the summit."[9]

Things got interesting at the base of the summit. "Here we found real danger awaiting us. The broken rocks of the peak, loosely piled on top of one another and almost perpendicular for nearly 300 feet, seemed ready to topple and fall on us every minute. However, without accident, all registered on the summit by 11:30. Never was a luncheon eaten with more magnificent surroundings," added Parsons.[10]

During the outing that lasted nearly three weeks, the group ranged far and wide, hiking to Cathedral Lake, Bloody Canyon, and Lembert Dome, which jutted into the sky opposite the encampment. Some of the members even ventured into the Grand Canyon of the Tuolumne.

A daily highlight of the first outing was the evening campfire program. Colby had arranged for a half-dozen professors from Berkeley and Stanford to address the group and share their knowledge. "At the large campfires every evening the grave and the gay prevailed by turns. Professor Dudley of Stanford gave some delightful talks on the forestry of the region. Dr. C. Hart Merriam of the U. S. Biological Survey, who was in that region with his family for the summer, joined our encampment while we were there. He told of the bird and animal life of the Sierra. John Muir, our honored and popular president, turned the pages of Nature's book for us," Parsons noted.[11]

As the outing came to a close, the campers packed up and drifted away. Camp Muir was dismantled on July 29, but a new institution had been born. Before the participants departed, they vowed to come back again.

The outing, most agreed, had been a huge success, paying many

Edward T. Parsons, top, and William E. Colby, below, guided the development of the early Sierra Club.

dividends. Among other benefits, it resulted in a newfound sense of discovery and adventure for a large number of urban dwellers exposed to the natural beauty of the Sierra high country for the first time. They recognized that they could not only survive, but thrive in the wilderness world. More than anything, the 1901 outing brought Sierra Club members together and provided a focus and mission they had not known before.

In 1902, the Sierra Club outing moved to Kings Canyon, but it routinely returned to the Yosemite high country in subsequent years. Over the next decade, the outings grew in size (coming to be as large as two to three hundred people), and became a key activity in the club's program. They also helped make the Tioga Pass region known to a growing number of mountain lovers.

In 1904, a group of fourteen Sierra Clubbers was organized by Edward Parsons to traverse the length of the Tuolumne River Canyon from the meadows to Hetch Hetchy Valley.

William Frederic Badè, in

The Muir Gorge section of the Tuolumne River Canyon, pictured here, provided a real challenge to the Sierra Club party led by Edward Parsons in 1904.

describing the canyon, observed that "For a long time it was considered impassable. In places the walls rise in almost vertical precipices to a height of more than five thousand feet. Though the canyon is scarcely more than thirty miles long, the fall of the river within that distance amounts to five thousand two hundred feet. It would be hard to imagine a wilder career for a river than that upon which the Tuolumne enters during this part of its course. Captain Clarence King, after a futile attempt to follow it through the cañon, is said to have pronounced such an undertaking impossible for any 'creature without wings.'"[12]

Clawing its way down the gorge, Parsons' group inched along. "The second day we passed through what is probably the wildest and deepest part of the cañon. The river now had gone stark mad. One who has not seen the Tuolumne during this part of its course would hardly deem a river capable of such acrobatic feats, such head-long abandon."[13]

On the fourth day of their journey, the tired and tattered adventurers reach Hetch Hetchy. "Our clothing was mostly shreds, and our shoes,

Top: Parsons Memorial Lodge was built by the Sierra Club in 1915 as a shelter for outings and other club activities. Photo courtesy of James Snyder.

Bottom: Soda Springs at Tuolumne Meadows and the adjacent Parsons Lodge were owned as part of a private inholding by the Sierra Club for many years. The property was sold to the National Park Service in 1973. Photo from the Stellman Collection courtesy of the California State Library.

in not a few cases, had to be excused from further service. But we had conquered the cañon, hitherto traversed by only a few hardy explorers, and had brought with us a rich store of memories," wrote Badè.[14]

The 1915 outing represented what the Sierra Club described as a "radical departure" from the usual high trips. It was a somewhat somber year, for the club was mourning the loss of its extraordinary outing leader, Edward Parsons, who had died a year earlier.[15] The program ran all summer, starting with a camp in Yosemite Valley that moved to the high country. To ease the trek to Tuolumne Meadows, the outing committee located a smaller camp at Tenaya Lake, which allowed the participants to make the trip in smaller sections. From the lake, the outing participants moved on to the main camp, a newly-acquired section of land at Soda Springs in Tuolumne Meadows.

The new "campground" came into being when the Sierra Club secured title to John Lembert's 160 acres around Soda Springs. The group made plans to construct a lodge on the property to serve the outings and other club programs. Construction of "Parsons Lodge" (named in memory of the revered leader) began later that year.

Another devastating loss had occurred the previous year when club president John Muir died on Chrismas Eve. Though he succumbed to pneumonia, many followers attributed his death to his disappointment over the loss of Hetch Hetchy Valley. To recognize Muir's many contributions to the Sierra, a proposal was advanced to develop a hiking and equestrian trail named for the great conservationist, with a route that would run along the crest of the Sierra. Thus, the John Muir Trail came into being, extending from Yosemite Valley to Mount Whitney and passing along the wagon road and through other areas that the departed Muir held dear.[16]

The Sierra Club appreciated the role that the rustic wagon road had played in the development of its programs and membership. In 1915, it joined with the Mather mountain party to celebrate the acquisition of the Tioga Road, which would become one of the more significant roads in the nation (see Chapter 8). While making no reference to the access the road afforded, club president Joseph N. LeConte noted that "the outings have steadily grown in size and perfection of organization, until now they stand as the most popular single feature of the club," and a model for other mountaineering clubs.[17]

For those who had trudged up the Mono Trail, the arrival of the

With a couple of spare tires, a tankful of gas and a lot of resolve, the intrepid motorist of the late 1920s might travel the Tioga Road in style. Photo from the Stellman Collection courtesy of the California State Library.

automobile brought promise as well as problems. The tiring tramps along the old trail were coming to an end. In 1916, LeConte made his first automotive foray along the purportedly repaired Tioga wagon road. It was a motoring adventure of epic proportions. LeConte and his family were accompanied in another car by his long-time mountaineering friend, Jim (J. S.) Hutchinson. For such a daring journey, there was safety and support in numbers.

LeConte and Hutchinson realized in advance that the "road" was little more than a widened mountain trail, better suited to pack animals and trampers than to tin-lizzies. The route was unpaved, unsigned, and ill-prepared for the approaching motorcade. Washouts, slides, patches of snow, mud holes, and downed trees provided ample road hazards and challenges. The group finally reached Tuolumne Meadows, then camped for a few days and readied their vehicles for the final push over the summit.

On the departure morning, LeConte got off first and reached Tioga Pass with little problem. "At the summit we waited and waited for Jim. It was over an hour before he came in. He had been delayed by another car, stuck in the mud, where it could not be passed. We went down to a place below Lake Tioga where there was a fierce mud hole. Several other cars were there, and the people were throwing in rocks to give a bottom. We all plunged through it, however, in safety. . . Then we went down the wonderful state road to the bottom of Lee Vining Canyon."[18]

Despite the obstacles, LeConte would return again and again. In the summer of 1918, he found the road in as poor a condition as ever. Over the winter hundreds of wind-thrown trees had toppled onto the road. The usual winter damage from slides and washouts caused other delays. LeConte's motorized caravan was forced to follow the repair crews up the road. Day by day they moved along, camping at night wherever the road workers did. He realized later that it would have been easier and faster to hike; from Crocker's Station it took nearly a month to reach Tuolumne Meadows.[19]

John L. Williams, a popular Yosemite author of the early 1900s, observed that "the Sierrans testify their love of the mountains by spending a month each summer among them. It was my privilege a few years ago to join the club's large party at their camp in Tuolumne Meadows, and there learn how 250 men and women, drawn from all the professions, lawyers, teachers and business men, students, doctors, preachers, were able, after a day's climb, to gather about a huge campfire and jest away their weariness in songs. Ah, those mountain firesides, after the long marches over the snow-fields, or across the passes, or down the cañons!" he enthused.[20]

Notes

1. David Brower, ed., *Sierra Club Handbook* (San Francisco: Sierra Club, 1957), 1.

2. Lincoln Hutchinson, "Wagon-Trips to the Sierra," *Sierra Club Bulletin* III, no. 1 (February 1901): 215-16.

3. J. S. Hutchinson, Jr., "Round Mount Dana," *Sierra Club Bulletin* III, no. 4 (June 1901): 320-23.

4. Ibid.

5. Ibid.

6. E. T. Parsons, "The Sierra Club Outing to Tuolumne Meadows," *Sierra Club Bulletin* IV, no. 1 (January 1902): 19-22.

7. Ibid., 21.

8. Ibid., 22.

9. Ibid.

10. Ibid.

11. Ibid.

12. William Frederic Badè, "The Tuolumne Cañon," *Sierra Club Bulletin* IV, no. 4 (June 1905): 287-296.

13. Ibid.

14. Ibid.

15. Parsons, "Sierra Club Outing," 22.

16. Hal Roth, *Pathway in the Sky* (Berkeley: Howell-North, 1965), 23-29.

17. Joseph N. LeConte, "The Sierra Club," *Sierra Club Bulletin* X, no. 2 (January 1917): 135.

18. Joseph LeConte journals, Bancroft Library, C-B 452; Vol. 33, 1907-16.

19. Ibid., 1917-22.

20. John L. Williams, *Yosemite and Its High Sierra* (Tacoma and San Francisco: self-published, 1914), 113.

CHAPTER 8

STEPHEN MATHER
PAVES THE WAY

Few of the thousands of visitors who make their way over Tioga Pass each year notice the small stone marker beside the Tioga Road a few feet inside the park boundary. That marker memorializes a man whose work was critical to the development of the Tioga Road, Yosemite National Park, and the National Park System. That system now embraces more than 350 parks, monuments, historic sites, seashores, and recreation areas, and serves as a model for preserves around the world.

A bronze plaque set in the stone at Tioga Pass reads: "This tablet commemorates the successful labors of Stephen T. Mather, Director of the National Park Service, in securing for the people the Tioga Pass Road. Dedicated to the enduring memory of a faithful public servant by the members of the Brooklyn Daily Eagle, National Park Development Tour, July 20, 1924." What the marker fails to note, however, is that the Tioga Road symbolizes the birth of the National Park Service, and served as its crucible.

Stephen Mather's trail to the Tioga summit followed a circuitous path. He was born, raised, and educated in California. He made his first trip to Yosemite as a ten-year-old in 1877. Upon graduation from the University of California at Berkeley in 1887, he worked as a reporter for the *Chicago Sun* for five years. After meeting his future wife, June Thacker Floy of New Jersey,[1] Mather joined the Pacific Coast Borax Co. as what would now be classified as a marketing director. He and a partner soon took control of the company, and Mather became wealthy in the process.

Though his work took him away from California, Mather's love affair with the mountains drew him back to the Sierra. In the early 1900s he learned about the Sierra Club from Berkeley and Bay Area friends, and began to participate in the club's outings. In 1905 he ascended the summit of Mount Rainier on a club trip.[2] His unique combination of charisma and conscience was revealed to the Sierra Club members who came to know him. "Mather was a striking alloy of drive and amiability. He had a horde of interests, and he mixed among them with a zeal that crackled. His fire

Opposite: National Park Service Director Stephen T. Mather believed so much in the importance of the Tioga Road that he contributed financially to its acquisition.

Stephen T. Mather assumed directorship of the national parks in 1917. He served through the presidential administrations of Wilson, Harding, and Coolidge, but the matter of his politics was never inquired into by any party.

was indescribable and absolutely unique," his friend Francis Farquhar observed.³

In 1912 Mather met John Muir while on a family outing in the Kern River Canyon. By then, Mather had become an avid mountaineer, and had developed a preservationist's philosophy and a deep respect for the great natural beauty of the western parks. When Mather made a visit to Yosemite, Sequoia, and three or four other national parks in 1914, he was appalled by the neglect and lack of facilities.

Mather had reason to be concerned. The concept of a park bureau had been broached well before Mather's time, beginning in 1864, with the creation of the Yosemite Grant, which ceded Yosemite Valley and the Mariposa Grove of Big Trees to the state of California. In 1872 Yellowstone National Park was established to protect the geysers and great natural features of the Wyoming Territory. Sequoia, Grant Grove, and a larger Yosemite became national parks in 1890. In short order, Mount Rainier, Crater Lake, Glacier, Rocky Mountain, and Mesa Verde National Parks were added to the list. While big parks such as Yellowstone, Sequoia, and Yosemite had received protection from the cavalry, the other twelve units were all but ignored by the General Land Office, the agency charged by the Department of the Interior with handling the new parks. The fifteen national parks and eighteen national monuments had no unified focus, direction, or support. Each area operated independently.

Mather complained to Interior Secretary Franklin Lane, a long-time friend and fraternity brother from his college days at Berkeley. Lane's jocular response is now famous: "Dear Steve, if you don't like the way the national parks are being run, come on down to Washington and run them yourself."⁴

Mather had never worked for government and felt some aversion to joining the bureaucracy. But Lane persisted, going so far as to offer Mather the position as assistant interior secretary. "I cannot offer you rank or fame or salary—only a chance to do some great public service," Lane pronounced.⁵ Mather accepted the challenge, and by 1915 he was hard at work, providing new leadership and direction for the embryonic collection of national parks.

One of Mather's first acts was to hire as his assistant Horace Albright, another Berkeley friend and alumnus, an attorney, and a Sierra Club member. Albright was about half Mather's age and had been working for the interior secretary as a clerk, using his expertise in land and mining law. Mather informed Albright that his new job was to help build the park system—and to keep Mather "out of jail."⁶ Mather next scheduled a three-day National Parks Conference on the University of California campus (attended by auto clubs, tourist agencies, and government officials) to develop goals and a collective vision for the parks with the advice of those who best knew them.

Slowly Mather's plan began to take shape. Crucial to his management approach was public support for the parks, based on finding a balance between preservation on one hand and use and enjoyment by the public

on the other. Unlike John Muir and the Sierra Club, Mather felt that the best way to preserve these natural resources was to make them known and accessible. Out of that appreciation, he believed, care and protection would follow. While conservation was his over-arching goal, he felt strongly that visitor comfort should play an important role in guiding park management. "Scenery is a hollow enjoyment to a tourist who sets out in the morning after an indigestible breakfast and a fitful sleep on an impossible bed," Mather told the conference.[7]

As the summer of 1915 approached, Mather made plans to gain new park support. He and Albright gathered a select party of nineteen influential individuals who could mold public opinion and force government action, and scheduled an introductory trip to the national parks of the high Sierra. The group included congressmen, journalists, and other movers and shakers, and subsequently became known as the "Mather Mountain Party." Perhaps the most influential member was Gilbert S. Grosvenor, director of the National Geographic Society, editor of its magazine, and an enthusiastic fan of the parks. The group assembled in Visalia, motored to Sequoia National Park, and then undertook a ten-day horseback trip from Giant Forest to Mineral King, then across the Sierra crest to Lone Pine on the eastern side. The outing was a mind-expanding experience for the easterners—and the occasion for Mather to explain his vision for the national parks, including an expanded Sequoia National Park.

From Lone Pine, the group drove north to Bishop, where Mather and Albright met many of their old Sierra friends, along with representatives of several auto and travel clubs. The next day, the mountaineers drove north toward Mono Lake, making their way up a rough and rugged Sherwin Grade—a primitive county road that would one day become state Highway 395. At Deadman Hill, the cars ran out of power (or traction)

In 1915, Stephen Mather (shown at far left), then assistant to the Secretary of the Interior, brought a group of prominent conservationists to the Sierra to promote its national parks. To his left is National Geographic editor Gilbert H. Grosvenor, who made the picture with a delayed-action trigger. Photo courtesy of the National Geographic Society. Copyright National Geographic Society.

and had to be towed over one steep section by work horses. At Mono Lake, the motorcade turned west and began the long, rough climb up the newly-completed canyon road, toward Tioga Pass.

Years later, Albright recalled the party's ride up Lee Vining Canyon in an open touring car: "Our . . . Studebaker, was driven by Will L. Smith, a groceryman from Bishop. . . Now Smith had been around this old road off and on during the preceding weeks while government crews were improving it, and stated that he knew every turn. It wasn't long before we prayed he was right. He wanted us to see all the sights, so sometimes he would stand up in his seat, turn around and point this way and that, but never stopping the car. Now two-thousand-foot precipices on the left and rock cliffs on the right were the only alternatives to the narrow, one-lane rut we were driving on. We novices to Sierra roads were terrified.

"Whenever Smith stood up, I poised at the open door, foot ready on the running board to leap when the car went over. [Emerson] Hough was right behind me, clutching my coat, ready to jump in tandem. After three or four of these heart-stopping moments, Hough sobbed hoarsely in my ear, 'Goddam this scenery-loving sonofabitch.' As for [Ernst] McCormick, he was frozen in his seat, later saying he feared for his life, that any movement or sound he might make would be the end of us all."[8]

Both Mather and Albright had been familiar with the Great Sierra Wagon Road for some time. They saw the wagon road not just as a way to lure motorists to the park—especially those headed for the approaching world fairs at San Francisco and San Diego. More importantly, they believed that better access to Yosemite would help build support for the idea of an improved park system.

In 1914, Mather had learned that the owners of the toll road, heirs to the Swift Packing Co., were willing to sell their interest in the thoroughfare for $15,500 if a quick cash sale could be arranged. He moved promptly to secure an option, but faced

Stephen T. Mather descending Lembert Dome at Tuolumne Meadows in 1921.

many obstacles before actual transfer of the road to the government could be made. Complicating the transaction was the fact that the route was in need of major repair, and this would require even additional money. How, doubters wondered, could the director get the necessary capital from a suspicious and often parsimonious Congress? To fund the purchase, in 1915 Mather wrote a personal check for $5,000 and executed a promissory note in his own name for another $7,500. Contemporaneously, the state of California agreed to buy the section of the road east of the park boundary (for $3,000), and to the west,

Tuolumne County accepted responsibility for the Big Oak Flat segment.

Mather lobbied Congress for support and was rewarded when a law was passed in 1915 that authorized the acquisition of the wagon road through gifts of land and money. The resourceful Mather solicited as many donations as possible, hoping to cover his own expenditures (and triggering questions from concerned critics). He eventually regained a major portion of his seed money. Finally, the high road was donated to the government, and long-needed repairs were made. Mather's personal contribution to the purchase of the Tioga Road earned him the nickname of the "millionaire mountaineer."

As the the mountain party from Bishop made its way towards Tioga Pass on July 28, 1915, a dedication ceremony, planned by Sierra Club leaders William Colby and Clair Tappan, awaited the group. At the summit, the half dozen cars in the Mather caravan were met by the assembled Sierra Club members, who had stretched a ceremonial ribbon across the roadway. Mather cut the ribbon to officially open the new Tioga Pass Road.

In Mather's remarks, the Assistant Interior Secretary pointed out that the transfer of the road to the national park marked the end of private exploitation of the roadway and the beginning of toll-free entrance to Yosemite. Mather noted that the date marked the twenty-fifth anniversary of the creation of Sequoia, General Grant, and Yosemite National Parks, and expressed his hope that one day the three Sierra parks might be combined into one national park.

Then members of the party placed a stone on the boundary line of

Wrapped in an American flag, Stephen Mather dedicated the Tioga Road as a toll-free entrance to Yosemite in 1915. He broke a champagne bottle full of water from the Pacific Ocean to symbolize the movement of water and people over the Sierra crest. Photo courtesy of the National Geographic Society. Copyright National Geographic Society.

Horace Albright, hired by Stephen Mather to be his assistant in the Department of Interior in 1915, was instrumental in the creation of the National Park Service in 1916. He became its first assistant director.

Yosemite. Mather broke a champagne bottle full of water from the Pacific Ocean against the rock to symbolize the movement of water and people across the Sierra crest. To record the event, National Geographic's Grosvenor photographed Mather wrapped in an American flag, as the government party and Sierra Club members looked on. Returning to the cars, the group then motored down to Tuolumne Meadows and the Sierra Club encampment near Parsons Lodge at Soda Springs. There the club hosted a hearty dinner followed by the now-traditional campfire, where more speeches were given detailing hopes and dreams for Yosemite and a greater park system.

The next morning, as the group began breaking up, Mather made one final address, this one from the back seat of an open touring car. "Now I want you to know that our job is not over. It is just beginning. Think of Sequoia as incomplete until the Kings River area is added; until Mount Whitney and its soaring granite appendages are under care of a national park, until the magnificent Giant Forest is out of private hands. And Yosemite—virgin timber and toll roads in private hands, lovely flatlands still owned by early squatters and never forget Hetch Hetchy! These must be restored to our country. Those are just two parks. We have many others and they all need protection. We must acquire and care for vast areas not under our control at this time. But most of all none of this will mean anything unless we have a safe haven for these wilderness places. We must have a National Park Service! Everyone of us must pull our oar," he declared.[9]

Mather's stirring sermon at Soda Springs had a profound effect on his audience. Colby and the other Sierra Club leaders, still smarting from the loss of Hetch Hetchy to the City of San Francisco and the recent death of their spiritual leader, John Muir, headed home, revitalized and recommitted to their mission of preservation.

Despite Mather's best efforts to reserve the first automobile crossing of the restored Tioga wagon road to his 1915 "Mountain Party," his delegation was pre-empted by an earlier group of motorized visitors. Nearly three weeks before in early July, the Fred Lester family of San Jose drove their Mitchell touring sedan over the still-under-repair road. At Tuolumne Meadows they had to ford the run-off swollen Tuolumne River near Soda Springs.

"They heard on July 8 that the Tioga Pass Road was about to open, and they left Yosemite Valley after lunch and drove as far as Tuolumne Meadows to camp. The next morning they were at the Tuolumne River and had to wait while the workmen completed the ford, using mules and Fresno scrapers. They passed through the ford on the morning of July 9 while the workmen waited to make sure they didn't get stuck, and then drove down to Lee Vining," June Lester recalled years later.[10] Thus Tioga Pass was first breeched by the horseless carriage.

Besides opening the Yosemite high country to auto traffic, the Tioga Road purchase helped establish strong ties between the Sierra Club and the park service. From its founding, the club's focus had been on Yosemite and the Sierra. Not surprisingly, five of the first six directors of the National Park Service had been Sierra Club members.[11]

Where the club was not directly involved, its kindred cousins took up the cause. In the Pacific Northwest, the Mountaineers of Seattle and the Mazamas of Oregon rallied around the park service banner. In the Rockies, the Colorado Mountain Club mounted the charge. In the east, it was the famed Appalachian Mountain Club that lent its backing to the park service agenda. In the period after World War I, the National Parks Association, the Izaak Walton League, and the Wilderness Society joined the park push.

The 1916 *Sierra Club Bulletin* contains Mather's account of the Tioga Road story. He wrote as well his hopes for the greater park system and for an agency of professionals to run it. He referred to the club's importance to the parks. "The Yosemite National Park, in which the Sierra Club is more vitally interested than any of the others, has seen much interesting development during the past year. . . I want to thank the officers of the Sierra Club, particularly your president, Professor Joseph N. LeConte, and your secretary, Mr. William E. Colby, for the assistance they have given me in working out the various problems in this park," Mather wrote.[12]

Returned to Washington, Mather continued to press his "park service" agenda. He and Albright envisioned a park agency led by professional rangers and experts (free of partisan politics and personal patronage) to fend off the exploiters and extractors. They believed that the agency should be separate and independent, unconnected to the previously established U.S. Forest Service.

Mather and Albright drafted legislation, crafting a bill that incorporated the philosophies of Muir and Frederick Law Olmsted, Jr., the son of the great American landscape architect and park planner, and their Sierra Club friends.[13] They also courted the press in an effort to spread their park service message. Newly-made friend Grosvenor was convinced to devote the entire May 1916 issue of *National Geographic* to the national parks.[14]

Congressmen William Kent and John E. Raker of California and Reed Smoot of Utah introduced the park service legislation in August, 1916. Albright assumed the responsibility for pushing the bill through Congress. Despite many challenges and proposed changes (including one to allow sheep grazing within the parks), the measure was approved the same month. Within a short time, the National Park Service was organized as the ninth bureau of the Department of Interior, with a budget of $19,500 for the salaries of five permanent employees.[15]

The function of the National Park Service was to "promote and regulate the use of the Federal areas known as national parks, monuments and reservations . . . to conserve the scenery and the natural and historic objects and the wild life therein, and to provide for the enjoyment of the same in such manner and by such means as will leave them unimpaired for the enjoyment of future generations."[16]

Mather was designated director, Albright, assistant director, and Frank W. Griffith of New York, the chief clerk of the new National Park Service.

More land units were placed under the organization's umbrella, and by 1919, the system included seventeen national parks and twenty-two monuments, and embraced over six million acres of land. In his first report to Interior Secretary Lane at the end of 1917, Mather noted an increase in national park patronage to 487,368 visitors that year[17]—a reflection of the burgeoning travel and tourism industry in the U.S. Mather praised the efforts of the automobile clubs, highway associations, and other organizations that had promoted park visitation, and cited the value of encouraging "park-to-park" travel.

One of Mather's biggest concerns was finding consistent and adequate park funding. With the creation of the National Park Service, the financial needs of the less well-known parks became more clear. But as World War I expanded, the park service chief found it increasingly difficult to obtain funds for the fledgling park system. While he had secured $30,000 for the initial repairs to the Tioga wagon road, his requests for another $75,000 to make additional improvements went unheeded.[18]

In drafting the new park legislation, Mather, Lane, and their associates went to great lengths to separate the park service from the forest service, which had been established nearly a dozen years earlier. In the process they defined a national ethic of preservation as opposed to the utilitarian conservation promoted by Gifford Pinchot.

Horace Albright succeeded Stephen Mather as Director of the National Park Service in 1929. While his tenure lasted only until 1933, in those four years he more than doubled the number of areas managed by the agency.

This ethic is reflected in the words of the statute: "The Service thus established shall promote and regulate the use of the Federal areas known as national parks, monuments, and reservations, hereinafter specified by such means and measures as conform to the fundamental purpose of said parks, monuments, and reservations, which purpose is to conserve the scenery and natural and historic objects and the wild life therein and to provide for the enjoyment of the same in such manner and by such means as will leave them unimpaired for the enjoyment of future generations."[19]

Mather envisioned the day when the larger parks could pay their own way. "I believe the time will soon come when Yellowstone, Yosemite, Mount Rainier, Sequoia, and General Grant National Parks, and probably one or two more members of the system will yield sufficient revenue to cover costs of administration and maintenance of improvements," he suggested.[20]

Development in Yosemite demonstrated Mather's management approach based on use and access. In 1916, the Desmond Park Service Co., a park concessioner, was given the green light to build "four chalet camps," at Harden Lake, Tenaya Lake, Merced Lake, and Tuolumne Meadows. The firm also was authorized to build new hotels in Yosemite Valley and at Glacier Point.

Mather dedicated himself to improving park access and accommodations. In his 1920 report he noted that the "most notable accomplishment" of that year was the establishment of the National Park-to-Park Highway.[21] Where there were not roads, Mather looked to the railroads to provide transportation and overnight lodging.

The need to develop trails and build ranger stations also was seen as important. In Yosemite, a ranger's outpost was constructed near Crane Flat in 1915; a year later a similar facility was constructed at Tuolumne Meadows. In 1917 a trail was built to Waterwheel Falls, followed by a footpath over Tuolumne Pass that linked Tuolumne Meadows with Merced Lake.

Enos A. Mills, in a 1917 article in *Your National Parks*, observed that Mather's efforts in the Tioga Road matter were of enormous importance to the future of the park system.[22] By today's environmental standards, however, Mather is seen by some to have been a director of tourism or a publicist for the parks, and he has been accused of seeking and promoting an unholy alliance with developers and commercial interests at the expense of natural systems. His work to bring luxury hotels to the parks (and thereby entice more park visitors) seems more subject to criticism than do the steps he took to provide improved access. His reform of the concessions system also served the parks well, although he failed to define what was necessary and appropriate to a park experience. Were luxury hotels and upscale dining facilities needed by park visitors? In all likelihood, neither Mather nor Albright ever imagined that a day would come when increased park visitation might compromise the concepts of preservation and protection.

Nevertheless, Mather's altruism and personal support of the park service set a standard for the nation. The country benefited repeatedly from his expenditure of his own wealth. On numerous occasions he underwrote projects Congress was unwilling to fund. Mather's methods were not always uncontroversial. In 1917, he barely escaped a political firestorm when he bailed out the failing Desmond Company in Yosemite, and then collected the loan. Over time, however, his stewardship and generosity inspired a culture of park philanthropy in the United States that resulted in the creation of Grand Teton National Park, Death Valley National Monument, and a host of other national treasures. In the National Park Service, Mather helped fashion a model for government service and attracted some of the nation's most dedicated public servants.

When Stephen Mather and Horace Albright decided in 1914 to

Stephen Mather and Washington B. Lewis, Yosemite superintendent, survey the Tioga Road, one of Mather's many legacies in the national park system, in 1925.

tackle the parks, they agreed to spend a year together, and then move on. Mather's tenure with the National Park Service lasted fourteen years. When he died in 1930, he was succeeded by Albright, through whom his devotion, dedication, and management philosophy prevailed for another decade. Albright retired in 1933. For the remaining fifty-five years of his life, he worked to ensure Mather's legacy.

It had been Yosemite that inspired Stephen Mather's tireless efforts to create a national park system, and throughout his life, Yosemite remained his favorite of the national parks.[23] George B. Hartzog, Jr., who served as NPS director from 1964-1973, observed that "Mather and Albright saw *use* as the engine to drive public support for preservation and expansion of the system. Their challenge was to build a park system. . . To a remarkable degree they succeeded."[24]

Notes

1. Robert Shankland, *Steve Mather of the National Parks* (New York: Alfred A. Knopf, 1951), 19-21.

2. Michael Cohen, *The History of the Sierra Club, 1892-1970* (San Francisco: Sierra Club, 1988), 40.

3. Shankland, *Steve Mather*, 8.

4. Horace Marden Albright and Marian Albright Schenck, *The Mather Mountain Party of 1915* (Sequoia N.P.: Sequoia Natural History Association, 1990), 3.

5. George B. Hartzog, Jr., *Battling for the National Parks* (Mt. Kisco, N.Y.: Moyer Bell Limited, 1988), 80.

6. U.S. National Park Service, *Vocation Plus Avocation Equal Preservation* (Washington, D.C.: U.S. Department of Interior, 1991). The is a N.P.S. 75th anniversary pamphlet.

7. Shirley Sargent, *Yosemite and Its Innkeepers* (Yosemite: Flying Spur Press, 1975), 47.

8. Albright and Schenck, *Mather Mountain Party*, 32.

9. Ibid., 33-34.

10. "Fred and June Lester's Tioga Pass Journey of 1915," recounted by Ron Olmstead, 15 October 1999; written account in the Yosemite Research Library.

11. "The Sierra Club on the National Scene," in David R. Brower, ed., *The Sierra Club—A Handbook* (San Francisco: Sierra Club, 1957), 11.

12. Stephen T. Mather, "National Park Notes," *Sierra Club Bulletin* X, no. 1 (January 1916): 98-101.

13. Edwin Bearss, telephone interview by author, 22 February 1991. The N.P.S. historian stated that "Olmsted, Mather and Albright all had a hand in it, reflecting their concept of what a park service should be. It probably included Muir's philosophies, but emphasized the legal training of Horace Albright."

14. National Geographic Society, *National Parks Portfolio* (Washington, D.C.: National Geographic Society, 1916). Reprinted by Charles Scribner's Sons for the Department of the Interior.

15. Cohen, *History of the Sierra Club*, 43.

16. "National Park Notes," *Sierra Club Bulletin* X, no. 3 (January 1918): 362.

17. Ibid.

18. Hartzog, *Battling for the National Parks*, 81.

19. The National Park Service Organic Act (16 U.S.C. 1 2 3, and 4) consists of the Act of August 25, 1916 (39 Stat. 535) and amendments thereto.

20. "National Park Notes," 97.

21. Stephen T. Mather, *Report of the Director of the National Park Service to the Secretary of the Interior for the Fiscal Year Ended June 30, 1920, and the Travel Season 1920* (Washington, D.C.: U.S. Government Printing Office, 1920), 37.

22. Enos A. Mills, *Your National Parks* (Boston and New York: Houghton Mifflin Co., 1917), 96.

23. Shankland, *Steve Mather*, 128.

24. Hartzog, *Battling for the National Parks*, 81.

CHAPTER 9

A New Turn in the Tioga Road

The new government-owned Tioga Road brought immediate change to the high country of Yosemite National Park. Not long after Stephen Mather helped dedicate the restored route, car counts on the road doubled and then doubled again. In 1915, its first year of public ownership, the former wagon road was traveled by 350 cars, 190 of them coming from the east side.[1]

It was an auspicious start for the scenic trans-Sierra route. As the beauty and accessibility of the Tioga region became known, a growing line of motorists headed for the park highlands. In that formative period, it seemed that most Californians with "tin Lizzies" wanted to test themselves —and their vehicles—by crossing the highest pass in the state. During 1917, 1,792 cars crossed over the pass before the winter curtain came down. Even America's entry into World War I failed to slow the pace, as 1,951 cars drove through the Tioga Pass gate in 1918.

For many of these early motorists, the road loomed as a high adventure and tested the driving skills and endurance of both human and machine. Increased use and lack of maintenance took their toll on the road, however. While some limited repairs were made, road conditions became progressively worse. Many motorists were put off, seeing the route as little more than a nearly-impassable wagon road. When Joseph Grinnell and Tracy I. Storer were conducting their research on the animal life of Yosemite in 1917, for example, they reported that the road had seriously deteriorated and was not fit for travel in their eyes. The two scientists chose to use pack animals to reach their Tuolumne Meadows destination.[2]

Funding requests for maintenance from the new director of the National Park Service, Stephen Mather, were ignored repeatedly, subordinated to the needs of World War I. Even the state was hard pressed to maintain the eastern section of the road up Lee Vining Canyon. The winter avalanches, spring snowmelt, and summer thunderstorms became annual headaches. Some motorists complained that they could hardly follow the road, clogged as it was by fallen trees, rock slides, and other debris.

Opposite: Early motorists were confronted with a Tioga Road that was narrow, steep, and curving, and conditions that produced overheating, vapor lock, and other mechanical failures.

Left: Car counts through the Tioga Pass gate grew from 350 in 1915 to 1,951 by 1918.

Right: Use of the Tioga Road by motorized vehicles was very controversial and sparked a multi-year debate over whether automobiles should be permitted on the route.

"The most frightening road in the state," charged one early motorist. "The road should be repaired or closed," suggested another. In commenting on the grade and alignment, a third critic wrote that the "road was built for the teams of a mining company, with the happy disregard of all mining roads for grades and no expectation of ever serving automobile travel."[3]

The complaints were disquieting, given events leading up to the road's re-opening. The initial proposal to permit cars to use the Tioga Road had been the subject of a long and often rancorous debate. For years, opinions had been split over the advisability of allowing automobiles into the park. The first car had sneaked into Yosemite Valley in 1900. Once the horseless carriage lost its novelty, it was viewed with suspicion in many quarters, and opposition arose.

The initial arguments focused on the unavoidable conflict between motor vehicles and animals on park roadways. Philosophical and ethical questions also arose. In 1907 Major Harry C. Benson, the commanding cavalry officer, chose to ban all cars from the park after Interior Secretary James Garfield concluded that Yosemite's roads were too "steep and narrow" to accommodate both horse teams and automobiles.

Benson's ban was immediately denounced. In 1912 the argument over horseless carriages reached its peak when representatives of various auto clubs gathered in Yosemite Valley for the National Parks Conference. There they met an anti-auto faction that was ready for a fight. One opponent summarized a common criticism: "[O]ne cannot really enjoy fine scenery when traveling at a rate of 15, 20 or 25 miles an hour. If you want to enjoy the beauty of such landscapes as the Yosemite presents, you must see them slowly. Fine scenery is seen best of all in walking, when one can stop any moment and enjoy any special point of view."[4] "Do not let the serpent enter Eden at all," he urged.

The auto clubs countered that cars had every bit as much right to enter the park as horses—and that it was a better way to visit Yosemite. Even John Muir tacitly supported motorized travel. "[Under] certainly precautionary restrictions, these useful, progressive, blunt-nosed mechanical beetles will hereafter be allowed to puff their way into all the parks and mingle their gas-breath with the breath of pines and waterfalls, and from the mountaineer's standpoint, with but little harm or good . . ." he reluctantly concluded.[5]

A year later in 1913, the new interior secretary, Franklin K. Lane, rescinded the vehicle ban, noting that he wanted to "make our parks as accessible as possible." As a result, autos again were admitted to Yosemite, but limited to use of the Coulterville Road. In addition, motorized travel was subject to a multitude of restrictions, not the least of which was a speed limit of six miles an hour, except on straight stretches, where a maximum of ten miles an hour was permissible. Ironically, horse-drawn wagons and saddle horses retained the right of way.

The door had been opened, and within a few years, the cars poured into the park in remarkable numbers. Even a $5 entrance fee imposed on the mechanical monsters did nothing to slow the trend. A new day, to be dominated by increased automobile use, had dawned for Yosemite and the national parks.[6]

Some of the earliest motorized crossings of the Tioga Road probably occurred following the completion of its Lee Vining Canyon section in 1913, though the Mather Mountain Party is generally credited for the first auto crossing in 1915.[7] After being exposed to the remarkable beauty and near vertical terrain of Lee Vining Canyon, many visitors urged its inclusion within the adjacent national park. In his 1915 report, Yosemite Superintendent George V. Bell urged that the land bordering the road be added to the park. "Lee Vining Canyon . . . is in the opinion of many people not equaled by the Grand Canyon for its impressiveness as to depth, ruggedness, and other scenic beauties."[8]

With the introduction of the very popular and affordable Model T Ford, more motorists (in addition to the auto clubs) called for improvements and the provision of support services along the Tioga Road.

The Lee Vining Canyon section of the Tioga Road was improved for automobiles in 1913. The first motorized crossings over the route probably took place in that year.

Leevining Canyon

Many believed that the highest route in the state, featuring some of the most spectacular scenery in the nation, deserved better treatment. Outposts of civilization began to appear along the road. The establishment of Desmond Park Service Company camps at Tenaya Lake and Tuolumne Meadows made those locales overnight destinations. Ranger stations were built at Crane Flat and Tuolumne Meadows to respond to the increased visitation. In 1918, growing use levels prompted the establishment of an entrance station on the Tioga Road at Aspen Valley.

During most of the summer of 1919, the road remained closed because the National Park Service could not find funds to make needed repairs. As noted earlier, the road conditions were so bad that the 175 participants in the Sierra Club outing that year hiked from Yosemite Valley to Soda Springs in Tuolumne Meadows. Still, the autos kept coming. One club member wrote: "A routing of forty automobiles a day past the park check-station . . . indicates this year's volume of travel. During the club's [eighteen-day] stay at

Top: The Tenaya Lake "Hiker's Camp" was built in 1924 and served visitors until 1938, when it was moved to May Lake. Photo courtesy of Marilynn Guske.

Bottom: The road up Lee Vining Canyon was built into the side of the cliff in several locations. Not only did it consist of only one lane, but also there were no guard rails.

the Springs the Tuolumne River banks were dotted with auto camps, which extended far up Dana Fork and were beginning to creep up Lyell Fork. One's first impulse is to resent this intrusion into Nature's heart, intimacy with which, one instinctively feels, should be reserved for those who can achieve it by physical endeavor. Upon reflection, however, one can but rejoice when increasing numbers of one's fellow-men find healthful pleasure in Nature's gifts."[9]

One early visitor described his experience in crossing the Tioga Road in his Model T Ford in the 1920s as no small undertaking. "We didn't get to the pass until late afternoon, then we had to drop into low gear to get down Lee Vining Canyon; that was the worst part. We didn't have any fear of the road but we did have a lot of respect. We took it slow and easy . . . but there were some people there that didn't want to drive down that east side. The road was only one lane, and there was no guard rail, even at the worst

places. Around the blind curves the motorists would sound their horn in case another car was coming the other way. The uphill driver had the right of way . . . and often some one would have to back up the hill to let the other guy get past. It was pretty hairy," Elzy Benson reported years later.[10]

To a great extent, Tioga Pass and the high park road remained far removed from the woes of Washington, D.C., and the poor road conditions and lack of maintenance persisted as nagging problems. On several occasions, park rangers observed visitors cutting away downed trees or making other repairs to the road so they could proceed to Tenaya Lake or Tuolumne Meadows.

The call for the road's repair or replacement became louder. "Bought five or six years ago and given to the government by the public spirited director of the national parks, Mr. Stephen T. Mather, [the Tioga Road] has since received such partial repairs as the inadequate park appropriation made possible, and been used by a tide of motor travel which bears convincing testimony to the need of modern roads from Yosemite Valley to the upper country. If the Congressmen responsible could but once be driven by automobile over this antiquated road, on its tedious way to the High Sierra, there might be a prompt ending of the neglect which has so long left the valley lacking proper connection with its hinterland," one traveler remarked.[11]

To contend with increased travel over the Tioga Road, a ranger station was built near Tenaya Lake (as well as at Crane Flat and Tuolumne Meadows).

Recognizing the potential of the tourist trade made possible by the modernization of the Tioga Road, Lee Vining merchants and others located on the east of the Sierra pushed the park service to keep the road open as long as possible each year. In the 1920s, the spring opening of the road was celebrated with a "fish fry" sponsored by Lee Vining business owners. Photo courtesy of Marilynn Guske.

Another commentator, Yosemite writer John L. Williams, espoused a road that would start at Happy Isles and continue up the Merced River Canyon past Vernal and Nevada Falls, skirt the foot of Clouds Rest, and cross boulder-strewn Forsyth Pass. Finally dropping down to Tenaya Lake, the proposed route was some two-thirds shorter than the Tioga Road to the same point.

"The new road most needed in the park, therefore, is by common consent, a well-graded modern highway which will avoid this long detour, and connect directly with the Tioga Road at Tenaya Lake. Such a road, by enabling the automobiles quickly to reach Tuolumne Meadows, will double the possibilities of pleasure in every visit to Yosemite," Williams wrote.[12] He complained that the sixty-one-mile road did a poor job of connecting Yosemite Valley with the high country. Oddly, Williams failed to consider the impact of the alternate route on the famed Mist Trail and other scenic areas of the park.

By the summer of 1920 twelve-passenger motor stages began making day-long trips between the scenic wonders of Lake Tahoe and Yosemite Valley.[13] This new trend in travel did not go unnoticed at Monoville and Hammond's, where the locals began to appreciate the potential profits that the park-bound traffic represented.

Lee Vining at the time was little more than a collection of ranches intersected by a dirt road, isolated for four or five months a year by snow. In 1926 Chris Mattly, a native of Switzerland who had come to the Mono Basin as a young boy, acquired three parcels totaling ten acres of land near the site of Lee Vining's long-gone sawmill. Unlike many other area residents, Mattly had not sold his property to the Los Angeles Department of Water and Power in the early 1900s. He decided to subdivide his three parcels, which subdivision created the foundation for the town of Lee Vining.

In the first year Mattly sold ten lots for $50 each. A resident named Gus Hess built the first local business, a garage and gas station, a year later. Lee Vining, named for the original settler in the region, was becoming a reality. A grocery store, bar, and restaurant followed soon after. The town took on more legitimacy in 1928, when a post office was established. But it was park visitation over the Tioga Road, the development of hydroelectric plants, and the addition of road maintenance facilities that eventually gave the town and the basin the economic push they needed.[14]

By the mid-1920s there finally seemed to be agreement, even on the part of the National Park Service, that realignment and reconstruction of the Tioga Road were necessary. What tipped the balance for the

Up until the start of World War II, open touring cars shuttled over Tioga Pass during the summer season. Operated by the park concessionaire, the cars made daily trips between Yosemite Valley and Lake Tahoe with a luncheon stop at Lee Vining.

Until the mid-1930s the Tioga Road passed considerably north of its present route, winding from Crocker's Station (shown above) through White Wolf to Yosemite Creek.

park service was the recognition that visitation had become a key factor in the politics of the national park system. Visitation drove budgets, appropriations, and other factors.

As the pressure for a better road mounted, Mather made repeated visits to Yosemite and "his road." In 1926, he inspected a suggested realignment with Superintendent Washington B. Lewis. Several other proposals were studied and then rejected by conservationists, engineers, and interested individuals. Collectively they agreed that the Tenaya-Tuolumne-Tioga Pass corridor was a unique resource, and needed to be carefully treated. Because of the sensitivity of the project, the park service felt some measure of consensus was necessary. Accordingly, it organized a special advisory board to recommend a preferred route. It was led by Frederick Law Olmsted, Jr., son of the great American landscape architect.

At the time, the Tioga Road wound from Crocker's Station (also known as "Sequoia") up the south fork of the Tuolumne River to Carl's Inn and then to Aspen Valley and White Wolf, crossing Yosemite Creek two miles downstream from the present bridge. It then followed parts of the old Mono Trail, moving off the present-day alignment below May Lake and around Snow Creek, down to Tenaya Lake. Continuing, it followed much the same course it does today to Tuolumne Meadows, before taking a slightly lower route through Dana Meadows to the pass and down to Lee Vining.

Two alternative routes were developed for the realignment: the High Line and the Low Line. When the construction project was given the go-ahead by the federal government, the park service worked to gain the approval for the new routing from various constituents, including the Sierra Club. In the summer of 1933 the NPS provided the club's executive committee a guided tour of both the preliminary routes. The High Line would run from White Wolf around Mount Hoffmann, through the Ten Lakes Basin, and rejoin the existing road at Tuolumne Meadows. With a few exceptions, the Low Line would follow the existing road, with a major realignment at Yosemite Creek to decrease the grade. Both alignments would allow the road to meet higher highway standards with widening, paving, and gentler grades.

After conferring, the Sierra Club's board of directors went on record in opposition to the High Line route. Increased snow removal, incursions into previously undisturbed areas, and, surprisingly, the need for trans-Sierra travel were among the board's considerations.[15]

Though the major realignment did not occur, many improvements to the Tioga route took place during the 1930s. The California Division of Highways made limited upgrades to the eastern end of the route, widening and rerouting the section between Ellery Lake and Tioga Pass.[16] The park service began the realignment of the road from Crane Flat to White Wolf in 1935. That eliminated the circuitous Aspen Valley and Carl's Inn routing. In 1937 the section of the roadway through Tuolumne and Dana Meadows was moved to minimize its impact on these fragile environments and to reduce its visual impact on the scenery.

Before its partial realignment in 1935, the Tioga Road passed through Aspen Valley, shown here.

The latter two projects were funded in large part by the City of San Francisco as a sort of "payback" for the advantages it had gained in Yosemite's Hetch Hetchy Valley. Under the Raker Act (which had authorized the damming of Hetch Hetchy and the construction of power-generating facilities to benefit San Francisco), the city was obligated to build recreation facilities at Hetch Hetchy and to provide roads and trails around the reservoir. Once the dam was operational, however, the city reneged. After some rather heated debate between San Francisco officials and the park service, the matter was resolved at the congressional level. The resolution took form in the city's agreement to fund a new section of the Tioga Road.

With the advent of World War II, park visitation to Yosemite plummeted; with gas rationing, visitor counts dropped over 40 percent. For a time the road issue was forgotten, as travel over the Tioga Road decreased to an even greater degree.[17] But when the war ended, park use returned to substantial levels again, and travelers rushed back to Tenaya Lake, Tuolumne Meadows, and Tioga Pass. They were reminded that the road still needed improvement. While debate over the two proposed alignments continued, the focus shifted to the middle twenty-one miles of the road between White Wolf and Cathedral Creek, its last unimproved section. Considerable discussion ensued over the appropriate alignment, level of disturbance to the park, and road and shoulder width.

There was not universal acceptance of the need for realignment, however. Some members of the Sierra Club became concerned that the improved road might make it too easy for the public to gain quick access to every corner of Yosemite. They had seen the impact of increased visitation on Yosemite Valley and other heavily used areas of the Sierra. Not surprisingly, the club found itself divided over preservation and recreational use of the trans-Sierra corridor.

About the same time, a band of "young Turks," led by climber and club activist Richard Leonard, began to push for a change in the club's bylaws. The organization's original purpose had been to "explore, enjoy and render accessible" the Sierra Nevada, but Leonard and other members felt the club should rather "explore, enjoy and preserve" the mountains—a position that required a marked philosophical change.

Many of the old guard gathered around president William Colby, the venerated outing section chairman. He also was a member of the Yosemite Advisory Board, which had studied the various road alignments. Colby believed the proposed High Line route through Ten Lakes Basin and north of Mount Hoffmann and Polly Dome would be a mistake because it would invade and impact that wilderness. But he also felt it would be inconsistent for the club to reverse its previous position that favored realignment.

From Colby's perspective, the "anti-road" position would create a public relations nightmare for the club, casting its members as elitists and exclusionists. A small but vocal minority, led by Dr. Harold Bradley and Ansel Adams, asserted that improving the road was inappropriate. Both were quite passionate about the issue, which they felt deserved the Sierra Club's foremost attention. In 1951, Bradley earned a spot on the club's board of directors, and at meetings he regularly voiced his anti-road sentiments.

At the heart of the objection of many Sierra Club members to the Tioga Road realignment in the 1950s was the damage they believed would be created by this stretch of the roadway along Tenaya Lake and also at Olmsted Point.

The Sierra Club had other concerns that some board members felt were of higher priority than the Tioga Road. It was battling controversial trans-Sierra road projects at Minaret Summit, Kings Canyon, and Sequoia National Forest. The club also was changing the emphasis of its work, assuming a national profile, vision, and agenda. After the war, it called for a massive rebuilding and renovation program for the national parks, as well as for the creation of new parks, primitive areas, and regions of wilderness. The club argued that conditions within the national park system were deplorable, and that the government was not providing the level of stewardship that the nation's most important lands deserved. Not wanting to be seen as working against their broader goals, the directors were slow to address the Tioga Road controversy. A rift developed within the board, and for years the club waffled on the matter. When the Sierra Club board finally got around to voting on the issue in 1954, the result was a split vote and no action taken.

This view below Olmsted Point shows the extent of the blasting and rock removal that was required to accomplish the realignment of this stretch of the Tioga Road in the late 1950s.

Congress responded to Sierra Club concerns, and in 1956 appropriated $484 million to rehabilitate the national parks under a rather ambitious federal project known as Mission 66. The name was selected to signify an intended completion date of 1966. A total of $22 million from the appropriation was earmarked to be used in Yosemite. In August 1956 National Park Service Director Conrad Wirth made a tour of Yosemite to decide how the money would be allocated at the park.[18] Among the approved projects were the rebuilding of Yosemite Valley campgrounds "and reconstruction of twenty-one miles of the Tioga Road.

While most Sierra Club members and park supporters seemed to favor the broader goals of Mission 66, many had serious reservations about some of the proposed improvements—a problem compounded by Wirth's inability to address critical questions about them. Among the projects that most disturbed the club were the Tioga Road construction and the flooding of Dinosaur National Monument on the Green River, and Wirth did a poor job of defending them.[19]

What was most controversial about the work on the Tioga Road was that it would create a new route around Olmsted Point and Tenaya Lake, a process that would require extensive blasting and ripping away of the granite landscape. Despite considerable opposition, however, the National Park Service and the Bureau of Public Roads approved the new alignment and began work. As jack hammers and bulldozers began gouging the land in 1957, charges and countercharges flew from those on opposite "sides of the road." Extensive blasting quickly severed the historic ties that had been forged at Tioga Pass years earlier between the Sierra Club and the park service. The Tioga Road, perhaps the most revered road in the nation, had become its most controversial.

Photographer and Sierra Club director Ansel Adams emerged as one of the most outspoken critics of the government. He characterized Mission 66 as little more than a "gigantic road building program designed to open the parks to development."[20] As for the Tioga Road alignment, Adams

As he watched the Tioga Road realignment take place, photographer Ansel Adams accused the National Park Service of using heavy-handed construction techniques and of destroying the very resource it was charged with protecting.

During the controversial realignment in the late 1950s, road crews had to blast extensive amounts of granite. Here a power shovel loads a large section of rock on to a dump truck near Tenaya Lake.

complained about the lack of public meetings, the unclear routing, and the impact of heavy equipment on a fragile setting. He was particularly concerned that construction would destroy one of his favorite areas—the giant slabs of granite around Tenaya Lake.

Gradually, Adams concluded that the Sierra Club's traditional approach of moderation and concession-making (their "Dream World of Compromise") was not working. By early 1957 Adams became so estranged from some of the club's directors that he offered to resign his position. As the road project rolled forward, Adams became more vocal about the damage he believed it would cause. He bombarded government officials with letters and used his reputation and connections to attack the project and enlist supporters. "The battle is joined," he wrote on July 11, 1958.[21]

During the summer of 1958, Adams and club director David Brower toured the Tioga work site and were appalled at what they perceived to be heavy-handed construction techniques. With photos and words, Adams criticized the project; much of the November 1958 issue of the *Sierra Club Bulletin* was devoted to his article entitled "Tenaya Tragedy."[22] Among his many charges was that the park service was destroying the very resource it was charged with protecting. At one point, Adams' assault caught NPS Director Wirth's attention. For a short time, he suspended construction while the government restudied the problem

Rumors circulated that during their inspection of the road work, Adams, Brower, and other opponents pulled out survey stakes, hoping to derail the project. For decades both men sidestepped questions regarding this purported "ecotage," but years later Brower noted that "it could have happened." Eventually, both men became disillusioned with the Sierra

The ribbon cutting for the new Tioga Road at Olmsted Point featured, from left, John C. Preston, park superintendent, Conrad L. Wirth, Director of the National Park Service, John C. Carver, Assistant Secretary of the Interior, H. T. Gunderson, a federal highways project engineer, Lawrence C. Merriam, regional park director, and Fred Bagshaw, an assistant director of public works. Photo courtesy of the Fresno Bee.

Club, Adams moving his support to the Wilderness Society and Brower forming Friends of the Earth.[23]

In many ways, the Sierra Club contributed to the mess that developed over the Tioga Road reconstruction. For nearly three decades, the club had run hot and cold on the controversy. Not only did some club members support the concept of improved, through-park access, but also the split vote by the board of directors underscored the club's lack of consensus on the issue. When the only "official" requests from the Sierra Club were for further studies and more information, the government felt justified to move the road project forward.

Dr. Edgar Wayburn, another board member, cited the lack of information on the project from the park service and the Bureau of Public Roads. While the Sierra Club had added to the confusion and delays by not taking a position, many felt that Wirth and the National Park Service had not detailed the ruinous construction standards beforehand. "The club has always been a good friend with the park service and we wanted to support the program, but when it came to the Tioga Pass road, we simply felt that the park service had to provide more information," Wayburn noted years later.[24]

Director Wirth defended the park service actions: "There were changes made in the plans for the Tioga Road which took into consideration several of the suggestions made by the conservation people. . . I think the

Dignitaries listen to speeches on the reviewing stand at Olmsted Point during the dedication of the realigned Tioga Road on June 25, 1961. In a gesture symbolizing his objection to the project, Sierra Club representative Edgar Wayburn chose not to dress in the obligatory suit. Photo courtesy of the Fresno Bee.

final decision was a good decision which took into consideration the many problems confronting us. No road ever reconstructed in the National Parks has had the detailed study and consideration that has been given to the Tioga Road. The route and standards were under intense study for 31 years," he noted.[25] In retirement, Wirth went even further, claiming the Sierra Club was "looking for a cause" when it opposed the road.[26]

The Sierra Club was still smarting when the new Tioga Road section was completed in 1961. The National Park Service, Bureau of Public Roads, and the state Department of Transportation issued the usual press releases, touting the benefits of the new stretch of mountain roadway. Sierra Club representatives were invited to attend the official dedication at newly-designated Olmsted Point on June 25. Edgar Wayburn, the group's president, had been camping in Tuolumne Meadows; he showed up wearing his grubby camping clothes. "All of the others on the review stand had on suits and ties. I probably stood out like a sore thumb. My wife said later that my appearance was a visual statement as to what the club thought about the new road. . . The Sierra Club missed the boat on that one. We should have gone to court and fought it out," Wayburn reflected.[27]

In the years following, some National Park Service employees have voiced their disappointment that the Sierra Club didn't put up a stronger fight. Herb Ewing, the grandson of Gabriel Sovulewski and Mather District ranger at Tuolumne Meadows from the 1950s through the 1970s, had complaints that went beyond the road's construction and alignment. "The park service brought in a modern highway that brought people to Tuolumne Meadows like you couldn't believe. But there was no support system to take care of those people. There was no water or sewer system for all those people. It was a terrible mistake. The park service had the horse before the cart," Ewing said in 1986.[28]

Carl Sharsmith, the venerable Tuolumne Meadows ranger-naturalist and alpine botanist, also believed the road was a mistake. He opposed reconstruction of any kind. Like many others, he thought the old road served as an effective control because it discouraged those who were unwilling to deal with the difficulties of high country travel. Sharsmith believed the new road made it too easy for all to see the magic mountains. "I said it then, and I say it now. That road was a mistake; it made it into a high speed highway," Sharsmith declared.[29]

Ansel Adams was damning in his final analysis of the project. "The Tenaya tragedy stands as an example of what must never happen again in the national parks or other wild areas. The only way we can prevent further depredations is to join firmly in a demand for an immediate moratorium on all construction developments in the national parks until a new and

freshly oriented study can be made by competent individuals and groups. . .
The bulldozers of bureaucracy have bypassed the gentle persuasions and
advice of our conservation spokesmen. The fruits of controversy are
tragically revealed at Tenaya Lake. We need to rededicate ourselves. We
have nothing to lose but our wilderness, and nothing to gain but the
satisfaction of seeing as much of it as possible preserved for the time to
come," Adams wrote.[30]

The twenty-one-mile section of the Tioga Road was no sooner
completed than the state of California began to upgrade the stretch
of the road on the eastern slope. Three contracts were let in the mid-
1960s, the result of which was a two-lane route all the way from Lee
Vining to Tioga Pass. By that time, the communities on the Sierra's
east side had come to realize that much of their economic life was
dependent upon the road. Between Bridgeport and Bishop the business
community became more vocal and political, asking then demanding
that the highway be opened earlier in the spring and closed later in the
fall. Through the years, a handful of optimistic merchants, putting hope
before reason, have urged that the road be kept open year-round.

In a 1954 letter to Yosemite National Park Superintendent John

*The road from Tioga Pass to Lee Vining
was widened to two lanes in the mid-1960s,
though the route still remained treacherous
and exposed. Photo courtesy of the California
Department of Transportation.*

C. Preston, Marjorie M. Gripper, the president of the Lee Vining Chamber of Commerce, pointed out that: "Conservatively, 50 percent or more of the business of Lee Vining is derived from tourist travel over Tioga Pass."[31] She went on to demand that the road be cleared as early in the spring as possible. Preston observed to a pair of visiting newsmen that if Gripper could have "put as much heat" on the Tioga Pass snow pack as she had on his superintendency, the road would have been opened much earlier, indeed.[32]

Over the years, the political pressures related to the trans-Sierra route have not subsided. Repeatedly, the National Park Service has found itself faced with the difficult task of balancing the economic interests of gateway communities and the tourism industry against the protection of park resources. Despite its early efforts at preservation and stewardship, the park service has demonstrated a somewhat inconsistent Tioga Road policy that has reflected the demands of modern-day life and politics.

In his book, *Yosemite—The Embattled Wilderness*, former Tuolumne Meadows ranger Alfred Runte observes that the park service "was caught between two opposing forces. It had helped encourage both, but only one—preservation—was unquestionably a legitimate purpose of national parks. The other force, commercialism, had been courted in the interest of building up visitation."[33]

Demand for access from both ends of the popular trans-Sierra route shows no sign of abating. Managing the use of the Tioga Road is one of the ongoing challenges with which the National Park Service must grapple in the twenty-first century and beyond.

NOTES

1. Keith Trexler, *The Tioga Road—A History, 1883-1961* (Yosemite: Yosemite Natural History Association, 1980), 20.

2. James Snyder, conversation with author, Yosemite Valley, California, 1972.

3. *Superintendent Report of 1917.* Yosemite Research Library.

4. James Bryce, "Should Cars Be Allowed in Yosemite?," in David Harmon, ed., *Mirror of America* (Washington, D.C.: National Park Foundation, 1989), 126.

5. Hank Johnston, *Yosemite's Yesterdays* (Yosemite: Flying Spur Press, 1989), 15.

6. *Report of the Superintendent of the Yosemite National Park to the Secretary of the Interior, 1915* (Washington, D.C.: U.S. Government Printing Office, 1915), 12-15.

7. *California Highways and Public Works* (January–February 1966): 7.

8. *Yosemite Superintendents Reports*, vol. 2; 1915 report, p. 20.

9. Charles A. Noble, "The Sierra Club Outing of 1919," *Sierra Club Bulletin* XI, no. 1 (January 1920): 15.

10. Elzy Benson, interview with author, Fowler, Calif., 7 February 1985.

11. John L. Williams, *Yosemite and Its High Sierra*, 2d ed. (Tacoma and San Francisco: self-published, 1921), 60-61.

12. Ibid., 61-62.

13. Trexler, *The Tioga Road*, 22.

14. Lily Mathieu LaBraque, *Man From Mono* (Reno: Nevada Academic Press, 1984), 11-14.

15. "Relocation of Tioga Road" in "Notes and Correspondence," *Sierra Club Bulletin* XIX, no. 3 (June 1934): 85-88.

16. Trexler, *The Tioga Road*, 17.

17. "Yosemite Park Travel Declines Because of War," *Fresno Bee*, 12 October 1941, B-1.

18. Ron Taylor, "Yosemite Expansion Will Ease Tourist Congestion," *Fresno Bee*, 27 August 1956, B-1.

19. Michael Cohen, *The History of the Sierra Club, 1892-1970* (San Francisco: Sierra Club, 1988), 138.

20. Ansel Adams, *Letters and Images, 1916-1984* (New York: New York Graphic Society, 1988), 259, 260.

21. Ansel Adams, "Tenaya Tragedy," *Sierra Club Bulletin* XLIII, no. 9 (November 1958): 1-5.

22. Ibid.

23. David Brower, conversation with author, Kings Canyon National Park, 17 April 2000. Virgina Adams said her husband was upset enough over the road to do so. See Kenneth Brower, *Yosemite—An American Treasure* (Washington, D.C.: National Geographic Society, 1990), 178.

24. Cohen, *History of the Sierra Club*, 139; and Edgar Wayburn, phone interview by author, 17 January 1991.

25. Trexler, *The Tioga Road*, 26.

26. Conrad Wirth, telephone interview by author, 22 January 1992.

27. Edgar Wayburn, telephone interview by author, 17 March 1991.

30. Herb Ewing, interview with author, in *Fresno Bee*, August 1987, "Parks in Peril" supplement.

31. Carl Sharsmith, telephone interview by author, 12 December 1991.

31. Adams, "Tenaya Tragedy," 4.

32. Marjorie M. Gripper, letter to John Preston, 19 January 1954. In the Yosemite Research Library, File D-30, Part 1, Tioga Road.

33. John Preston, conversation with author, Yosemite Valley, California, early 1960s.

34. Alfred Runte, *Yosemite –The Embattled Wilderness* (Lincoln and London: University of Nebraska Press, 1990), 194.

CHAPTER 10

WINTER TALES FROM TIOGA

Seasonal changes in the Tioga region have added to the richness and color of the history of the trans-Sierra route. About mid-November the great white curtain rolls down over the high country corridor, and the land is transformed into a winter wilderness. For the next six months, the high country lies under a frosty mantle of snow and ice.

Almost nothing is known of the challenges faced by early Indian inhabitants of the Tioga area, caught by an early winter storm. The accounts of the suffering endured by the Joseph Walker party during its October 1833 crossing of the Sierra—one that tested even the hardy mountain men—provide only a suggestion of the conditions in the mountains when they are severe.[1]

Fifty years later, the first vanguard of miners met the wicked winter atop the snowy Sierra. "[W]hen the Storm King of Winter is abroad in the Sierras [*sic*] and the snow is whirling through the air with a velocity of more than 100 miles per hour and a density so great that one cannot see his own feet, the scene is appalling, and more so as the eastern side of this sharp ridge, over which you may be hurled bodily at any moment, is a precipice of more than a thousand feet," related one early argonaut.[2]

For those first year-round residents, the winter represented the season of the unknown. The snow and cold, accompanied by chronic shortages of food and supplies and the unpredictability of the high country weather, added to the isolation and hardship. In January of 1881 miners Ben Dettman and Tom Moore departed Monoville on the east side of the Sierra for the Mount Dana Mine, by way of Bloody Canyon. In those days before weather forecasting, mountain travelers had no way to predict winter storms that might unleash their fury with unexpected and frightening consequences. The trip started with clear and crisp days, but the two soon ran into trouble as a storm swept over the Sierra. For five days they fought their way up the canyon, over a snow-covered trail and through "a fearful storm." The miners stumbled on until they came to an empty cabin, where they took refuge.

Opposite: Jules Fritsch skis the slopes above Tuolumne Meadows in the late 1920s in this photo by a young Ansel Adams.

The winter conditions were harsh and severe given the exposure at the Great Sierra Mine. During the winter of 1881-82, the snow was waist deep around this cabin at the mine.

Meanwhile, at the nearby Tioga Mine, concerns for the safety of Dettman and Moore mounted, and a search party was organized—just as the two men made their way into camp. "Our people were very glad to learn that the travelers had safely arrived at their destination, and many a glass of whiskey was sacrificed in celebration of their good fortune. It is very risky business rambling around these canyons in winter," the celebrants and survivors noted.[3]

During one particularly severe freeze in the winter of 1881–82, three workers at the Great Sierra Mine were seriously injured in an explosion of blasting powder. Someone had set six sticks of frozen explosives next to a wood stove to thaw; the powder ignited with devastating consequences. Once the injured were pulled from the wreckage, a messenger was dispatched to Lundy for medical aid. The *Homer Mining Index* reported that the courier made the eleven-mile trip in four and a half hours "on foot without snowshoes [skis], and most of the distance through waist deep snows."[4]

A week later the paper observed that "the three men injured by the powder explosion at the Great Sierra Mine last week are doing well, and all of them are recovering rapidly. George M. Lee is able to be around as usual, but cannot be induced to sit down. . . The fragments of the demolished stove struck George in the rear, below the belt and numerously. The most seriously injured, James M. Kickham had been hit by 200 fragments; after two weeks treatment at Tioga, it was decided that he should be moved to Lundy for additional treatment, which was done by making a stretcher over what the miners called 'Norwegian snowshoes,'" the early newspaper reported.[5]

In the high mining camps, the snow, cold, and isolation took their toll. Few miners lasted more than one or two winters. Avalanches were a particular danger. "Neither language nor the painter's art can convey to the mind of the most imaginative anything like a true conception of the appalling scene the inhabitants of these vast mountains witnessed during the days and nights of terror through which they passed last week. On March 9 and 10, 1882, sixteen inches of snow fell; the 11th was a clear day. But by the 15th, six feet of snow had fallen in Mill Creek Canyon and seven to eight feet in the higher mountains."[6] At approximately 11:00 p.m., as most residents of the mining camps lay in their beds, a series of avalanches tore down the mountainsides at several locations between Tioga Pass and Lundy. The huge snow slides demolished and buried buildings, and entombed their sleeping occupants.

At Bennettville an avalanche buried twenty-one men in the miners boarding house. Many managed to crawl out of the wreckage, digging with little more than their bare hands and feet. The frantic cries of those

trapped inside led to other rescues. Some were freed only after broken
beams and splintered boards were chopped away. The stunned survivors
were directed to the few standing cabins. The snows continued throughout
the night, touching off additional slides—and fears.

In nearby Lake and Lundy Canyons, the slides caused even greater
havoc, destroying several buildings and trapping dozens of inhabitants.
When rescuers turned out to help there, they were hampered by enormous
drifts, more falling snow, and the threat of additional avalanches. J. C.
Kemp, manager of the Great Sierra Co., mounted a search for three of
his crew who had been buried in the slide helping to transport mining
equipment over the crest to Bennettville. At one point he offered to
provide skis for anyone who would participate in the recovery of the dead.[7]
The rescue operations went on for several days, which were punctuated by
even more storms. By the time the storms finally had passed, at least four
people, including the three involved in transporting the mining machinery
to Bennettville, had been killed. Several others were not accounted for.

The Tioga and Lundy mines were located in avalanche-prone areas,
and recorded numerous slides over the years. The mines suspended
operations between 1884 and 1888, and for the next two decades there was
little winter activity in the Tioga area. Around 1911, following the initial
construction of the Lee Vining Canyon road, a handful of trappers and
poachers made cold-season trips up from Mono Lake.[8]

*Park snow removal methods have come a
long way since the 1920s when clearing the
road entailed considerable hand labor. Photo
courtesy of Charlotte Ewing.*

One near disastrous incident occurred around 1913,[9] when George LaBraque, a member of a pioneer Mono Basin family, and three of his friends were trapping fox and pine marten around Tioga Pass.[10] The four set up a cabin near Rhinedollar Lake and ran a trap line toward Mount Dana and then over to the old Tioga Mine. The prized pelt was that of the elusive silver fox, a cross between the common red and black foxes, that had become extremely valuable.

Because the trapping was poor, LaBraque and companion Evert Matty decided to try their luck inside the park. They made their way over Tioga Pass on skis and down to Tuolumne Meadows, just as a big storm swept over the crest.[11] By the time they reached the meadows, it was blowing a blizzard. "The storm hit us suddenly; we were buffeted by heavy winds and swirling snow. We were in a blizzard so fierce we could hardly see where we were going, and by then it was too late to turn back. We tried to follow the road, but the snow was so deep and the blizzard so violent this was out of the question," LaBraque wrote.[12]

They discarded their packs and searched the storm-obscured landscape for what they called the "main park cabin," the recently completed Sierra Club lodge at Soda Springs. They located the chimney of the snow-covered building as night fell. Digging down to the entrance, they found the door locked.

Tired and freezing, the two trappers forced the lock. They started a fire, discovered a cache of food, and thus were able to survive the storm. After three days the weather broke, and the pair beat a difficult retreat to their Tioga base camp. While they returned empty-handed, they were alive, much to the amazement of their friends, who had given them up for dead.

Hibernation and isolation were the rule for the Tioga high country each winter until the late 1920s,

Top: An early snowplow makes its way up the snowy Tioga Road as a passenger vehicle follows behind.

Bottom: The snow banks were remarkably high near Tioga Pass when the road opened in 1928.

when developments in and around Yosemite set in motion many changes. The completion of the all-year highway from Merced to Yosemite Valley in 1926, coupled with the construction of the Ahwahnee Hotel a year later, prompted the Yosemite Park & Curry Company, the main park concessionaire, to look for ways to increase the numbers of their winter guests.[13]

At the time, the public's interest in winter sports was on the rise, both in the United States and Europe, as indicated by the founding of the Winter Olympic Games in 1924. Dr. Donald Tresidder, the head of the Curry Company, and his wife Mary (Curry) Tresidder hoped to capitalize on this trend and create a winter sports program in the park.

The couple visited several of the leading winter resorts in Europe. On their return home they formed the Yosemite Winter Club in 1928 to "encourage and develop all kinds of winter sports."[14] Mrs. Tresidder observed that, "Winter sports seemed to give some hope of spreading a thin layer of guests over the lean days. We were more hopeful than that as a matter of fact. We had ourselves been infected by the deadly ski virus, as we saw Yosemite with its background of beauty as an outstanding winter place."[15]

With the support of acting park superintendent Horace Albright, the company launched an ambitious campaign to bring visitors to the park during the winter season. A large skating rink, a toboggan slide, a ski hill, and other winter recreation facilities were established in Yosemite Valley. The Tresidders imported and hired several European skiers and skaters, with the goal of making Yosemite the winter sports capital of North America. Among the transplanted winter athletes were Ernst DesBaillets of France and Jules Fritsch of Switzerland.

It was, however, a young American mountaineer from Big Creek named Orland Bartholomew who first called attention to winter travel in the Sierra with a remarkable exploit that is still unrivaled in the Yosemite area. In an epic adventure that spanned three months and 300 miles, Bartholomew skied alone from Lone Pine to Tuolumne Meadows to complete a winter-long exploration of the Sierra.[16] Crossing Donohue Pass and skiing down Lyell Canyon, Bartholomew arrived in Tuolumne on April 1, 1929, to become the first person to ski the length of the still uncompleted John Muir Trail—a feat some historians call the greatest ski trek of all time.

During his ninety-day trip Bartholomew camped in the snow at night, endured buffeting storms and avalanches, and relied on a series of food caches placed the summer before. Along the way, he made over 400 photographs of the mountains—the first of the Sierra high country in winter—inspired to some extent by the initial success of his Sierra Club compatriot, Ansel Adams.[17] Adams, who was working as a publicity photographer for the Yosemite Park & Curry Company, also joined the growing ranks of high country skiers, making subsequent winter forays into the snow-covered mountains around Tuolumne Meadows.

Bartholomew kept a daily record book of observations. On April 1 he noted: "Min. temp. 14. Ave. depth snow Donohue Pass 2.5 ft., Lyell Fk. Tuolumne at 9,500 feet, 3 ft. . . Ditto at mouth Rafferty Creek. Cloudy all day. Birds—Nutcrackers, Chicadees. Animals—Coyotes, Porcupines." Snow too frozen to record small animals. Away at 8 and over Donohue. Lunched at upper end of meadows in Lyell Fork of Tuolumne and then dropped down to the mouth of Rafferty Creek. Travelling excellent on account of cloudy weather."[18]

Winter sports enthusiasts travel on cross-country skis through the snow-covered forest near Tenaya Lake in the early 1930s. Photo by Ansel Adams.

Alone and unaided, Orland Bartholomew skied through Tuolumne Meadows in the spring of 1929, completing his winter-long trek along the crest of the Sierra Nevada. Photo courtesy of the Bartholomew family.

In the late winter of 1928-29 Dr. Donald Tresidder made a trip with
Ernst DesBaillets and Jules Fritsch and a few other friends to Tuolumne
Meadows. They returned with glowing accounts of the ski terrain. That
summer, a ski cabin was built near Snow Creek, above the rim of Yosemite
Valley at the top of the Tenaya Zig-Zag Trail. It became known as the
Snow Creek Lodge. The Curry Company also secured permission from
the park service for winter use of the ranger cabins at Tenaya Lake and
Tuolumne Meadows, and equipped them as ski huts. Its plan was to
encourage hut-to-hut ski touring, similar to that practiced in Europe. The
cabins were located about a day apart. The company promoted three-day
and week-long package ski tours, hoping to lure visitors with the winter
splendor of Tenaya Lake, Tuolumne Meadows, and the Yosemite scenery.

To start the trips, horses carried guests' skis and gear to the rim of
Yosemite Valley. Each ski hut had bunks for sixteen people, a wood cook
stove, and an outdoor privy—spartan accommodations even by standards
of the day. Fritsch and other staff members served as guides, cooks, and
companions, leading the skiers from one cabin to the next. Along the way
the experts instructed the newcomers in the intricacies of the telemark turn
and other ski techniques.

During the first winter of operation, 1930, a mere fifty-six skiers visited
the Snow Creek cabin. "We have already spent several thousand dollars
in the construction of ski houses and the purchase of equipment to make
possible the inauguration of ski tours. We realize we are entering a pioneer
field in the United States and that we cannot expect any direct financial
returns for many years. We do believe, however, that High Sierra ski tours
will add a great deal of interest, romance and color to winter sports in
California," Don Tresidder wrote.[19]

*Mary Curry Tresidder, shown here in 1939,
was a winter sports enthusiast responsible in
large part for the development of the winter
ski hut system in Yosemite.*

The outings were ambitious trips that ranged up and down the slopes
of the surrounding mountains. They led to many ski mountaineering feats,
including the first winter ascents of several summits, starting in 1930 with
Mount Watkins, Mount Hoffmann, Tenaya Peak, and Mount Dana from
the Tuolumne and Tenaya cabins. On other trips skiers traveled over routes
that lead to Tioga Pass and Vogelsang Pass.

Mary Curry Tresidder was especially supportive of the ski huts, and
would have been their best customer had she and her husband not owned
much of the concessions operation. She once observed that during the
five winters the ski huts were operational, she spent a total of five months
skiing among them. Her favorite trip was to Tuolumne Meadows, where
a dozen or more inviting slopes could be found.[20] The Tresidders often
took friends along, including some of the foremost skiers of the day.
Also among their trip-mates was a young Ansel Adams, the company
photographer. His promotional photographs both captured the skiers in
action and highlighted the beauty of the high country.

In the late 1930s and early 1940s, the trans-Sierra ski scene was
sustained by ski mountaineers from the Sierra Club, led by Dave Brower,
Bestor Robinson, and the Harold Bradley family. In the wake of World
War II, a handful of skiers continued their touring ways, with most of the

Top: The Ostrander Ski Hut, built by the Civilian Conservation Corps, was another part of the effort to popularize winter sports in Yosemite. It opened in 1940.

Bottom: This cabin at Snow Flat was one of several built during the 1930s in an effort by the Yosemite Park & Curry Company to introduce hut skiing to Yosemite. Photo by Ansel Adams.

Yosemite action centered at the Ostrander Lake Ski Hut. In 1947, Doug Coe of Oakhurst made a ski trek over Tioga Pass using the snow-covered roadway as his route. "I made it by myself . . . that haul from Lee Vining over the Tioga Pass just about killed me. So did a blizzard. All I could do was climb into my sleeping bag—4½ pounds of down—and let the snow cover me up. I was well insulated. But three days in a sleeping bag is not much fun," Coe recalled years later.[21]

Despite the efforts of the Tresidders and their Yosemite concession, hut skiing and touring in the park failed to take off. Even the spectacular beauty of the snowbound Tioga corridor couldn't generate enough business to make the ski huts successful. The Sierra Club tried to encourage touring, but it seemed unable to sell the sport to its members and others. While the Ostrander Ski Hut would help sustain Nordic skiing, there had been a shift to a preference for downhill skiing. In response, the Yosemite concessioner focused its attention on Tempo Dome and Badger Pass, where mechanized lifts made their appearance in 1935.

In the end, the spectacular slopes of Mounts Hoffmann and Dana could not compete with mountains that were ski-lift equipped. Inevitably, the success of downhill skiing at Badger Pass forced the closure of the huts. Today the Snow Creek cabin sits mostly unused by ski mountaineers, though it has recently been rehabilitated, while the Tenaya hut was removed to make way for the new highway. A cabin in Tuolumne Meadows still sees occupation by winter backcountry users, many of whom come over Tioga Pass from the east side.

Another winter activity in Yosemite's high country was initiated in the mid-1920s, when the first snow surveys of the Tioga area were undertaken. In 1926, the National Park Service began measuring snow depths at Dana Meadows, Tioga Pass, Ellery Lake, and Saddlebag Lake. It wasn't until the 1930s that the California Cooperative Snow Surveys Program began making stops at Tuolumne Meadows, Fletcher Lake, Snow Flat, Tenaya Lake, and Gin Flat.[22] The purpose of the surveys was to obtain information on the spring snowmelt for the use of downstream water users on both sides of the Sierra.

Park rangers also made their own measurements for more immediate application, according to Carl P. Russell, author of several early articles in *Yosemite Nature Notes.* The rangers recorded the snow depth, according to Russell, "for the purpose of foretelling roughly what the summer condition of the famous waterfalls of the park are to be and to gain advance information on the approximate dates of the opening of high trails, roads and camping spots."[23]

Henry J. During, an early park ranger, made several of the initial survey trips into the winter wilderness. The surveyors traveled on skis and used the park's winter cabins. Their goal was to make measurements on April 1, because figures from that date tended to reflect the maximum snowpack.

A party of skiers takes a luncheon break atop Mount Watkins in the early 1930s. Photo by Ansel Adams.

On one difficult and demanding ski trek to Tuolumne Meadows in 1931, During took a head-first fall near Fletcher Lake, landing face down in the snow, almost knocking himself unconscious.[24]

The high country snow surveys continued at a minimal level through the Depression and World War II. Gradually, established "snow courses," defined measuring sites, were established along the Tioga Road and elsewhere. From these locations precise and repeated measurements were made at scheduled intervals, allowing hydrographers and other experts to calculate the amount of snow melt that might be available to thirsty Californians.

In 1956, Thomas "Tommy" Tucker, the Mather District ranger, enjoyed one of the more memorable assignments of his forty-year career when he took part in a ten-day snow survey along the backbone of the Sierra.[25] Tucker had originally planned to do the survey with a surplus World War II half-track vehicle, known as an M-7, that belonged to the California Department of Water Resources. After repeated breakdowns, the M-7 was parked and abandoned near Crane Flat. Instead, Tucker and rangers Ken Ashley and Glenn Gallison made the trip on skis, leaving from the valley and heading up the Tenaya zig-zags, breaking their way through deep, fresh snow to the Snow Flat snow course.

The next day the group skied to Tuolumne Meadows, taking the snow depth measurements at Tenaya Lake and Tuolumne Meadows along the way. After a layover day in Tuolumne, the three men pushed their way up to the Fletcher Lake snow course. The next day's leg to Tioga Pass was memorable for its terrible weather conditions.

"The wind was so fierce that it created a ground blizzard, a white out, so that we could hardly see where we were going. It was bitter cold and the snow was freezing to our eyebrows. Up near the pass, we could see the snow banner blowing off the summit of Mount Dana, stretching out two to three hundred feet. When we finally got to the Tioga Pass Entrance Station, we decided to spend the night there, but found the ranger cabin totally covered with snow."[26]

Using their hands to dig, the three rangers burrowed down into the snow and finally located the eaves of the cabin, under which a shovel had been stored. To minimize their work, they dug down to a window on the side of the building, which they broke out to gain access to the cabin. Tucker became concerned that the deepening snow might again cover the window and block their exit. By removing an inside door and passing it through the window to the outside, the men managed to deflect the snow and maintain their escape route. To complicate matters, Tucker's old leather ski boots were coming apart at the seams. A search of the station yielded some paper clips that were straightened and used as wire for makeshift repairs to the boots. Before completing the excursion, the three skied to Ellery Lake, then Saddlebag Lake (passing through several avalanche areas) for more measurements.

"That was one of the toughest things I have ever done. I was so damn tired that evening that I barely made it back to Tioga Pass, where we spent another night. I made other ski trips over the same terrain at later times; but none stood out so vividly as that ten day period I spent with Glen and Ash in January of 1956," Tucker recalled years later.[27]

Beginning in the 1960s through about 1990, the state provided the park service with a Tucker Sno-Cat,[28] a special vehicle designed for snow travel. Crews left Crane Flat early in the morning and quickly make the trip up the snow-covered road to Gin Flat, where the first course was surveyed with a device known as a Mount Rose snow tube. The next measurement stop was Snow Flat, from which point groups followed the alignment of the old Tioga Road to Tenaya Lake, thereby avoiding the avalanche-prone area east of Olmsted Point. After recording depths at the Tenaya Lake course, crew members continued on to Tuolumne Meadows, reaching their cabin by nightfall.

Park employees, ferried by helicopter to the site, conduct a survey on the Tuolumne Meadows snow course.

The Tuolumne Meadows, Dana Meadows, and Tioga Pass snow
courses were surveyed the following day. Locations east of Tioga Pass were
handled by snow surveyors from Southern California Edison Company,
the giant southland utility, because those locations are in a different
hydrologic basin.

The snow surveys require considerable work. They must be made in
varying snow conditions, often involve travel in storms, and sometimes
result in mechanical problems. But they are also rewarding for those who
make them. The trips provide the rangers involved rare opportunities
to see the Tioga corridor resplendent in its winter mantle. "This is
what rangering is all about," observed Ron Mackie of the NPS during
a 1984 survey. "How many
people get to see Tuolumne
and Tioga like this?"[29]

The surveys are made February
through May, with the April 1st
check still considered the prime
measurement, since it tends to
reflect the maximum accumulation
of snow for the winter. By that time
the courses along the Tioga Road
usually have an average snow depth
of seven to eight feet, with a water
content of about thirty inches.
Variance can be enormous, however.
During the record years of 1969 and 1983, the snow depth reached
twenty-two feet and had a water content of nearly seven feet—the snow
melt would have left the high country under seven feet of water (had it not
run off)! At the other extreme, in the drought winters of 1976 and 1977,
ranger Ron Mackie drove up the Tioga Road in a four-wheel drive vehicle
with park service veteran Herb Ewing to measure the few inches of snow.

Top: A snow survey crew at the course near
Tioga Pass.

Bottom: Snow surveyors in a Tucker
Sno-Cat stop to investigate the stability of
the snow slope in the avalanche-prove stretch
of the Tioga Road east of Olmsted Point.

Snow surveying techniques have continued to evolve. In 1985, the state
installed the first electronic monitor device, known as a "snow pillow," at
Tuolumne Meadows. It provides more frequent readings than are possible
through manual measurements. In 1990, the park service discontinued the
use of motor-powered conveyances (snowmobiles, jeeps, etc.) for traveling
to snow courses to take measurements.

A variety of motorized winter vehicles have traversed the Tioga Road
over the years. In the 1960s, a handful of recreational snowmobilers
(unregulated at the time) used the snow-covered route. As the activity
grew, snowmobile clubs from the east and west sides of the Sierra
frequented the park's high country and the area east of its Tioga boundary.
But in 1976, with the increased popularity of cross-country skiing and
showshoeing, the park service banned snowmobiling from the roadway.
This set off a major controversy. The desire to see and know the winter
world of the Tuolumne Meadows and Tioga Pass area pushed some users
to extremes. While most of the snowmobilers obeyed the park service

A park ranger stands next to the enormous snow bank left by snow plows working to open the Tioga Road following the heavy winter of 1983. Photo by author.

regulations, some operators ventured into remote areas, far distant from the snow-covered roadway.

The recreationists argued that they were not harming the environment with their machines. The National Park Sevice cited the noise produced by the devices, snowmobiler conflicts with skiers, and alleged incidents of off-road travel. The Sierra Snowmobile Club, directed by Fresno plumber Bud Weber, put up a strong fight. Several appeals were made, but the ban was maintained and has remained in force ever since. In one gesture of protest, a group of Lee Vining snowmobilers drove into Tuolumne Meadows, where its members were arrested for violating the park's ban. Most area snowmobiling is now done on the east side of the Sierra.

Increased winter use of the Tuolumne-Tioga corridor by cross-country skiers and showshoers became an issue that the park service could not ignore. Each year, winter climbers trying to push the limits got lost or ran into trouble, forcing extensive and expensive NPS search-and-rescue operations. In the fall of 1975, Judy and Randy Morgenson were installed as the first winter rangers at Tuolumne Meadows.

Before the road was closed, the husband and wife team were transported to the meadows with their food and equipment, then took up residence in a winterized ranger cabin. At the same time, the old Tuolumne Meadows ranger station was converted for use as a shelter for winter travelers. During the winter of 1975-76, over 500 mountaineers visited the area.

By the winter of 1979, the Yosemite Natural History Association, the non-profit organization that assists the park service with a wide range of programs and support services (now known as the Yosemite Association), began to offer "trans-Sierra" winter seminars. Participants in these week-long outings began at Lee Vining and entered the park at Tioga Pass.

At night the groups utilized backcountry cabins along the way. Shortly thereafter the Yosemite Winter Club initiated its own annual outing over the Sierra, allowing its members to enjoy the majesty of the snow-covered high country each winter.

Over the years, the annual opening of the Tioga Road each spring has become a much-awaited event. Until the twenty-one-mile section of the road was completed in 1961, the road did not open until Mother Nature melted the snow on the roadway.

Even today, the process of clearing the road each spring can be a titanic chore. Usually in mid-April, crews from both the park service and Caltrans begin the snow removal, using giant rotary plows and other equipment. During "big winters" (such as 1969, 1978, 1983, and 2005), when twenty feet of compacted snow has accumulated in the deeper sections, bulldozers are sent ahead of the giant rotary plows to break up the frozen crust, then push or blade back the dislodged snow to the auger-blowers of the rotary plows. When the snowpack is heavy, the park service often requires a special congressional appropriation of $100,000 or more to finance the operation.

On the east side, the Caltrans crew has a relatively short section to plow. "Compared to the park, we've got the easy part—but it's not always that easy," remarked one veteran of the snow removal wars. "We usually have seven or eight miles. They've got over forty." For Caltrans, one of the more difficult areas, the Blue Slide, lies along the section east of Warren Creek. At this spot, the snow removal is complicated by rock that has been swept into the roadway during the winter and hidden by the snow. These rockslides can easily damage the swirling augers of the rotary plows.

Inside the park, the avalanche-prone sections east of Olmsted Point and at the crossing of the South Fork of the Tuolumne River bring

Cross-country ski trips across the Sierra crest over the Tioga Road gained real popularity in the 1970s. A public cabin for winter travelers is still maintained in Tuolumne Meadows. Photo by author.

great hazards to workers removing snow. As one veteran park employee observed, "The designers forgot winter when they got the Tioga Road to this point." To reduce the danger, the park service has tried to hasten the snow melt by various techniques, including dumping inert charcoal in these sections. In recent years park crews even covered the Olmsted Point section with black plastic sheeting in an effort to heat the underlying snow.

Normally the two snow removal crews plow only their areas of responsibility and no further. As a result, the Caltrans crew is usually first to the summit. But in heavy winters, the Caltrans machines have been known to slip inside the park and give a helping hand. In 1983 when park workers were battling twenty feet of frozen "Sierra cement" near McSwain Summit, their Caltrans counterparts pushed their plows well past Tuolumne Meadows.

The fall closing of the Tioga Road brings different problems. For the past twenty years or so, the park service has imposed a late-season overnight parking ban to prevent autumn backpackers and campers from being caught by snow. During the many seasons veteran ranger Ferdinand Castillo occupied the small Tioga Pass entrance station, he observed an unorganized band of Tioga Pass "regulars," who wanted to be among the last over the road in the fall. It was part of the road's following, he quipped.

A century after the first miners spent the winter in the Tioga mining camps, Marilyn Muse and Jim Harper spent the big winter of 1982-83 as the winter patrol rangers at Tuolumne Meadows. "It was a long winter with a record-breaking amount of snow falling in the Tuolumne Meadows area and the Sierra in general. Between October 30, 1982 and May 31, 1983, we received 600 inches of snow," Muse observed.[30] Though not all fifty feet were on the ground at one time, the snow fell in prodigious quantities.

Every season along the Tioga Road is different. For some the fall road closure marks the change of seasons more than any other natural phenomenon or event. For others, it defines the start of a waiting period and begins the countdown to that day when once again they'll be able to return to their beloved high country.

Tuolumne Meadows winter rangers Jim Harper and Marilyn Muse spent the winter of 1984 in this cabin, far removed from the bustling world beyond the park. Photo by author.

NOTES

1. Bil Gilbert, *Westering Man—The Life of Joseph Walker* (New York: Atheneum, 1983), 134.

2. Douglass Hubbard, *Ghost Mines of Yosemite* (Fredericksburg, Texas: Awani Press, 1958), 23 (Chapter 15).

3. *Homer Mining Index*, 5 February 1881.

4. Hubbard, *Ghost Mines of Yosemite*, 5 (Chapter 4).

5. Ibid.

6. Ibid.

7. William B. Berry, interview with author, Reno, Nevada, 17 April 1987. The ski historian emeritus for the U.S. Ski Association said that skis or Norwegian snowshoes were relatively common items in the mining camps around Tioga Pass during the late 1800s.

8. Lily Mathieu LaBraque, *Man From Mono* (Reno: Nevada Academic Press, 1984), 77-85.

9. LaBraque's 1913 date is apparently in error. Gardisky did not arrive on the scene and the Sierra Club's building was not built until after 1915.

10. LaBraque, *Man From Mono*, 77-85.

11. Ibid.

12. Ibid.

13. Mary Curry Tresidder, "Story of the Snow Creek Lodge," manuscript dated October 1952. Copy in Yosemite Research Library, Box 979.447, T-4, #33.

14. Shirley Sargent, *Yosemite and Its Innkeepers* (Yosemite, CA: Flying Spur Press, 1975), 118.

15. Mary Curry Tresidder file, Yosemite Research Library.

16. Gene Rose, *High Odyssey* (Clovis, Calif.: Panorama West Books, 1987): 147-150.

17. Ansel Adams, letter to Orland Bartholomew, 27 October 1929 (author's collection).

18. Rose, *High Odyssey,* 154.

19. Dr. Donald Tresidder, letter to Dr. Rea Ashley, no date, reprinted as Appendix #1 in Mary Curry Tresidder, "Story of the Snow Creek Lodge," 4.

20. Mary Curry Tresidder, "Story of the Snow Creek Lodge," 7.

21. Omer Crane, "148 Years of Skiing for Badger Pass Oldtimers," *Fresno Bee,* 5 March 1978, C-1.

22. Linda Wedel Greene, *Historic Resource Study: Yosemite,* vol. 2 (Washington, D.C.: U.S. Department of the Interior, National Park Service, 1987), 728-29; *Water Conditions in California,* Fall Report, October 1983, California Cooperative Snow Survey Bulletin 120-83 (Sacramento: California Department of Water Resources, 1985).

23. Carl P. Russell, "Why Are Snow Surveys Made?," Yosemite Nature Notes, VI, no. 3 (31 March 1927): 19.

24. Henry J. During, telephone interview by author, 14 August 1991.

25. Tommy Tucker, letter to author, 18 August 1991.

26. Ibid.

27. Ibid.

28. The manufacturer was not related to Tommy Tucker.

29. Ron Mackie, conversation with author, Tioga Road, 7 March 1984.

30. Marilyn Muse, "Natural History Observations for Tuolumne Meadows, Winter 1982-83," report in Yosemite Research Library.

CHAPTER 11

TALL TALES
FROM TIOGA

The stories that go with the "old" Tioga Road are as colorful and varied as the high route itself. Every Sierran traveler can relate an adventure from a crossing of California's highest pass. Old-timers tell yarns about early drivers who became so terrified at the route that they "froze at the wheel." Reports, such as the one that called it "tantamount to committing suicide" to tackle the one-lane wagon road, have naturally been embellished over time.

Some of the best Tioga accounts are fish stories. A few years after Stephen Mather's mountain party came up the east side, Bill Banta, an early Mono Basin pioneer, got together with some young friends. They decided to try their fishing luck at Saddlebag Lake. "It was 1919 and we made the trip up in a Model T Ford. There was no town of Lee Vining in those days, but the state had finished a bridge across the [Lee Vining] creek, and the narrow dirt road up the canyon toward Tioga Pass. At Saddlebag they were finishing off the small dam that raised the lake. The fishing was the best I had ever experienced. We got two five gallon cans full of trout. They were so big that their tails flopped over the top of the cans," Banta recalled.[1]

Increasing visitor use of the Tioga Road brought the need for summer rangers in the high country. In 1927, Eva and Charles McNally, newlyweds from Stockton, arrived at Tuolumne Meadows to become the first seasonal rangers at the small outpost. At that time, Charles recalled, it was a long day's drive from the Central Valley to the high country. Crocker's Station, Carl's Inn, and then Aspen Valley marked the "peopled places" along the old wagon road in the 1920s. After that the road climbed up to White Wolf and over McSwain Summit before dropping down to Yosemite Creek.

"We got the job because a friend or ours knew park Superintendent [W. B. "Dusty"] Lewis. They wanted to know if I had a pistol and knew how to use it—you had to have your own pistol then. Then they had me take an oath, then they issued me a badge—with a $5 deposit—and that was it. The only training I had was on the job," Mr. McNally explained.

"The first summer we worked as seasonal rangers—a husband-and-wife

Opposite: The entrance station at Tioga Pass has been a welcomed and welcoming landmark for many years.

team at Tuolumne Meadows under chief ranger Forest Townsley. I did everything from ride patrol, man the entrance station, and work fires and searches. It was anything that came along, but most of it was answering questions from the visitors. It was a great camping area even then. People used to drive all over the meadows, camping wherever they wanted. It was okay then because there weren't the crowds that came after the war," McNally reflected years later.[2]

He recalled several incidents when those unfamiliar with the route became paralyzed at the wheels of their cars and refused to move. In such cases, a ranger or another volunteer driver would take over and drive "the victim's car" to his or her immediate destination. There were numerous accidents, but McNally could recall no fatalities on that original section of road during his summers at Tioga Pass.

"The old road, particularly the Lee Vining Canyon section, had the reputation as 'the most frightening road in America,'" he noted. "But the people respected that old road; they took their time with it. There was a lot of backing up and pulling over to let the other guy by, but there weren't a lot of serious accidents."[3]

With the establishment of Lee Vining in the mid-1920s, the road's reputation grew. Pioneer Bill Banta observed that even with the road's rather frightening notoriety, he could recall only two fatal accidents in his lifetime spent in the area. During the reconstruction of the 1930s, when a maintenance facility was located at the Warren Creek crossing, a pair of road workers came down to Lee Vining for a night on the town. After too much to drink, they tried to drive back to camp, but went into the creek and drowned. In the other accident, a young construction worker died after backing a dump truck off the road during the reconstruction of the 1960s.[4]

Even the gloom of the Great Depression did little to slow the migration over the high mountain road. The car counts for 1929 and 1930 were healthy and nearly identical—13,292 and 13,571. Some old-timers contend that the depression actually spurred park visitation, as camping

The old Tuolumne Meadows gas station had one of the most scenic settings in the country. Lembert Dome served as its dramatic backdrop.

Eva and Charles McNally stand on the porch of the Tuolumne Meadows Ranger Station. Note that she is wearing a service revolver at her waist and a ranger badge pinned to her argyle sweater.

and touring were less expensive than resort vacations or foreign travel. In fact, in 1931, the first full year after the stock market collapse, Tioga Pass had its then record-high visitation of 18,674 cars, a figure that would not be exceeded for the next fifteen years.

Sterling Cramer, whose career with the Yosemite Park & Curry Company spanned thirty-five years in jobs ranging from ticket clerk to vice president, said the 1930s were the years of discovery for car campers. Early in that decade Cramer left Yosemite Valley, after working all Saturday, and headed for Tenaya Lake, where he was to join his family in the campground. The Tioga Road at that time went from Crane Flat to Carl Inn and followed the old wagon road alignment.

By the time Cramer reached White Wolf, it was dark. A couple of miles beyond, the lights on his Model A Ford failed and he found himself in the darkness of the red fir forest, unable to see the road. For an hour he sat there, hoping another car would come by, but none did. Soon thereafter, however, a big August moon moved out of the trees and bathed the high country in moonlight. Cramer cranked up his coupe and drove to Tenaya Lake "by moonbeams," arriving shortly after midnight—and without encountering another car.

Top: Engineers and road workers inspect the framework of a trestle during the 1926 reconstruction in Lee Vining Canyon. Over the years this rugged terrain has posed recurring challenges to road builders.

Bottom: The early Yosemite Creek grade stretch of the Tioga Road was both narrow and steep. Here it is shown in 1927.

A few years later, Cramer and his wife were returning to the valley from another Tioga trip when something went wrong with their car's transmission near Yosemite Creek. He found himself limited to the use of "high gear" only. That, he joked, wasn't the gear of choice for the Tioga Road. "You seldom ever shifted into high, especially on the twenty-one-mile section," he mused years after.[5]

Leroy Rust, the late park postmaster with Yosemite roots back to the 1800s, recalled how his grandfather, who had once hauled freight into the valley by mule wagon, served as the road foreman during the days when the Crane Flat cut-off was being constructed. One morning he experienced some discomfort with his false teeth and removed them, setting them aside as the road work went on. At lunch time, when Rust went to eat lunch, he couldn't quite remember where he had set his dentures. Recognizing basic priorities, he immediately suspended construction and sent the crew along the roadway to look for his false teeth. Well into the afternoon, the missing dentures were located. Only then could lunch be had—and the road work move forward.[6]

Yosemite author Shirley Sargent's introduction to Yosemite came by way of the Tioga Road in 1936. "My dad was an engineer working on the new Tioga road for the Bureau of Public Roads. We spent two enchanted summers along the road. The first summer we were at Tuolumne Meadows in an abandoned CCC [California Conservation Corps] camp in a sixteen-by-sixteen-foot tent. It was a pioneer existence, with tents, outhouses, and Coleman lanterns. There was no refrigeration. The workers used to keep their beer packed in snow that they hauled down from Tioga Pass."[7]

Sargent had her first lesson on wildlife protection there. "I had a sling shot and one day one of the early ranger naturalists, Duane Jacobs, came up to me and asked me if I had ever thought how I would feel if I killed a bird or squirrel with my sling shot. He did it so tactfully and I was so impressed that I went up to the top of Lembert Dome and threw it away . . . and immediately regretted it, but it was my introduction to conservation."[8]

In the mid 1940s, Hal and Eva Berglund acquired Al Gardisky's old fishing camp from his heirs and opened Camp Tioga, later known as Tioga Pass Resort. Like those before them, they became imbued with the spirit of the place, as they lent their energies to the accommodation of the passing parade of travelers. "We got to know many of the old-timers who had come up the east side in the days when it was a real adventure. The part that used to amaze me concerned their stories on the bridge or viaduct section of the old road below Ellery Lake. In the early days, that section was nothing more than a couple of boards across a ravine, and the drivers had to be guided onto those boards so the car's wheels would line up in order to get across. It was no place for a timid driver."[9]

The Berglunds had their own adventures, particularly with summer thunderstorms. "We had some real gully washers. Both below and above the resort. Sometimes the road would be closed for weeks at a time. The area known as Blue Slide was particularly troublesome," Hal Berglund recalled.[10]

John Bingaman, who served the park service as a ranger between 1918 and 1956, had his share of adventures and adversity along the roadway. After an early winter storm forced the closure of the pass in late October of 1950, Bingaman and another park ranger had to escort a Curry Company tow truck that was hauling a disabled car to Crane Flat. Snow and strong winds buffeted them as they retreated down the road. Near the junction with the May Lake trailhead road, they were stopped by wind-thrown trees that blocked the road, forcing them to get out a saw and cut the trees out of the way. It was not the only roadblock they were to clear that day.

"We sawed some twenty to twenty-five fallen trees before reaching White Wolf. It was snowing and blowing hard most of the afternoon. We had only a crosscut saw and were beginning to get tired and cold. The wind we estimated was about forty miles per hour. We were traveling slowly between White Wolf Meadow and Smoky Jack when a red fir tree fell across the road in front of us. This stopped us as there was no way to get around. We were just debating what to do when, with a swish and crash, a five foot thick fir tree fell on top of Ranger Brown's car mashing it almost to the ground. It was a close call for all three of us. Sizing up the situation, it seemed the best thing to do would be to unhook the tow truck and use it for our transportation as the other two cars were hemmed in. We drove it around the trees and up a small bank of the road to get through. The four wheel drive finally made it around the two downed trees and back on the road," Bingaman related.[11]

Arthayda Quick, widow of Yosemite seasonal ranger-legend Clyde Quick, had a mountain of memories tied to the Tioga Road, spanning the twenty-five years the Quicks worked in Yosemite. She remembered the joys of motoring up the old dusty road as it ran from Carl Inn and up through Aspen Valley, before the Crane Flat realignment was made in the 1930s, and learning about the road's rich and colorful past.

There were many motoring incidents and a few accidents—like the

TIOGA CREEK AT CAMP TIOGA
TIOGA - YOSEMITE HIGHWAY P.O. LEEVINING, CALIF.
FRASHERS FOTO - POMONA

Top: Tioga Creek as it flows past the location of then Camp Tioga. Photo courtesy of Stanley Valim.

Bottom: Al Gardisky was the founder of Camp Tioga, an early fishing camp that developed into the popular year-round facility known as the Tioga Pass Resort. Photo courtesy of Neil Kelly.

time the driver of a pickup truck lost his brakes on the grade down from McSwain Summit—and lived to tell about it. "My son once came down the grade in a snow storm with logs tied behind his car to keep it from sliding off the road," she noted. "There weren't many serious accidents. Very rarely was anyone ticketed or taken to the hospital. There were dents and disgruntled drivers and complaints when they got to the ranger station."[12] Her husband, other rangers, and some visitors figured a way to deal with the difficult driving on the one-lane road. Since the road was "narrow, steep, and crooked," they would drive it at night so they could see the headlights of the approaching cars.

During the late 1950s, when the twenty-one-mile section was being realigned, the Quicks occupied the Yosemite Creek Ranger Station, which gave them a front row seat to the controversial construction project. "All of us listened with dismay to the domes being scarred across their faces in the name of progress, and yet we knew that even the little old road had too many cars on it. It was a beautiful little road, and you had time to see it as you had to wait for lots of cars, maneuvering to meet in a wide place; many dents happened, many cars overheated and stalled. It was a road that affected the heart and soul," she added.[13]

In 1954, Richard and Dee McLaren and their two young daughters arrived at Tuolumne Meadows, where Richard would work as assistant district ranger to John Bingaman. While he was out rangering, Dee had to maintain some manner of family life in a tent cabin. "Occasionally I would drive down to Lee Vining and pick up a few groceries. On one occasion I left just as one of those afternoon thunderstorms was building. By the time I got down the road it was really coming down—like a flash flood. I did my shopping and started back up the road when it soon became apparent that there were problems ahead. Then some of the road people stopped me and told me that the road was out.

"I managed to get back to Lee Vining and phone the valley and get word to my husband. Then I found out that the road was out in several places and couldn't be repaired for several days. Sonora Pass was also closed. As a result I had to drive all the way around through Reno to get back to Tuolumne Meadows. That one bag of groceries cost me a 300-mile trip," McLaren reminisced years later.[14]

Dorothy and Lee Verrett of Santa Barbara spent their summers in the Sierra, also. As school teachers, they enjoyed the fringe benefit of long summers, and they piled up nearly forty of them in the Sierra, dividing

Top: The Tioga Pass Resort is used by automobile-borne travelers in summer and skiers in winter. Photo by author.

Bottom: Ranger John Bingaman in 1950.

their loyalties between Reds Meadow and Tuolumne Meadows. For ten summers in the late 1950s and early '60s, Lee served as caretaker at Parsons Lodge, where they became seasonal fixtures.

While Lee Verrett told a series of entertaining bear stories, Dorothy personally experienced the ultimate bear incident. "We were staying in a little cabin at Tuolumne Meadows. At one point during the Columbus Day holiday, I noticed that the 'bruin baffle' on the building where the campers stored their food was open, so I went to close it. As I did, out burst a mother bear and her two cubs. She motioned to the cubs to run and then turned on me. I was attacked, but I was so astonished that I couldn't move; she pinned me to the tree and held me there until she saw her cubs were up a tree."[15]

Despite that incident, Dorothy's fondest Yosemite memories are tied to the Tioga Road. She recalls entering the park with the retreating spring snows and departing with the advancing October storms. "During our years at Tuolumne we saw the northern lights on a couple occasions. Some of the people thought it was a forest fire it was so bright. Those summers were very special times. My husband loved to drive the Tioga Road; he couldn't get enough of it. He died in 1977 and he wanted his ashes scattered at Tuolumne Meadows. The high country gave us memories to last a lifetime. That's what I live on now," she said.[16]

The Saddlebag Lake Resort, located about three miles northeast of Tioga Pass, had its own loyalists. In the twenty-six seasons following

Top: *A ranger car passing through Tuolumne Meadows soon after the Tioga Road was cleared.*

Bottom: *Seasonal ranger Frank Givens on horse patrol near Tuolumne Meadows in 1932.*

Top: It's easy to see why the road up Lee Vining Canyon has been subject to washouts and rockslides over the years.

Bottom: A number of maintenance and construction projects slowed traffic on the Tioga Road over the years. Here cars wait while an oiling operation is undertaken in September, 1938.

World War II when they ran the resort and ferry service, Mavis and Chuck Grover experienced many ups and downs in the Tioga Pass area. There were heart attacks, auto accidents, lightning-caused deaths, and other misfortunes, of course. But those tragedies were insignificant compared to the happy and enjoyable times they, like most Tioga travelers, knew. Fabulous fishing trips, high country outings, and special occasions such as mountain weddings became part of the Grover's extraordinary world.

Mavis Grover recalls one incident when a solitary, middle-aged man arrived at Saddlebag without any apparent agenda. For the first few days he remained detached from the rest of the guests. "He would come into the store for a few things, but was never outgoing; most of the time he just moped around. But over the space of the next week he gradually became more active and involved. Gradually he started talking to us and some of the others, and he took a greater interest in the area.

"Toward the end of his stay, he came into the store and told me that he had come there with the idea of committing suicide. But after a few days to reflect, he came to realize that there was a way out. The mountains had given him time to think out his problems, and he now realized he could go back home and face his problem," she recalled.[17]

Now retired, the Grovers, like many other mountain merchants, acknowledge that their resort business was more a labor of love than of financial reward. "Oh, we made money every once in a while, but the real profit was in the wonderful experiences we had there," Mavis added.[18]

Ruth Ewing, the widow of Mather District Ranger Herb Ewing, has her own Tioga history, reaching back over the thirty years her husband patrolled the Tioga Pass corridor after World War II. "We went up before the road was open, up through that tunnel of snow, and we would stay there until the snows returned in the fall. When my son Bob was only five months old we were living in a tent at Tuolumne—for the entire season.

Saddlebag Lake sits in a granite-rimmed bowl well above tree line on the crest of the Sierra Nevada.

Eventually we moved into the little patrol cabin, but that wasn't much better. The facilities were terrible: shared bath facilities, and someone was always walking in. We wanted a shower; working with the horses you had to have a shower or bath. But the park service said 'no' because it would be unsanitary to have a shower in the kitchen, the only other room. But what did it matter because the kitchen sink is where we bathed anyway."[19]

She said that the rangers' wives were taken advantage of. "They got two employees for the price of one. We were always expected to roll out the red carpet for any VIP that came along, providing them food and booze we couldn't afford to buy for ourselves. I remember the time some eastern senator from the appropriations committee came up and we were supposed to take care of him. He was on a freebie anyway, staying at the Ahwahnee, and we did what we could, but he really galled us when he said we should be paying the government for the pleasure of working there.

"Almost every night there was a problem. People out of gas, bear problems, or the motorist who had hit a deer. They were always coming up and shining their flashlight in our faces, looking for a ranger. I remember one occasion when one couple brought in a deer they had hit with their car. It was too far gone and the only thing we could do was put it out of its misery. Herb had to take a hammer and end its suffering because he didn't have a gun. He had always wanted a gun for such emergencies, but they wouldn't give him one."[20]

Mrs. Ewing tells a story of the old road from the post-World War II period, when a long line of motorists became stalled by vapor locks—a recurring problem at high altitude with the cars of that era. Rangers Herb Ewing and Carl Danner were called on to respond. After reaching the cars, the two men told the drivers to let their motors cool and instructed their passengers to get out and walk to the next rise, in an effort to lighten the vehicles and reduce the likelihood of the motors overheating again.

Herb Ewing, Mather District Ranger for many years, spent multiple summers in rustic accommodations at Tuolumne Meadows. Photo by author.

"A long line of people were walking up the grade, and it was very hot. Word finally got to Herb that former President Herbert Hoover was one of those who had been told to walk up the road. Hoover was quite elderly by then; anyway, Herb related this to Danner. When Danner heard the former president of the United States was among those walking up the road he jumped back in his car and drove up the road until he located Hoover and offered him a ride.

"Danner then drove Hoover to the top of the hill whereupon Hoover got out and offered up his thanks. 'Thank you, thank you very much, Mr. Forest Ranger.'" Danner was furious at being called a forest ranger. He said it was no wonder the park service never got any money during Hoover's administration. 'He didn't even know the difference between the National Park Service and the U.S. Forest Service,' Danner said."[21]

Both Ruth and her husband thought that arrangements for employees and visitors at Tuolumne Meadows were inadequate. The new road brought in more visitors, but without the support facilities to accommodate them. Still, Ruth had fond memories of the experience. "I loved the mountains and we had some wonderful times. We always seemed to have ice cream parties or watermelon feeds—we had all the snow in the world. And we had some great pot luck dinners, but it was not easy. The people we met were great."[22]

Ranger Carl Danner in a casual horseback pose in 1949.

After about sixteen summers, Ruth Ewing had had enough, and in 1969 she accepted a job with the post office in Yosemite Valley, while her husband continued to hold forth at Tuolumne Meadows until 1977. He retired that year, and the couple moved to a ridge-top residence near Groveland, where they could look east to the mountains and their beloved Tioga Pass.

There are hundreds of other stories about the remarkable relationships that people have developed with Yosemite's high country over the years. Almost all demonstrate the passion that the Tioga region generates in those who come to know it.

Perhaps the ultimate love affair was that involving Ferdinand Castillo, the veteran Tioga Pass entrance station attendant. For nearly forty seasons and until his death in 1993, Castillo (known as "Ferd" by many) reigned as the sentinel at Yosemite's eastern gate. Every spring he would follow the snow plows to "his" outpost, and there he would shovel the snow from the entrance station and nearby office that served as his residence. Then for the next six months he would devote his energies to the passing parade of visitors and to protecting Tioga Pass (about which he was very possessive).

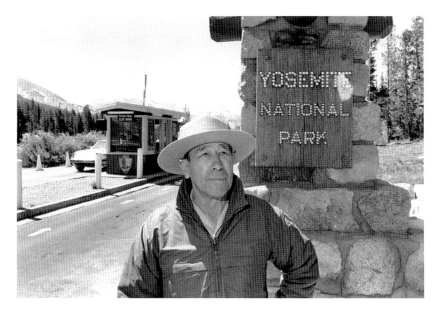

Ferdinand Castillo, a fixture at the Tioga Pass entrance station for over thirty years, became so attached to Tioga Pass that he treated the area around it as his own. Photo by author.

Castillo's devotion to the pass took many forms. He kept copious records regarding the weather and visitor numbers. His love for the mountains seemed to compel him to share them with others. As foreign visitation surged in the 1970s, Ferdinand learned to detect accents, and he picked up a smattering of several different languages. "What country are you from? Germany? Ah, ser gute, Deutschland. Gute reise," he would say. His experiences motivated him to press the park service to provide visitor information in several languages.

There were times, however, when Ferdinand didn't understand any language or job-related directive. During the 1980s, when his supervisor, district ranger Bob Johnson, arrived after the first major snowstorm to close the road for the reason, Castillo chose not to acknowledge the situation. "Ferdinand tried everything he knew to delay closing the pass. It would be snowing like mad and he would insist that the weather was going to get better. It was a real hassle for us to get him out of there. He could find more excuses not to leave. We almost had to drag him out of there," Johnson recalled.[23]

As protector of the pass, Ferdinand developed an enthusiastic group of fans—many of whom he really didn't know. What they shared in common was a love for the Yosemite high country and Tioga Pass, and Castillo embodied those locations for them. It was these "groupie campers" who provided him food and transportation, knowing he didn't drive or keep any kind of kitchenware. But he had his detractors, too—those put off by his over-zealous demeanor. Ferdinand watched the area around Tioga Pass with an overprotective and eagle eye, often remonstrating wandering visitors with "Stay out of the meadow. Don't trample the wildflowers."

Carl Sharsmith gave meaning to higher education, Sierra style. For nearly fifty summers, the Yosemite high country served as his classroom, and park visitors were his students. A professor of botany at San Jose State and one of the nation's foremost alpine botanists, Sharsmith also was the park's longest-tenured seasonal interpreter.

At the end of the school year Sharsmith would jump in his old Ford convertible and head up the Tioga Road to Tuolumne Meadows and his high country tent-frame home. There he reigned as Yosemite's most venerated ranger-naturalist, leading hikes to Mount Dana, Glen Aulin, Lyell Canyon, and other locations. Visitors flocked to his wildflower walks and overnight hikes, seeking to discover the magic of his alpine world.

As the high country patriarch, Sharsmith inspired a long line of admirers who regarded the high country as their mountain cathedral. Sharsmith followed in

Three classic high country characters: Ferdinand Castillo, Carl Sharsmith, and Nic Fiore. Photo by author.

the footsteps of early pathfinders and Tioga icons, such as John Muir, Little Joe LeConte, and William Colby. Carl Sharsmith died in 1994, but his spirit still inhabits the alpine meadows, forests, and peaks of his beloved Yosemite.

Another Tioga legend is Nic Fiore. Up until 2003, when health problems interceded, Fiore served as the manager of the High Sierra Camps, based at Tuolumne Meadows. For many Yosemite lovers, Fiore had the "ultimate job." During the winter months he ran the Badger Pass ski school, introducing thousands of visitors and their children to the art of downhilling. With the late spring closure of the ski area, Fiore would turn his attention to readying the High Sierra Camps. Depending on the winter, the abbreviated high season could range from two to three months. From Glen Aulin to Merced Lake, Fiore would oversee the high camps, literally running from one to the other, sharing his love of the high country with others.

Today, a new generation of Tioga titans is on the scene. One Tuolumne Meadows fixture is Martha Miller, who over the past thirty-plus years has run first the White Wolf Lodge, then Tuolumne Lodge (the only High Sierra Camp accessible by road). On the National Park Service side, seasonal park ranger Fred Koegler has patrolled the Tioga Road for more than forty summers.

Over the years, legions of appreciative visitors and employees have explored and enjoyed the trans-Sierra route, each with different experiences and stories. The lore of the Tioga region will continue to grow as the area's timeless qualities are discovered by each new generation.

Long-time high camp manager Martha Miller at White Wolf Lodge. Photo by author.

Notes

1. Bill Banta, conversation with author, Lee Vining, 14 January 1992.

2. Charles and Eva McNally, interview by author, Fresno, 17 February 1991.

3. Ibid.

4. Bill Banta, conversation with author, Lee Vining, 14 January 1992.

5. Sterling Cramer, interview by author, Wawona, 3 October 1990.

6. Leroy Rust, conversation with author, Wawona, 3 November 1989.

7. Shirley Sargent, conversation with author, Foresta, 6 September 1991.

8. Ibid.

9. Hal Berglund, telephone interview by author, 1990.

10. Ibid.

11. John W. Bingaman, *Guardians of the Yosemite—A Story of the First Rangers* (Lodi, Calif.: END-KIAN Publishing Co., 1970), 47.

12. Arthayda Quick, conversation with author, Fresno, 1992; and Arthayda Quick, letter to author, 17 February 1992 (in Yosemite Research Library).

13. Ibid.

14. Dee McLaren, conversation with author, Clovis, 25 June 1991. Dee McLaren is the widow of Richard McLaren.

15. Dorothy Verret, telephone interview by author, 23 February 1981.

16. Ibid.

17. Mavis Grover, telephone interview by author, 12 June 1990.

18. Ibid.

19. Ruth Ewing, interview by author, Pine Mountain Lake, Calif., 17 October 1991.

20. Ibid.

21. Ibid.

22. Ibid.

23. Bob Johnson, conversation with author, Yosemite, 12 September 1989.

CHAPTER 12

TIOGA TRAILS AND TURNOUTS

The Tioga Road passes through one of the world's great wonderlands. Many a first-time traveler whose introduction was simply driving the route has returned repeatedly to experience the countless elixirs of the Tioga world. For along its winding way, the high country course touches dozens of trailheads that lead beyond such recognized attractions as Tenaya Lake and Tuolumne Meadows. The rewards of a day hike or backpack are shimmering high-altitude lakes, peaceful alpine meadows, mountain peaks overlooking stunning vistas, and forests alive with flora and fauna unique to the Sierra.

From its western beginning at Crane Flat in Yosemite, where it turns off the Big Oak Flat Road, the Tioga Road swings gradually to the east towards the crenelated roof of the Sierra. Every turn reveals another high country gem, each with its own beauty and history. The varied and unusual place names assigned to the landmarks suggest earlier times, events, and visitors. At Gin Flat, a serene sub-alpine setting, a barrel of booze (gin, of course) reportedly fell off a passing freight wagon, but was recovered and emptied by grateful herders or cowboys.[1]

Today Gin Flat provides a nice stopping spot and is the turnoff for the popular Tamarack Flat Campground, which also serves as the trailhead for several outstanding hikes. One route winds down to the Big Oak Flat Road, while another heads off for the north rim of Yosemite Valley and El Capitan. The hardy hiker can move back in time by following the rough remains of the old Big Oak Flat Road to Yosemite Valley. It was along this death-defying stretch that the first wagons made their way to the enchanted valley, but it is no longer maintained as a road or trail. For those willing to do a little pathfinding, the rugged route offers some spectacular vantage points. Some rough off-trail scrambling through boulders is rewarded at the old overlook known as Rainbow View. When the light is right, a colorful arcing bow appears in the mist of Bridalveil Fall.

About a mile beyond Gin Flat, the Walker Party Overlook marks another milestone in Yosemite's human history. The location

Opposite: A open-topped touring car hugs the inside lane as it starts its exposed descent down Lee Vining Canyon.

Siesta Lake, set in a glacial cirque, is slowly filling with sediment.

commemorates the first group of Euro-Americans to view Yosemite Valley. As they look out over the scenery, visitors can imagine the hardships and privation the great mountain man, Joseph R. Walker, and his men endured as they struggled through the unmapped, roadless wilderness in the fall of 1833. They faced early snows, grizzly bears, cold, hunger, potentially hostile Indians, and the unknown. Though the actual route taken by the Walker party is uncertain, historians believe that the adventurers may have passed near this spot on their trans-Sierra route.

Three miles beyond, the dancing and dashing waters of the South Fork of the Tuolumne River greet the Tioga traveler. The South Fork Bridge is a great place to stop in the early season to witness the magic of the spring run-off as it booms down the mountainside. Both sides of the bridge offer spectacular viewing. In late summer the run-off slows and the river's trickle is just a hint of its impressive springtime flows.

Up the road, ancient red firs line the route, almost touching the sky. They convincingly support John Muir's thesis that they are, indeed, "the noblest" in the Sierra forests. Nestled among the red firs are the remains of the old Smoky Jack Campground. Smoky Jack was the nickname for one of Muir's early employers, John Connell, who ran sheep in the area.[2] Allegedly, Smoky lived primarily on beans, which he poured into his pockets each morning as he sauntered off with the sheep—with increasingly odiferous consequences.

Siesta Lake, about a mile to the east of Smoky Jack, illustrates that the trans-Sierra route is still undergoing geologic transformation. Eons ago, a receding glacier left a tumble of boulders known as a terminal moraine, creating this scenic, cirque-bound lake. But over the years, sediments back-filled the drainage, and the lake became a pond. Sometime in the future it will become Siesta Meadow. The reader would be well-advised to see it now; another 100,000 years and it may be too late. Along the Tioga Road, nature is continually at work, revising the sublime beauty of the unparalleled landscape.

Beyond Siesta Lake, the White Wolf turnoff leads to the historic White Wolf Lodge and Campground. The original Great Sierra Wagon Road came this way, and a pair of homesteaders from Groveland, John D. Meyers and his wife, settled and built a home here. After World War I, with the arrival of the first motorists, the couple began offering meals and overnight accommodations. Their business thrived, and they added a dozen tents. Some historians suggest that Meyers used White Wolf as a base for his cattle. After the National Park Service acquired the land, he used the Stanislaus National Forest and herded on the Cherry River range until about 1940.

How did the name White Wolf originate? No one really knows, but it is believed that the designation has an Indian origin.[3] Today White Wolf has a large following, both as a concession for lodging and meals and as a park service campground. It also serves as a jumping off spot for Harden Lake and the northern approach to Lukens Lake, for the Grand Canyon of the Tuolumne, and for the Ten Lakes Basin.

During John Muir's first summer in Yosemite, he spent considerable time in the Yosemite Creek drainage herding sheep.

Three miles further along the Tioga Road a spur road forks off to the right, leading down to the popular Yosemite Creek Campground. Beyond this turnoff, the road passes the parking lot trailhead for the southern approach to Lukens Lake (on the left). The grade increases as the motorist approaches 8,147-foot McSwain Summit. It is here in winter that the Tioga snow pack is often the deepest and the snows the most enduring, being shaded both by the north-facing slopes and the tall stands of trees.

At turnouts beyond McSwain, the road offers outstanding views of Mount Hoffmann and the more distant Clark Range to the south, then descends to a bridge over Yosemite Creek. The Yosemite Creek drainage was John Muir's special country. In his

Left: *This sign, which no longer stands, marked one of the last remaining sections of the "old" Tioga Road. A few remnants of the unimproved road still exist.*

Right: *The Tioga Road allows hikers quick access to the trailhead for Mount Hoffmann. The Hoffmann Ridge, shown here, is near the geographic center of the park.*

classic *My First Summer in the Sierra*, Muir related the difficulty he and another herder had in trying to get their sheep to ford Yosemite Creek. Despite many efforts and tactics, the sheep refused to cross, leading Muir to conclude that "a thousand sheep do not have the brains of one fool human." Finally Muir carried one lamb across, and enticed its mother to follow. Then with the herd instinct, the rest of the flock plunged into the stream. Muir's ghost still stalks the forests and ridges of the Yosemite Creek drainage that hikers and backpackers explore.

At the crossing of Yosemite Creek, a heavily-used trail on the north side of the road leads to the Ten Lakes Basin, a popular hiking and backpacking area northwest of Mount Hoffmann. When it comes to access to backcountry trails, the Tioga Road is hard to beat. Ron Mackie, retired from the National Park Service in 1997 after thirty-two years in Yosemite, including eighteen years as the park's wilderness ranger, believes the trail system emanating from the Tioga Road is unequalled anywhere in the United States.

"There are thirty-nine maintained trails and probably at least that number of unmaintained trails along the Tioga Road. It has a hiking heritage that goes all the way back to the Indians. There are little-known trails to places such as Deer Park where John Muir camped. It's hard to choose the most spectacular ones . . . there are so many, places like Pate Valley, Clouds Rest, and Lyell Canyon. I don't know of any road in the park system that has a greater variety of trails and other points of interest than the Tioga Pass Road," Mackie observed.[4]

Not far up the road, on a long straight stretch, lies Porcupine Flat, a primitive campground without running water and very few amenities. For centuries, this mountain meadow served as the gathering spot for Indians on their annual seasonal migrations to and from the high country. The campground has become a popular spot for those who want a less-developed, unmodernized camping experience.

In this area unmarked trails fan out on both sides of the Tioga Road, offering the experienced hiker a variety of choices. North from the Porcupine Flat Campground, an informal trail winds out to a series of ridges and meadows. To the south, a marked trail leads downhill to North Dome and one of the finest views available of Yosemite Valley. Along the way the trail touches sections of the old Mono Trail; at other spots its offers tremendous vistas of Half Dome, Mount Starr King, and other spires of the Clark Range.

As the motorist proceeds eastward, sections of the old road intersect and are visible from the highway, winding in and out among the trees and providing glimpses of the route early travelers took through the mountains. About two miles beyond Porcupine Flat on the north side is the turnoff for May Lake and Mount Hoffmann. For many Yosemite lovers the best thing about the Tioga Road is the access it affords to Mount Hoffmann, regarded by Muir, Whitney, and others as the centerpiece of the park. The side road and nearby trail lead up near the Snow Flat winter cabin and towards the May Lake High Sierra Camp. From the lake today's hiker can retrace the two-mile route of early mountaineers to the base of Mount Hoffmann and up the rugged but rewarding 1,500-foot climb to the summit. The peak is at the geographic center of Yosemite and offers an amazing 360 degree view of the park's grandeur.

Top: The turnout at Olmsted Point, with its remarkable view to the south and west, is the most popular along the Tioga Road.

Bottom: The massive granite wall of Tenaya Canyon is revealed to the visitor who takes the time to venture off the road a bit. Photo by author.

Back on the Tioga Road, Olmsted Point stands out as the most popular turnout along the entire route. The vista provides tremendous views of Tenaya Canyon, the back side of Half Dome, and Clouds Rest. To the east, it offers a grand glimpse of Tenaya Lake and the spires and domes surrounding it. In the opposite direction, another spectacular portrait of high country ridges and ramparts is afforded.

At Olmsted Point visitors from all over the globe will be expressing their wonder in an array of languages, though "ooh" and "aah" seem to belong to the universal idiom. The vista point was named for Frederick Law Olmsted, the noted landscape architect famed for his work in New York's Central Park and elsewhere, who was on the board of the original commission to manage Yosemite Valley and the Mariposa Grove.

At Tenaya Lake, two miles past Olmsted Point to the east, the opportunities for rest and recreation are unmatched. The late Lanson

Left: The hiking opportunities in the vicinity of Tenaya Lake are varied and extensive.

Right: *A High Sierra Camp operated by the Desmond Park Service Company once graced the banks of Tenaya Lake. Photo courtesy of Marilynn Guske.*

Crawford of Fresno, an artist, hiker, and long-time Tioga Road aficionado, once observed that there are more hiking and sightseeing opportunities along the Tioga Road than any road in the entire national park system. Crawford claimed he could spend a week at Tenaya and hike every day without retracing his path. Besides the trail that loops the lake, there is access to the trails to Olmsted Point, May Lake, Polly Dome, and Sunrise. A number of unmarked cross-country trails leads to nearby summits and lakes.

One of the more spectacular unmarked paths starts directly across from the west end of Tenaya Lake and goes up the glaciated slope to a small dome topped by two wind-scuplted, whitebark pines. This vantage point was a favorite of Edward Weston, one of the great landscape photographers of the mid-1900s, who was guided there by his colleague, Ansel Adams.

The sandy beach on the east end of Tenaya Lake was once the site of a High Sierra Camp (long since removed) founded in 1916 by the Desmond Park Service Company. During August the beach takes on a bit of a Coney Island appearance, as hundreds of vacationers and visitors flock here to hike, picnic, boat, and swim. In February, it is a vastly different sight, as winter snows edge the frozen lake's surface and visitor-filled automobiles are only a memory.

Across the road from Tenaya Lake near the western base of Polly Dome, a trail leads north to the Polly Dome Lakes. In recent years, the granite dome has become a magnet for rock climbers, and it's not unusual to see dozens of climbers looking like human flies on its flanks. Up the road at marker T-26, the Ghost Forest gives testimony to the recuperative powers of natural systems. The lodgepole pine forest is returning to health after thousands of the trees were killed by needle miners (harmful insects) in the early to mid-1900s. At this marker another unmaintained trail, one of the so-called fishermen's routes, heads out to the south, snaking its way up the mountainside to Lake of the Domes and Cathedral Lakes.

As the Tioga Road proceeds east beyond Tenaya Lake, it passes through a fine forest of mountain hemlock, one of the few such stands in Yosemite.

Above: *Tuolumne Meadows is the largest meadow system in the Sierra Nevada and the hub of the Tioga Road corridor.*

Left: *The Tuolumne Meadows store, a canvas-covered structure, has long been a popular gathering place for hikers, climbers, and campers.*

The route also skirts the base of Fairview Dome and several other large granite hemispheres, including Medlicott Dome. This towering rock was named for Harry Medlicott, an early Tioga miner, road builder, and mountaineer. It is a fitting monument to a man who braved extreme weather conditions, avalanches, and other forms of adversity in the high country he chose to inhabit.

Next along the route is Tuolumne Meadows, the largest meadow system in the Sierra and the hub of the Tioga Road corridor. Besides a ranger station, campground, store, stable, interpretive center, and other facilities, Tuolumne Meadows is home to a lot of happy campers. During the summer months, "Downtown Tuolumne Meadows" becomes the Sierra's largest "tent city." No less than a half dozen major trails radiate from Tuolumne. Besides the Pacific Crest and John Muir Trails, alternate or secondary trails lead to Cathedral Lakes, Pothole Dome, Dog Lake, Elizabeth Lake, Glen Aulin, Vogelsang, and Fletcher Lakes. Favored day hikes include the walk up Lyell Canyon or the trip down along the Tuolumne River to Glen Aulin and beyond.

Top: Mount Dana dominates the skyline east of Tuolumne Meadows.

Bottom: An early open touring car affords its occupants an unobstructed view of Tioga Lake, just east of Tioga Pass.

East of the meadows, the imposing forms of Mount Dana and Mount Gibbs dominate the skyline. Farther east, Kuna Crest stands in profile, with Mono and Parker Passes beyond. Along the trails in this area are fading signs of the old wagon road and the remains of some of the mining cabins that were abandoned decades ago.

A short but steep hike from the Tioga Pass entrance station leads north to the Gaylor Lakes and the remains of Dana City and the Tioga Mines. Situated in a high basin, the two lakes have been popular day hike destinations for Yosemite visitors for years. Another route leads from the lower lake's western outlet, and down to a park service utility road about three miles west of the Tioga Pass.

The Tioga section of the popular *Yosemite Road Guide* identifies forty points of interest between Crane Flat and Tioga Pass. Veteran park rangers and long-time visitors know that there are many more, both inside and outside the park, filling the Tioga Road's diverse and unrivaled world. Tuolumne Meadows "regulars," who come back year after year, constantly discover new areas to hike and explore beyond the well-known trails and destinations.

Between Tioga Pass and Lee Vining, the hiking opportunities do not decrease. About a half mile east of the pass and south of the road, another unmarked route leads off around the west end of Tioga Lake. It winds its way up to a saddle leading to Glacier Canyon, Dana Lake, and the

small glacier lying on the rugged eastern face of Mount Dana. When the Tioga Road opens in spring, cross-country skiers often can be seen high on these slopes, squeezing that last bit of downhill action from the retreating snowfields.

Occupying a special place in the hearts of many high country fans is the venerable Tioga Pass Resort (known affectionately as "TPR"), located about three miles east of the park boundary and founded in the early 1900s. A couple of hundred yards east of the resort, the Saddlebag Lake road leads to a small campground that is the trailhead for the *pièce de résistance* of the eastern slope of the Sierra. A trail leads to the once-bustling community of Bennettville, home of the Tioga Mine. Here the modern day romantic can wander about the hills and reflect on the activities and challenges of the earliest miners.

The first stop on the Saddlebag Lake road is the Sawmill Walk-in Campground. On its western periphery a series of unmarked cross-country routes leads out toward a half dozen alpine lakes that dot the eastern slope of White Mountain. The adjacent area includes much of the Harvey Monroe Hall Natural Area of the Inyo National Forest, where overnight use is prohibited. Farther to the north lies Saddlebag Lake. For a fee, a boat transports hikers across the lake to a network of cross-country hiking opportunities towards Conness Lakes and Glacier and Steelhead Lakes, where the hardy hiker or backpacker can re-enter Yosemite National Park and reach McCabe Lakes.

Back on the Tioga Road and into the main Lee Vining Canyon, about two miles below the outlet of Ellery Lake, an old jeep road takes off to the north near Warren Creek. A state-operated road-maintenance camp was once located here. Today the site serves as a starting point for serious hikers who want to visit the Hoover Wilderness. Following a difficult trail

Left: *The Tioga Road starts at the bottom of Lee Vining Canyon, ascends gradually for a bit, then makes a steep and tortuous climb to Tioga Pass and Yosemite.*

Right: *The intimidating route of the Tioga Road up Lee Vining Canyon is shown here. Locating and constructing the road was a feat of skilled engineering. Photo courtesy of California Department of Transportation.*

Right: The driver of the first car over Tioga Pass in 1919 is rewarded with a snowball attack.

Below: The prospect of descending the Tioga Road through Lee Vining Canyon was a daunting one. Some drivers froze in terror behind their steering wheels. Photo courtesy of the California State Library.

up talus slopes, hardy hikers can reach Oneida Lake and either make their way back toward the Saddlebag road or, by turning east, venture down to Lundy Lake. Throughout this remote and rugged land, signs of the early miners' presence are everywhere.

Before the road in Lee Vining Canyon became two lanes in the 1960s, Dodge Point was a popular stopping spot. The scenic lookout served a dual purpose on the narrow grade. Besides its view of California's most scenic—and frightening—road, it provided a wide spot where opposing traffic could squeeze by. How was it named? A pair of young motorists was traveling the spectacular road in a Dodge, when the driver decided that he wanted to take a photograph. He stopped and moved his companion behind the steering wheel while he sized up the scene. Concluding that the picture would be more impressive if the car were pulled slightly ahead, he asked his friend to move it. Unaccustomed to the vehicle, he accidentally put the Dodge into reverse—and backed off the cliff.

The descent of the road through Lee Vining Canyon testifies to the bold engineering of Nathaniel Ellery, who first pushed the road up the rugged canyon. The steep cliffs were a formidable barrier, and even during the reconstruction of the road in the early 1960s, workmen were forced to rope up so they could take their jackhammers and pneumatic drills on to the steep canyon walls.

In 1987, the Mono Lake Basin was protected as part of the Mono Lake National Scenic Area.

In the bottom of Lee Vining Canyon, Lee Vining Creek meanders through a series of National Forest Service campgrounds. Popular with both campers and anglers, the creek is yet another beautiful Sierra brook that offers respite from the rush of modern life.

In 1986 about two dozen California bighorn sheep were re-introduced to Lee Vining Canyon by the Sierra Nevada Bighorn Sheep Recovery Program. After a difficult start and subsequent augmentation, the herd's numbers appear to be on an upward swing, although it will be years before the project can be termed a success. The sheep population seems to have stabilized after several years of serious predation by mountain lions. Occasionally, motorists will see the animals on the surrounding hills near Warren Creek, or, at times, right along the highway.

The Native Americans of the area still visit the Tioga region. In 1990, as part of the Yosemite centennial, native people from both Yosemite and the Mono Lake Basin re-enacted the historic migration across the crest via Bloody Canyon and Mono Pass. The trek has become an annual event, bringing renewed recognition to the ways of Tioga's original inhabitants.

As well, forest service archaeologists have found a significant Indian archaeological site below the Lee Vining district office, underscoring the long Native American presence in the Mono Lake Basin.

The Tioga Road ends at its intersection with state highway 395 in Lee Vining. Nearby lies the remarkable body of salt water known as Mono Lake. In recent years conservationists have focused on the plight of the lake by trying to restrict the water diversions out of the basin south to Los Angeles. They hope to maintain the lake level at 6,437 feet, and thereby preserve the ecosystem of the basin. In 1987, Congress established the Mono Lake National Scenic Area under the administration of the Inyo National Forest.

In recognition of the multiple scenic and natural resources near and adjacent to Yosemite National Park, some have called for the creation of a greater protected ecosystem that would transcend political boundaries and focus on the environmental health of the area between Mono Lake and the foothills of the western Sierra. Still others support the concept of a larger, unified national park, the so-called "Range of Light National Park." Such a reservation would span the Sierra, stretching from Lake Tahoe on the north, to south of Sequoia National Park. Significantly, the Tioga Road would be at the center of an expanded park.

Notes

1. Richard P. Ditton and Donald E. McHenry, *Yosemite Road Guide* (Yosemite: Yosemite Association, 1989), 41.

2. Ibid.

3. Linda Wedel Greene, *Historic Resource Study: Yosemite,* vol. 2 (Washington, D.C.: U.S. Department of the Interior, National Park Service, 1987), 689; and George H. Harlan, *An Island in Yosemite—The Story of White Wolf Lodge* (Greenbrae, Calif.: self-published, 1981).

4. Ron Mackie, interview by author, Yosemite National Park, 9 December 1991.

YOSEMITE

NUMBER 3
1961

TIOGA ROAD
1883 - 1961

The Tioga Road
A History, 1883-1961

by Keith A. Trexler, Park Naturalist

I t has been called the "road to broken dreams." Perhaps, though, its many miles of unexcelled scenic grandeur have fulfilled the desires, the deep-felt longing for a contact with nature's wilderness, even the dreams of many thousands who have passed over its often twisting, ever-changing course.

Before The Road

Trails have existed across the Sierra since the first large mammals came hundreds of thousands of years ago. Grazing animals—sheep, deer and even bear—move up the Sierran slopes to find tender young shoots as snow lines recede. Others travel over the passes seeking salt. John Muir noted that especially in rugged and inaccessible terrain the trails of "white men, Indians, bear, wild sheep, etc., be found converging in the best places."[1]

Next to appear were the pedestrian Indians, whose midden piles near El Portal show evidences of transsierran trade from at least as early as 2,000 BC.[2] Indians did not travel for pleasure; their purpose was trade. Acorns, berries, beads, paint ingredients, arrows and baskets were traded by the west slope Miwoks for the Eastern Mono's pine nuts, pandora moth larvae, fly pupae, baskets, rabbit and buffalo robes, salt and obsidian. Finds of these materials, not native west of the Sierra, help us trace the early Indian paths. Numerous highways of today, and the Tioga Road, follow these aboriginal trade routes.[3]

The Mono Trail, an Indian footpath from Crane Flat, through Tamarack Flat via Tenaya Lake to Tuolumne Meadows, was used by the first party of non-Indians to pass through what is now Yosemite National Park. Joseph Reddeford Walker and his party trekking over the Sierra, probably used the Indian pathway, evident even though many parts were covered with snow. The group endured great hardships and took over a month to make the crossing from Bridgeport Valley to the San Joaquin. They were undoubtedly the first white men to see the Giant Sequoias.[4, 5]

A visitor admires the plaque placed in 1924 to commemorate Stephen T. Mather's help in securing the Tioga Road for Yosemite National Park.

No records of man's use of the trails exist for the next 19 years. In 1852 1st Lt. Tredwell Moore and his troopers of the 2nd Infantry, pursued a group of Indians wanted for the death of two prospectors in Yosemite Valley, to Tenaya Lake and from there over the Mono Trail to Bloody Canyon. During the trip Moore noticed rich-looking outcrops and brought back some samples of gold to Mariposa. Among those who saw Moore's samples was Leroy Vining, of whom we shall hear more later.[5]

Moore's expedition reports interested James M. Hutchings in bringing the first tourists into the Yosemite Valley, and, according to Brockman, "public interest in mining opportunities east of the Sierra was kindled, resulting in the development and use of a trail in 1857, from Big Oak Flat through the Tenaya Lake-Tuolumne Meadows region. This route approximated the old Mono Trail and was a forerunner of the present Tioga Road."[6]

In 1852 Leroy (or Lee) Vining led a group of prospectors over the Sierra via Bloody Canyon and generally explored the region. Although Vining settled in what is now Lee Vining Canyon he apparently did no mining. Instead he homesteaded about two miles up-canyon from the present power plant and built a sawmill, thus being the first to settle in the Mono area. For a time he supplied lumber to the eastside mining camps, but his career ended in an Aurora saloon where he accidentally shot and killed himself.[8]

Although no rush followed Lt. Moore's discoveries, there was in 1857 an exodus from the Tuolumne mines to the Dogtown and Monoville settlements near Mono Lake.[5] Much of the old Mono Trail was used by the gold-seekers and the route was well blazed and cleared by Tom McGee "following very closely on the old foot trail." Bunnell makes the point that Indian trails were unfit for pack animals. He felt they "had been purposely run over ground impassible to horses."[9]

The early 1860s saw the coming of Josiah D. Whitney of the California Geological Survey. His description of the headwaters of the Tuolumne was published in 1865, with Tioga Pass (which he called MacLane's) being noted as 600 feet lower than the present route (Mono Pass) and perhaps a better transcontinental route.[10]

In the summer of 1858 a party from Mono Lake, including a woman and baby, visited Yosemite Valley. This group, perhaps the first to use the Tioga route purely for pleasure, journeyed over the Sierra via Tuolumne Meadows and Tenaya Lake, taking the Coulterville Trail to Yosemite Valley.[11] Other evidence indicates that the Mono Trail was being used for tourist travel, especially by hikers from Yosemite Valley heading for Tuolumne Meadows.[12]

John Muir's first visit to this spectacular country was in 1869 with a band of sheep. In traveling to the meadows, John and his charges followed the general course of the present Tioga Road.[13] In the same year J. H. Soper and E. G. Field with only blankets and a "supply of crackers and sardines" hiked over Mono Pass, met a sheepherder (Muir?) in the Meadows, and followed the trail out to Coulterville.[14]

By 1870 railroads had come to within a few miles of the west end of the Mono Trail. In 1871 Copperopolis was a terminus of the lines from San Francisco. Travel to Yosemite Valley was increasing. More than likely, visitors took side trips over the trail to Tuolumne but no records exist of their trials and tribulations. The Big Oak Flat Road reached Crocker's in 1871 and Yosemite Valley in 1874, but still there was no road to Yosemite's high country.[7] An economic boost was needed.

THE MINES

Although Lt. Moore's discoveries excited the Mariposa miners, nothing in the way of true mines seemed to come from the reports. Early in 1860 a prospecting party consisting of a justice of the peace, an ex-sea captain, a surveyor, a dentist and a professor was prospecting in the Bloody Canyon area. The dentist, George W. "Doc" Chase, remarked, while camped near Tioga Pass, that if they could but spend one more day in the area he could locate and claim "the biggest silver ledge ever discovered." The next day he placed a flattened tin can, on which he scratched the location notice with his knife, on Tioga Hill. The ore he carried out was never assayed as he and his partners arrived at Monoville just when the Aurora strike was made. Each made money but none ever returned to the "thundering big silver ledge" on Tioga Hill.[15]

Some 15 years later, William Brusky, Jr., while herding his father's sheep, found a rusty pick and shovel and a flattened tin can, on which he could make out, "Notice, we the undersigned" and the date 1860. Having heard of the lost mine, Brusky took ore samples to his father, who tested them and pronounced them worthless. Young Brusky did not discourage easily. The next summer he "sank a small hole in the ledge and procured some better looking ore." It was not until 1877 that an assay found the ore to be rich in silver.

Claims were not actually made until 1878 when nine were established and the Tioga Mining District organized.[15] The "city" of Dana, site of the Great Sierra Mine, was given a post office in 1880.[16] In 1881 the

At left center stands the crumbling remains of a rock cabin built by the ill-fated Great Sierra Consolidated Silver Company.

Great Sierra Consolidated Silver Company, financed with eastern capital, bought up all claims on Tioga Hill and started drilling a tunnel destined to go 1784 feet into the mountain, but never to produce pay dirt.[15]

On February 25, 1882 the Great Sierra Tunnel was begun by twelve miners working three 8-hour shifts. Soon it was evident that drilling machinery would be needed.[17] This was purchased and shipped to Lundy, on the east side of the Sierra. The *Homer Mining Index* reported: "The transportation of 16,000 lbs. of machinery across one of the highest and most rugged branches of the Sierra Nevada mountains in mid-winter where no roads exist, over vast fields and huge embankments of yielding snow and in the face of furious windstorms laden with drifting snow, and the mercury dancing attendance on zero, is a task calculated to appall the sturdiest mountaineer; yet J. C. Kemp, manager of the Great Sierra Consolidated Silver Co. is now engaged in such an undertaking, and with every prospect of success at an early day—so complete has been the arrangement of details and so intelligently directed is every movement. The first ascent, from Mill Creek to the mouth of Lake Canyon, is 990 feet, almost perpendicular. From that point to the south end of Lake Oneida, a distance of about two miles, is a rise of 845 feet, most of it in two hills aggregating half a mile in distance. The machinery will probably be hoisted straight up to the summit of Mount Warren ridge from the southwest shore of Lake Oneida, an almost-vertical rise of 2,160 feet. From the summit the descent will be made to Saddlebags Lake, thence down to and along Lee Vining Creek to the gap or pass in the dividing point to tunnel, a distance of about one mile, is a rise of 800 feet, most of it in the first quarter of a mile.

"The machinery consists of an engine, boiler, air compressor, Ingersoll drills, iron pipe, etc. for use in driving the Great Sierra tunnel. It is being transported on six heavy sleds admirably constructed of hardwood. Another, or rather a pair of bobsleds accompanies the expedition, the latter being laden with bedding, provisions, cooking utensils, etc. The heaviest load is 4,200 lbs. Ten or 12 men, two mules, 4500 feet of one-inch manila rope, heavy double block and tackle and all the available trees along the route are employed in snaking the machinery up the mountain. The whole being under the immediate supervision of Mr. Kemp, who remains at the

The remains of an air compressor sit outside the Great Sierra Tunnel. The machine and others like it powered the drills used to burrow into the unyielding rock.

front and personally directs every movement. It is expected that all sleds will be got up into Lake Canyon today, and then the work will be pushed day and night, with two shifts of men."

It took Kemp and his men more than two months, from March 4 until May 6, to move the eight tons a distance of about nine miles. It is said that Kemp's remark at the end of the back-breaking task was, "It's no wonder that men grow old!"[15]

The machinery was installed and put to work immediately upon its arrival at the mine. Meanwhile, on March 13, 1882, a post office had been established at Bennettville, company headquarters.[16] Miners swarmed to the area. More than 350 claims were located in the Tioga District alone. Bennettville was touted as an excellent location with ample room for 50,000 inhabitants, an abundant water supply and invigorating climate. [17]

Other claims were found. The May Lundy about 10 miles north of Tioga produced $3 million, though the Golden Crown, Mt. Hoffmann and Mt. Gibbs groups followed the Great Sierra example.[15a] In 1881 the Sierra Telegraph Co. built a line from Lundy to Yosemite Valley via Bennettville.[15]

On July 3, 1884 the boom was over. A financial "crisis" occasioned the Great Sierra's Executive Committee to suspend all operations and soon Dana City and Bennettville joined the silent ranks of fabled western ghost towns. Although more than $300,000 had been spent, as best we know no ore ever left the Sheepherder mine for milling.[15] But a road had been built.

THE GREAT SIERRA WAGON ROAD

Expectations of success and needs for large quantities of supplies coupled with the near disaster of hauling mining machinery over the snow led the Great Sierra Board of Directors to consider the building of a wagon road to the mines. Although trail routes had been established to the eastern railroads via Lundy and Bloody Canyon, the new road was to cross the Sierra from the west with goods to be hauled from the railhead

At the end of the Great Sierra Wagon Road, Bennettville, 1898.

at Copperopolis via the Big Oak Flat Road. Civil Engineer R. F. Lord in 1881 estimated the total cost to build a road from near Crane Flat to the mines at $17,000.[27]

In the fall of 1882 the company gave the go-ahead and Charles N. Barney was assigned as engineer with William C. Priest as his assistant. Both the survey and construction began at once. H. B. Carpenter and H. P. Medlicott conducted the road (and railroad) survey with a Mr. Hall and John V. Ferretti as chainmen. In addition to making the road survey the group was picking a line for a railroad "to make the shortest and most direct route from the east to San Francisco." Years later the pass was considered for part of the Union Pacific route.[23]

In July of 1882 the California and Yosemite Short Line Railroad had been incorporated in Sacramento to run from Modesto to Mono Valley via "old Lee Vining Creek or McLean Pass" with its "Principal place of business, Bennettsville, Tioga Mining District." J. C. Kemp, Van Eee, C. W. Curtis, O. H. Brooks and R. W. Woolard, all of the Great Sierra Consolidated Silver Co., organized the company with $5 million capital stock with $250,000 actually subscribed. California and Yosemite Short Line Railroad monies provided supplies, via Lundy, for the survey crew.[28]

The survey party advanced to White Wolf before snowfall. Work was resumed the spring of '82, and Tioga Pass was reached in July. The Bodie *Daily Free Press* noted that "Engineer Carpenter's . . . survey (was completed) for the California and Yosemite Short Line Railroad from McLean's Pass . . . to Mono Lake Valley" on July 20.[19] In August the *Free Press* commented on the fate of Tuolumne Meadows' hospitable hermit, John Lembert: "Now, however, the spirit of civilization in the person of John L. Ginn, Chief Engineer of the Yosemite Short Line Railroad, has planted the survey stakes of a railroad line within a hundred feet of the hermit's door, and it is a mere matter of time when his lonely reveries will be broken by the shrill whistle of the locomotive."[20] Chainman John Ferretti recalls meeting John Lembert who was living in a hut that to him "looked more like a bear trap than a place for human habitation" over Soda

Springs. Ferretti was somewhat awed by the hermit but found him friendly, though saddened by the advent of the road.

Another incident recalled by Ferretti concerns one of the survey party's mules. While camped on Yosemite Creek the mules had been stampeded by bears and one "had slipped into the little stream and hung itself." Later, on the return trip, Ferretti found the construction gang camped in the same spot with the dead mule only a few feet upstream from their water point.

After completing the survey through Tioga Pass, the surveyors tied in the mine locations and disbanded. John Ferretti joined the construction gang as a blacksmith's helper and general roustabout. His pay was augmented by pies, cakes and cookies slipped to him by Sing Lee, the camp cook. John's final act on the job included splitting his big toe with an axe. The "first aid man" applied "a large chew of tobacco, took a rag and tied it up, guaranteeing that it would be as good as new in a few days. At that moment . . . I severed my connection with the Tioga Road for all time."[21]

Construction progressed at an awesome rate. Nearly one-half mile of finished road was turned out by the 160 man crew for each day on the job.[22] The fall of '82 saw the road advance from Crocker's to as far as the present park boundary, about two miles.[21] On April 27, 1883 work was resumed "and it was carried forward without interruption or accident until finally completed September 4th, 1883." In 130 days the 56¼ mile stretch was completed at a cost of $61,095.22, or about $1,100 per mile.

From the columns of the August 11 *Homer Mining Index* we learn of construction progress and methods. "The Great Sierra Wagon Road is rapidly approaching completion. Harry Medlicott's graders from this side have reached the upper end of Tuolumne Meadows, while Priest's pick and shovel brigade from the other side are on Rocky Canyon Creek, leaving a gap between of little more than three miles, all of which is easy grading. Priest's powder gang, following the picks and shovels, reached Lake Tenaya Thursday and will skip the heavy blasting along the margin of the lake for the present and follow up to the Tuolumne River, after which one hundred blasters will be put on to finish the three-fourths of a mile along the lake. It is believed that freight wagons will reach Tioga by or before the end of the month. The construction of this road was a stupendous and costly undertaking and the Eastern capitalists to whose enterprise and public spirit the people of this county and coast are indebted for a great thoroughfare to a hitherto inaccessible but rich and extensive region, deserve to be remembered with gratitude."

According to one report[24] there were 90 white men and 250 Chinese in the employ of the company. Another alludes to 250 men[21] and a third a 160

John V. Ferretti

man crew of Chinese. We are certain that at least 35 Chinese were at work on the Tioga Road in '83 as a receipt for their hospital tax, paid for by the road company, is part of the Yosemite Museum collections.[26] Pay rates were phenomenal: the Chinese received $1.20 per day, the Caucasians $1.50.[25] The foreman, James Lumsden of Big Oak Flat, was most pleased when his wage was advanced from $1.75 to $2.00 per day in recognition of his making "changes of his own accord which the surveyors afterwards said were more practical." In addition all hands were supplied with excellent board.[24]

Soon after the Great Sierra Wagon Road was completed, "a big jollification was held in Sonora" with many prominent men of the day in attendance.[24] The road was built!

TRAVEL PRIOR TO 1915

But was it ever used for the purpose for which it was built? Probably not. No records survive to prove the point, but it is known that no ore was ever shipped out of the mines and special equipment purchased for use in the Sheepherder tunnel never got beyond San Francisco where it was sold at auction after the mines had closed.

Priest's report of August 4, 1884, "all clear from snow and being

On the old Tioga Road, about 1890.

repaired," leads us to believe at least some of the Great Sierra Silver Company's business was conducted over the route.[43] The last mention of the road in company records is dated 19 October 1884, more than three months after cessation of operations at the mines. "The road is in very good condition and will probably remain so during the winter and spring. Cross ditches have been put in all the way from Bennettville to Crockers, and I think $1,000 expended next year after the snow is gone will put it in as good a shape as ever."[44]

Although technically a toll route, no collection gates ever were set up and the road was used frequently by tourists, army troopers and stockmen. Little mention is made of the physical condition of the road until 1894 when the *Homer Mining Index* informed its readers, "A man who recently came over the Great Sierra wagon road reports it to be in execrable condition. It should be kept in tolerable condition if the company wishes to hold it; but, as a matter of real fact, it should belong to the Government and be kept in prime order, as an eastern outlet to Yosemite Park."[45]

However poor its surface, the Great Sierra Wagon Road was being used. One party remarked, "The road is very rough in places, but is not impassable." They recommended a light wagon be used in attempting the route.[46] Another group reported "fallen trees and washed-out roads had bothered us many times . . . but in no case had done more damage to us than to shorten our day's journey by five or ten miles." Their method of travel included unhitching the horses and transporting the wagon across "difficult" stretches with block and tackle attached to convenient trees.[47]

Official reports decried the condition of the road, intimating it was something less than a footpath, and a difficult one at that.[32, 52, 56] Replies from the attorneys of the owners, though admitting the road had not been kept in excellent condition, maintained that it was passable for its entire length by wagons and horse travelers.[33] This war of words continued for more than a quarter century.

The army superintendents were especially vocal. Captain A. E. Wood started the ball rolling in his first report (1891) saying that although trees were down across the road and that it was badly washed in places it made "a good mounted trail, and as such, is of much importance."[48] Later reports reiterate and expand upon Captain Wood's observations, and, in addition, urge the Interior Department to purchase the rights to the route.[49, 50, 51] It was noted that "The foundation shows excellent work, intended to be permanent."[50]

In 1896 a bill authorizing purchase of toll roads within the park was considered by the House but did not get to the floor for a vote.[58] The next year the cost of repairing the "extremely out of repair" road was estimated at $10,000.[51] Two years later a bill was introduced in Congress to authorize surveys for a new road from Yosemite Valley to Mono Lake which apparently duplicated the Tioga Road which was then considered impassable.[60] The Acting Superintendent in 1898 was of the opinion that the road was government property by default. "This is not a toll road and never has been; it has been abandoned by the builders for more than twenty

Army troopers patrolled the Tioga Road for twenty-five years.

years; if they ever had any rights they lost them by abandonment. The eastern half of the road is in such bad condition as to be hardly a good trail. I consider the Tioga Road the most important highway in the Park."[56]

By 1899 enough interest had been generated that the army was directed to clear the road for a Congressional commission inspection. Their report contains an excellent description of the road at the turn of the century. "The grades vary from 0 to 10 percent and the width from 10 to 20 feet. The road, however, was skillfully laid out and it may safely be said that most of it has a grade of only about 3 percent." It was "exceedingly well built, the bridges having fine stone abutments, and there is a particularly well-built section of sea wall along the shore of Lake Tenaiya." Most of the original surfacing was gone and the road was obstructed in numerous places by fallen trees. "It appears that no work in the way of maintenance has been done by the owner of the road for a number of years, though some slight work has been done by campers traveling over it." The commissioners estimated the cost of constructing a similar road to be $58,000, though the original outlay was found to be $61,095.22. Their final assessment was that the road was in fair condition, that its value was $57,095, that $2,000 would suffice to put the road in original condition and that the Federal Government should purchase the road as soon as practicable.[59]

Fate, most likely in the form of the sinking of the battleship *Maine*, interceded and though the bill was read in the House, it was never passed.[54] A second bill was proposed in 1901 to purchase all toll roads within the Park for $208,000, and it too failed of passage.[57]

In 1902 the Secretary of the Interior appointed a second committee to survey the park's toll roads. They, like their predecessors, urged immediate government control of all park roads.[61] Superintendents' reports for the years following upheld the committee's views, with one exception—Major W. T. Littebrant in 1913, in a notable example of shortsightedness, felt that trails and mules would be sufficient for park administration for the foreseeable future![62]

In 1911 the *Sierra Club Bulletin* under the heading "Old Tioga Road to be Acquired," noted that "The Government brought suit . . . to condemn an unused toll road . . . to make it part of the new system of roads through Yosemite National Park. W. C. N. Swift . . . is named as defendant."[63]

One of the most telling comments on the condition of the road is contained in a 1912 letter from Major W. W. Forsyth, Acting Superintendent of the park, to the Secretary of the Interior. "Several wagons passed over the road last summer, . . . but also last summer I had to order a gratuitous issue of rations to a destitute family who were moving by wagon across the park from the east side by the Tioga Road because their team became exhausted on account of the difficult road and their food supply gave out before they could get through."[64]

What of the owner's side of the story? Before answering we might well ask, as did Yosemite's acting superintendent in 1913, "who were the owners?"[65] At a Mono County sheriff's sale in 1888 W. C. N. Swift, as trustee, purchased the entire properties of the Great Sierra Consolidated Silver Company for $167,050.[15] For an additional $10, Swift obtained the Tioga Road toll franchise from W. C. Priest,[31] who remained in charge of the road.[66] The mine properties and road were sold for taxes in 1895 to Rudolphus N. Swift, and remained the property of his heirs until 1915.[67] All during this period the firm of Wilson and Wilson handled the affairs of the road's owners. Through them we hear the "owner's side of the story."

Immediately after Captain A. E. Wood's initial blast, Wilson and Wilson offered to the Secretary of the Interior an affidavit from Road Superintendent Priest. "That said road is about 20 feet wide on an average and that teams may pass with convenience, with few exceptions, throughout the entire length of said road, and that in the opinion of this deponent said road is the best road that has ever been built on the Western Slope of the Sierra Nevada."[68] The battle is joined!

Wilson and Wilson's tenor was not so positive some four years later. They noted that the road had not been abandoned, but "we confess that they (the owners) have been somewhat neglectful by reason of the slight travel . . . upon the road."[66] It was the attorney's opinion that the road would have been kept in repair had a road been completed down the eastern side of the Sierra.[59] "If and when that eastern portion is completed the owners intend to resume the collection of tolls." The law firm urged the United States to purchase all the toll roads in the park and was of the opinion that this would have already been done "but for the extreme difficulty of inducing Congress to spend money on any new project, especially one which necessitates a regular annual expenditure for maintenance."[69]

In answer to charges that since tolls were not being collected the road belonged to the government by default, Allen Webster pointed out that the owners had spent thousands of dollars in repairs and that toll gates were not erected because of light travel.[70]

As the debate progressed others were brought in to testify on behalf of the road. Mrs. H. R. Crocker, whose home and place of business was Crocker's Station, the western terminus of the road, commented in 1907 that there was considerable travel over the road this season and "all are unanimous in its praise. . . Travelers had no trouble in getting over the entire length with team and heavy wagon." She reported some repairs to the road, including replacement of the Yosemite Creek bridge which had been out for eight years, by persons in her hire.[71]

Later correspondence from Mrs. Crocker repeats her original points, with the added suggestion that "something should materialize towards its (the road's) permanent repair."[72, 73]

In 1908 Andrew P. Dron found the road to Soda Springs in "excellent condition." He noted that two or three bridges were out over small streams, "but their want is not at all felt." All of the fallen trees are out of the road and . . . taken as a whole I consider it a better road as it is today without any work on it, than the Ward's Ferry road . . . to Groveland." He made 38 miles in one day over the Tioga Road.[74]

With the suit of 1911 in progress further depositions were made. Mrs. Crocker was in the fore stating that "repair work (was done) in 1912 and the road opened as usual to travel. It has been opened and traveled by

Sunset Camp in 1936 located at the site of the former Crocker's Station.

YOSEMITE'S TIOGA COUNTRY

teams (both heavy and light wagons), people on horse back and pedestrians every year since its construction. It has never been closed to travel, except . . . when . . . blocked by snow. It is still in fair condition with the exception of two or three places at Lake Tenaya and Yosemite Creek."[75]

Swift's attorneys proclaimed that considerable sums had been expended on up-keep of the roads (though no documentation of the expenditures was presently available) and that the franchise standards, i..e. a *100 foot wide roadway,* had been lawfully maintained. They cited the fact that the counties through which the road passed had always accepted the company's tax offerings, implying that all the franchise conditions were being met. The reason advanced for non-collection of tolls was that the company did not receive enough in returns to keep a man on as tollmaster. Their final opinion was that the United States had no claim to the road except by lawful and fair purchase.[33] The suit was never pressed to completion and the debate remained unresolved until 1915.

Business Ventures

Soon after completion of the Great Sierra Wagon Road William C. Priest of Big Oak Flat, at the request of the Directors of the Great Sierra Company, was assigned the right to collect tolls by the counties of Mariposa, Tuolumne and Mono. Rates established were: Freight teams with two horses, $5; single horses, $1.50; passenger teams, each horse, $2.50; footmen, $1; horse and rider, $2; pack animals, $1.50; loose horses and cattle, 50¢; sheep and goats, 10¢ each.[29] A congressman quoted the rates as working out to 3½¢ per person per mile, comparing favorably with the 3⅓¢ on the Big Oak Flat Road, 3¢ on the Coulterville and 2¢ on the Wawona Road.[30] No records exist of toll revenues. The Swift heirs, successors to W. C. N. Swift's purchase of the toll franchise in 1888 for $10,[31] stated that though considerable sums had been spent on upkeep of the road no tolls had ever been collected.[33]

Other enterprises were more profitable. Since the early 1880s H. R. Crocker had operated "Crocker's Sierra Resort" stage stop on the Big Oak Flat Road, just west of the present park boundary. Mr. Crocker and his young wife with the help of ex-sea captain Allan S. Crocker, provided excellent board, clean rooms and diverse entertainments to Chinese Camp and Yosemite Stage Company passengers, private travellers, campers, and even Indians from a nearby Miwok Rancheria.

Crocker's Station was construction headquarters during the building of the Great Sierra Wagon Road and later provided a comfortable stopping place for those using the road for business and pleasure. Many well known names grace the Crocker register, among them John Muir, Stewart Edward White, Edwin Markham and Herbert Hoover. The resort was considered by many "the showplace of the road." Although sold by widow Crocker in 1910, the station continued to serve the Yosemite-bound until 1920, when several of the buildings were moved and the rest allowed to decay. [34]

Some ten miles northeast Jeremiah Hodgdon built, in 1879, Yosemite's first and only two story log cabin.[34] Unknown to Jeremiah, the cabin would

later house some of the builders of the Great Sierra Wagon Road, would
provide shelter for the cavalry patrolling Yosemite National Park,[38] and
in the 1920s become the center of a busy tourist stop on the Tioga Road.
In 1931 the Aspen Valley Lodge complex included the lodge, a rooming
house, store, gasoline station, auto repair garage, laundry, restaurant and
the old two story log homestead cabin in use as a storehouse.[35] A park
entrance station and ranger station were located nearby. With realignment
of the Tioga Road in 1937, profits dropped and closure of the facilities
was assured when public use of the old road was discontinued in World
War II. Private summer homes and a logging operation existed into the
1950s. Most of the land eventually became acquired for park purposes: the
homestead cabin was moved to the Pioneer History Center at Wawona.

Next stop on the line for the eastbound visitor was White Wolf, named
by a sheepherder who saw a white wolf there. Settlement at White Wolf
probably began with crude shelters for the Meyer boys and their ranch
hands. Little is known of early developments, but in 1930 it was reported,
"Mrs. Meyer is in charge of a believed-to-be well-paying resort." Twelve
tents, a main building which housed a dining room, kitchen and small
store, two tourist cabins, a power plant, and the ubiquitous gasoline station
comprised the assessable property.[35] Relocation of the road and the tourist
hiatus of the second world war brought the operations at White Wolf
to a standstill. After three years of very indifferent lessee proprietorship,
the Yosemite Park and Curry Co., in 1952, with government purchase of
the land and facilities, acquired the concession rights, and the following
year opened the rejuvenated unit as one of the High Sierra Camps. 1960-
1961 saw the improvement, by the National Park Service, of the public
campground and access road.

Between White Wolf and Tenaya Lake, a distance of nearly 20 miles, no
accommodations have ever existed, though camping was, and is, permitted

in designated spots along the road. On August 1, 1878 an enterprising Irishman and one-time Yosemite guide, John L. Murphy, homesteaded the meadows abutting the south end of Tenaya Lake and a small portion of the north shore. Thirty days later he planted 52 brook trout from the Tuolumne River; in 1882 a correspondent for the Bodie *Daily Free Press* reported, "the lake is swarming with fish, some already two feet in length." Mr. Murphy was established!

In 1881, Archie Leonard, destined to become one of Yosemite's first rangers, put on a ten-horse saddle train between Yosemite and Lundy.[39] Business must have been good for Leonard and Murphy as numerous articles proclaiming the virtues of the trip and its accommodations appeared in the Bodie and Lundy tabloids. One reporter opined, "Lake Tenaya is destined to become a watering place of note"[20] and Murphy's is a place "where good accommodations will be found, where the scenery is particularly grand, picturesque and beautiful, and trout are abundant."[40]

Another author commenting on "where to go and what to do" gives us an idea of what accommodations were like there. "The business of accommodating travelers at Tennayah has not yet reached sufficient dimensions to warrant the establishment of a fully modern-ized hotel. Mr. Murphy has . . . maintained a 'stopping place'. . . that will be found quite satisfactory to all comers who are not excessively hard to please, and that may have a more piquant interest to persons to whom the shifts and devices of mountain life are matters of some novelty."[42]

Murphy's hospice served as a stopping place for the Great Sierra Wagon Road surveyors as well as H. L. Childs' Bennettville to Yosemite Valley telephone line construction crew.[20] Later visitors included Helen Hunt Jackson, John Muir and Galen Clark. Nothing is known of the operation from 1890 to 1916 when the Desmond Park Company set up a tourist camp on the site of Murphy's place. The Yosemite Park and Curry Co., Desmond's successors, closed the Tenaya operations in 1938 in favor of a more isolated location at May Lake, thus establishing another of the High Sierra Camps.[39]

Although Tuolumne Meadows had been touted as an excellent camping spot since Lt. Moore's 1852 visit, little was done to oblige visitors to the area. Cabins were built in the 1880s by sheepmen using the meadows for summer pasture.[38] John Lembert's reign as the "hermit of the Sierra" extended over a period of about 10 years during which time he offered what hospitality and help he could to the wayfarer and tourist.[42] Lembert

White Wolf Lodge in 1931.

Lee Vining Canyon and the Lee Vining Grade, looking towards Mono Craters.

homesteaded the Soda Springs property in 1885,[41] though he had spent his summers there since at least 1882 and perhaps earlier. Hermit John left the Meadows in 1890 after being snowbound and losing his profitable angora goat herd. After Lembert's murder below El Portal in the spring of 1896, his brother sold the homestead to the McCauley brothers of Big Meadows. They in turn sold it to the Sierra Club in 1912;[41] three years later the Parsons Memorial Lodge was built.[39] The Sierra Club occupied the property until December 1973, when it was sold to the National Park Service for $208,750. The Club sold the property, because of "growing problems connected with managing the campgrounds, Parsons Lodge, and the nearby Soda Springs."[39a] "Neither the Club nor the Foundation are equipped or prepared to adequately meet the problems of running a campground within a public park, with all the problems—overuse, sanitation, policing—that attend such an operation."

The National Park Service operated the campground for three years, then closed it. The Yosemite Natural History Association presently provides information and interpretive services at Parsons Lodge.

Tuolumne Meadows Lodge was opened in 1916 by the Desmond Park Company and is currently operated by the Yosemite Park and Curry Co. In addition to the lodge there is now a store, restaurant and service station operated by the concessioner plus National Park Service ranger stations, campgrounds and a small museum. For the first few years of operation of the Tioga Road as a park route, the park entrance station was in the meadows; it has since been moved to Tioga Pass.

THE EAST SIDE

Even before the Great Sierra Wagon Road was completed, suggestions and surveys for routes down the eastern escarpment of the Sierra had been made. At first only horse trails over the Mt. Warren divide and down Bloody Canyon connected the Tioga mines with the Mono valley. In 1899 the California Department of Highways urged the building of an east side link in the Tioga route "to make Yosemite Valley, the high Sierras, and Lake Tahoe more attractive and accessible." A bill, authorizing appropriations for construction of the section was passed by the California legislature in 1897, but did not become law because of a technical error. Highway engineers recommended the Lee Vining Creek route as the best and estimated construction costs for a 16 foot roadbed at $30,000.[76]

Monies were forthcoming in 1899 and the Tioga Pass-Lee Vining line was selected. Construction began three years later.[77] By 1905 all but the five miles east of the pass had been finished. The cost—$39,000. One bid of $23,861 was received for the remaining section but work was delayed until an "understanding with the owners of the Tioga Road proper, regarding their non-resumption of the collection of toll" could be reached.[78]

The Sierra Club *Bulletin* of 1909 declared, "The new State road from

Mono Lake to Tioga Lake was completed last summer and is reported to be a monument to the skill of the State engineers. It has a maximum grade of seven per cent, and is a good road for automobiles. The old Tioga road (not now available to autos) . . . should be repaired without delay, so as to afford one of the most wonderful trans-mountain trips in the world."[79] Maps in 1910 Yosemite National Park booklets show the Tioga route as a through road to the east, despite the Park Superintendent's warning that the "road is in wretched condition."[80] In 1913 the California State engineer, asking if the Tioga Road was in condition for travel, noted that the east side road is "in excellent shape." Major Littebrant's reply was that "the Tioga Road through Yosemite National Park is impassable except for saddle animals."[81, 82]

During 1939 and '40 the Lee Vining Road between Tioga Pass and Lake Ellery was widened and realigned at a cost of $78,000. "The completion of this improvement is regarded locally as one of the highlights of the 80 years of man's struggle against the barrier of the Sierra at this crossing."[83] The State's plan for the Lee Vining grade in 1961 included realignment and widening.[84]

AUTOMOBILES ARRIVE

Although the first auto entered Yosemite Valley in 1900, it was not until 1913 that they were authorized legal entry. On August 16, 1913 the first auto permit was issued by Ranger F. S. Townsley. The car drove into the Yosemite Valley via the Coulterville Road (the only one open to autos) and was promptly chained to a tree.[6, 85, 86] According to Townsley, auto travel began in earnest in 1914 despite the more than 60 separate regulations aimed at limiting vehicular traffic in the park. Not only was one-way traffic the rule, but strict schedules had to be met. Fines of 50 cents per minute were assessed the hapless driver who dawdled along the way.[86] Top speed permitted, on straight stretches only, was 10 miles per hour, with 6 m.p.h. as the limit where curves were evident.[87]

In January 1915, Stephen T. Mather, an enthusiastic booster of auto travel in the National Parks, accepted the post of Assistant to the Secretary of the Interior. One of his first concerns in the new job was to make park travel easier. "A cash primer was called for to set the process off. Mather thought about this and had a familiar reaction. He hauled out his checkbook. For a curtain-raiser to his park's administration he wanted to make some noise—preferably in Yosemite, which had high hopes for 1915, California being set for two "international expositions." Casting about for an idea, he remembered the Tioga Road, a broken-down east-west thoroughfare, fifty-six miles long (and privately owned) that bisected the park. Since the Tioga Road was the only potential automobile route aross the 270 mile wall of mountain stretching from Walker Pass, back to Bakersfield, to Sonora Pass, south of Lake Tahoe, its resurrection would be both beneficial and widely acclaimed. Mather thought about all this and then began to show an inner turmoil, a characteristic mark of his approach to a weighty decision. He gave the impression of being carbonated.

A visitor stops her touring car to take in the view of Tenaya Lake from the Tioga Road.

His associates were startled, but when they learned what was gurgling in him, they politely pointed out that the government could not make repairs on a road it did not own, and even if it could, it would not. "I'll buy the road, have it repaired myself, and donate it to the government," said Mather. They smiled. The United States of America is not a university or charity foundation. Giving things to the government was almost as suspect as making bank deposits to the account of a Cabinet officer or placing a bomb under a Senator's front porch. Congress must examine and pass upon every gift. "All right," said Mather. "My motives are pure." He had a special provision drafted for the Appropriations Committee authorizing the Secretary of the Interior to accept any donations of money, land rights of way, etc., for the national parks. That, he did not doubt for a moment, would do it. Fitzgerald surprised him. The Congressman, sure that only a black-hearted briber would want to donate something to the government, tore the provision up.

"Mather had to look for help to the California Senator James D. Phelan and to an old Chicago friend, Congressman William Kent, then of Kentfield, California. The two Californians, with some difficulty, managed to wheedle Fitzgerald into relaxing long enough to approve a limited provision covering gifts to Yosemite, setting Mather free finally to go ahead on the Tioga Road, which, he learned, carried a purchase price of $15,500. He made up his mind to raise as much of that as he could by subscription and to contribute the balance himself."[88]

Bus travel over Tioga Pass to Lake Tahoe became popular in the 1920s.

Calling upon his friends, Mather began to accumulate the purchase price. Julius Rosenwald, a Chicago philanthropist, was good for $1,000; Thomas Thorkildsen of San Francisco donated another $1,000, while the Modesto Chamber of Commerce and Sierra Club collected about $6,000. Mather donated the balance.[88] He then arranged for the Tuolumne County Surveyor to begin clearing of the old road and asked William E. Colby, his friend and fellow Sierra Clubber, to purchase the road from the Swift estate as Mather, being a government employee, was not in a position to donate the road to the United States.[89] Authorization to accept the road came from Congress on March 3, 1915 and formal title was transferred to the U.S. on April 10, 1915 for a consideration of $10.[90]

Mather next organized the first of his famous "mountain trips," outings designed to convince the influential or wealthy participants of the need for more and better National Parks. Robert Shankland's description of the group's ride up the Lee Vining grade on their way to the dedication of the Tioga Road is a classic comment on that stretch of the highway. "Coming over the Lee Vining Road, they followed an interesting road—just a fraction more than one-car wide with an unfenced drop-off of as much as two thousand feet. Local men were at the wheels, and the one handling the open Studebaker that contained E. O. McCormick, Ermerson Hough, and Horace Albright had not yet, though a native, become bored with the scenery. He would glance ahead briefly to gauge the curves, then rise from his seat, twist around, stare off over the grisly precipice into the distance, and, with a hand he kept free for the purpose, point out features of the landscape. McCormick, up front, was mute with terror. In the rear, safeside door open, Albright and Hough sat crouched to leap. Albright was trying to keep one hand on the open door and one foot on the running board and at the same time hold off Hough, who was clawing at him and hoarsely whispering over and over: "G__ d___ that scenery-loving cuss, G__ d___ that scenery-loving cuss!" To their surprise, however, they made the top of the range. There Mather formally dedicated the Tioga Road to public use, breaking a champagne bottle filled with Pacific Ocean water at a spot where it would flow both east and west. The night was spent camping with the Sierra Club at Tuolumne Meadows, and the next morning the party started on its final run, to the Yosemite Valley. It broke up there on Thursday, July 29."[88]

The 1915 report of the superintendent of National Parks noted that the Tioga Road had been acquired, was being rehabilitated this summer and was formally opened July 28. "When same has been put in shape it will be the most popular pass for transcontinental tourists through the Sierra Nevada."[91] During the 1915 season 190 cars entered the park via Tioga Pass and the comment was made that a visitor to the park could now travel 260 miles of road, at elevations ranging from 2,000 to 10,000 feet, for the $5.00 entrance fee.[92]

The following year 578 westbound autos checked in at Tuolumne Meadows.[93] After more than $30,000 had been spent rehabilitating the old mining road it became apparent that the route needed a thorough reconstruction, with some realignment, to bring maintenance cost down to a reasonable level. Mather asked Congress for $75,000.[94] The money not forthcoming, park officials began maintaining the road as best they could.

Gabriel Sovulewski's construction reports, 1916 to 1922,[95] help us recreate the tremendous task of keeping the undoubtedly decrepit road in shape for auto travel. In 1916, 24 men and two teams of horses were assigned to the road which was "in many places badly washed . . . (with half mile sections) . . . almost destroyed by dangerous washouts." Yosemite Creek bridge was gone and was replaced by a "permanent" structure. In addition more than 30 trees were down across the road between Tenaya Lake and Tuolumne Meadows. By the end of the season the roadway was placed "in very good condition considering the state in which it was found in the spring." The public speaks "very highly of the park roads, and there has been nothing but praise for the Tioga Road, though conditions are far from satisfactory and not as we would like to have them."

Stephen T. Mather and W. B. Lewis studying road location in 1925.

During the 1918 opening, 1200 pounds of powder was used to blast 150 trees off a five mile section of the road. Later that season damage from thunder storms was frequent and costly, nearly $6,000 being spent to keep the road passable.

By August of 1922 Sovulewski considered the road in excellent condition. However that fall, severe storms undid all the work and soon it was evident that the road was being destroyed "faster than we could keep up with repairs." There was no question now, there must be realignment and reconstruction. Preliminary plans were laid in the late '20s, but the job would not be complete until 1961. Meanwhile the road was in ever increasing use.

Entrance stations were set up in Tuolumne Meadows and Aspen Valley in 1918. In the same year a *California Motorist* article praised the road but reproduced a map showing 20 per cent grades near May Lake. Top speed on straight stretches was 20 m.p.h., with reductions to 8 m.p.h. when ascending and 12 m.p.h. when descending hills.[96]

Steve Mather's annual report for 1918 praised the road in no uncertain terms. "Again last summer did the Tioga Road amply justify its purchase and presentation to the park system. Again did it prove the need and popularity of a motor gateway to the upper wilderness. . . Fifty or sixty automobiles a day traveled the Tioga Road last season" with many drivers making the complete trip to Lake Tahoe. "It will be noticed that Yosemite National Park as a park, that is, without any special consideration or use of the Yosemite Valley, also seems to be coming into its own. This is a good sign."[97]

The Tioga Road gained popularity throughout the 1920s. Each summer the opening of the road was attended by fish fries and celebrations with local dignitaries in attendance.[98] From about 1925 onward an intense interest in earlier opening dates, mostly on the part of businessmen from east of the Sierra, began. Park Superintendents were cautious, replying that early openings were too costly when considered in terms of the price of snow removal and increased maintenance.[100]

Newspaper and magazine ads of the day, as well as government produced leaflets, entreated every citizen to visit his national parks and especially to travel "the world's greatest mountain tour through Yosemite to Lake Tahoe."[99] The finest accommodations were available on the route as well as comfortable campsites and excellent trout streams.[101]

Everything was not as advertised, however. "All motorists with camping outfits are obliged to undress completely and be fumigated for a full hour." Hoof and mouth disease had struck California and the foregoing applied to those heading into Nevada from points west. The circular to all park personnel continued, "This information should be given to those inquiring regarding conditions along the road. Giving of this information is bound to result in discouraging travel east of Tioga Pass!"[102]

Another, not quite so personal factor was beginning to discourage travel over the Tioga Road. The nation's highways were being improved and expanded at an amazing rate and the motoring public was becoming accustomed to smooth well-paved thoroughfares with high gear grades and easy curves. The Tioga Road was not such a route. It remained an all-dirt road until 1937. It was as Gabriel Sovulewski put it, "only an old-fashioned wood-road."

RECONSTRUCTION

As early as 1925 consideration had been given to realignment and reconstruction of the Tioga Road. In that year Director Mather visited Yosemite to walk-out suggested routes with Park Superintendent Washington B. Lewis.[103] In the years following, various routes were studied and rejected, with the Park Service submitting each for detailed review by conservationists, engineers and other interested groups.

Among the consulting groups was the Yosemite Advisory Board whose three members were imminently qualified to pass judgement on the various proposals. Chairman of the Board Frederick Law Olmsted, Jr., whose father, the "Father of American Landscape Architecture," was

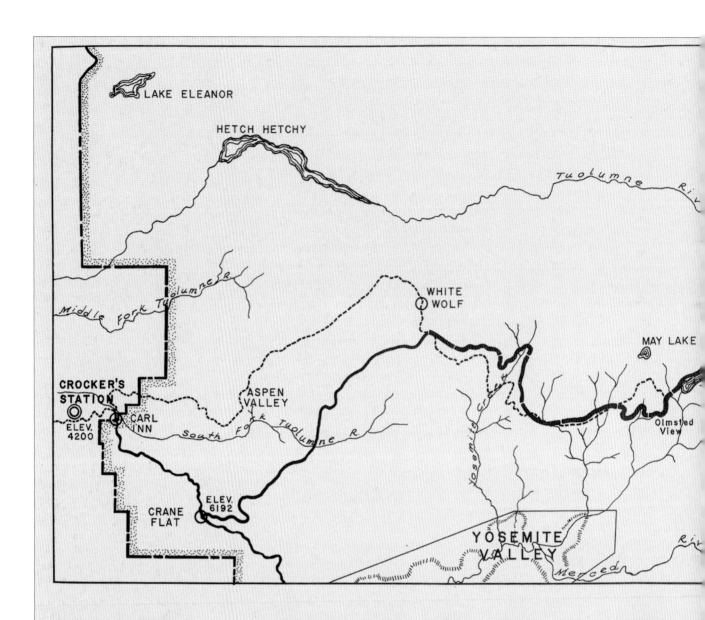

THE TIOGA RO

YOSEMITE NATIONAL PARK, CALI

L E G E N D

PARK BOUNDARY	
GREAT SIERRA WAGON ROAD	
SECTIONS REBUILT 1936-1939	
SECTION REBUILT 1958-1961	

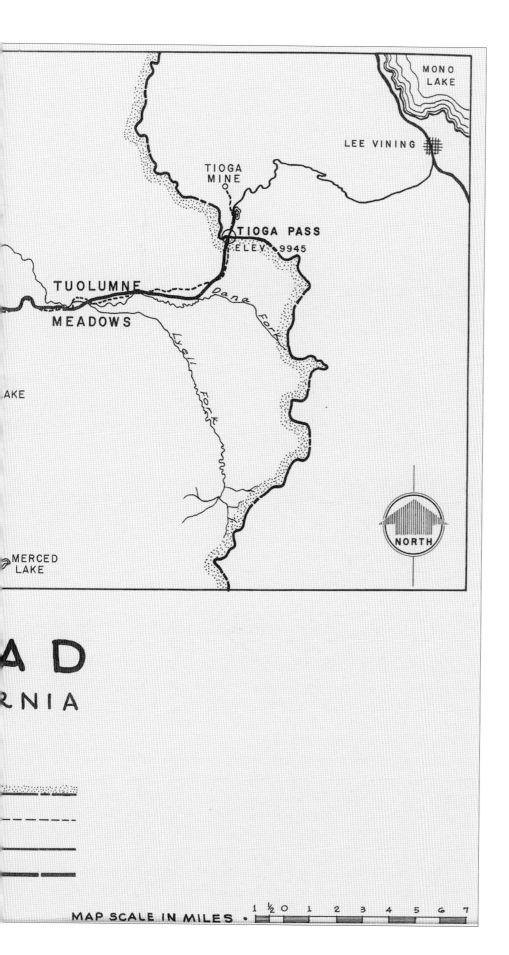

MONO
LAKE

LEE VINING

TIOGA
MINE

TIOGA PASS
ELEV. 9945

TUOLUMNE
MEADOWS

Dana Fork

Lyell Fork

AKE

MERCED
LAKE

NORTH

AD

RNIA

MAP SCALE IN MILES · 1 ½ 0   1   2   3   4   5   6   7

instrumental in the setting aside of the Yosemite Grant, was in his own right a world-famed landscape architect, an expert on parks and park development and former director of the California State Park Survey. (A prominent overlook on the new road has been called Olmsted View.) The second member of the Board, Duncan McDuffie, had served as Chairman of the California State Parks Council, was past president of the Sierra Club and recipient of the Cornelius Amory Pugsley medal for American Scenic and Historic Preservation. Professor John P. Buwalda, geologist and departmental chairman at California Institute of Technology, was the member of the group perhaps best able to advise on the Yosemite landscape, having done considerable scientific study in the area.

In 1932 a preliminary field survey was made with the tentative route marked and declared open for inspection. Several field trips were made by interested groups and by 1935 there was general agreement, including the concurrence of the Sierra Club,[104] that the present route of the realigned Tioga Road would be the one followed.

Meanwhile, work had begun on the eastern and western sections. In 1932 contracts were awarded for construction of the Tioga Pass to Fairview Dome section. Funds for the job, $250,000, were allocated from monies received from San Francisco as "rental" for the Hetch Hetchy area.[106] Fifty thousand dollars from the same source was to be made available for the Crane Flat to White Wolf portion, with work to begin in the spring of 1935.[107]

Paving of the 11.6 mile stretch of the new Tioga Road from Cathedral Creek through Tuolumne Meadows to Tioga Pass was completed in the fall of 1937 and for the first time in its history the one-time wagon road had a dustless section.[108] During 1938 the 21-mile McSwain Meadow (White Wolf intersection) to Cathedral Peak section of the unchanged bed of the Great Sierra Wagon Road was oiled for the first time,[109] and with the completion of 14.5 miles of new road between Crane Flat and McSwain Meadows on July 18, 1939, an era had ended.[110] Although nearly a quarter-century would elapse before the 21-mile central section of the old road was replaced, clouds of dust no longer obscured the vistas or irritated the adventuresome motorist.

Clouds of a different sort appeared on the horizon. World War II brought to a halt the further development of the road. Lack of maintenance funds during war-time caused the closing to the public of the Aspen Valley section of the old road.

A couple of "war stories" bear repeating. After the road was closed for the winter in 1942, a man with his wife and three children managed to plow his car through the drifts, after breaking the Tioga Pass gate. He was met by a ranger at Crane Flat and it was decided the best course of action for disobeying the road closure was to have the visitor return to the pass in his own car and repair the gate, a round-trip of 148 miles. "The visitor had intended to drive through the park without stopping, but he became so delighted with the trip back over the Tioga Road that he decided to stay in the park for several days longer. Ranger Givens, who accompanied the man to Tioga Pass, states that the man was a real lover of the mountains and that he enjoyed his punishment immensely. Not only was he taught respect for park regulations, but it is certain that this punishment left nothing but good will for the Park Service in his mind."[111]

After a hiatus of more than 50 years, cattle again were driven over the Tioga Road in 1943. Permission had been granted because rubber and gasoline shortages made truck transportation of the Aspen Valley herds an impossibility.[112]

Clouds Rest and Half Dome from Olmsted Point parking area.

POST WAR DEVELOPMENTS

Following World War II, travel to the parks resumed its upward trend and by 1950 use of the Tioga Road had increased more than 30 per cent above the pre-war level. Correspondence increased, too, both favoring and condemning the middle 21 miles of the Tioga route. While some feared damage to the park's scenic values would result if the route agreed upon in 1935 was built, many more feared the old road itself and worried about the more personal damage to themselves or their cars while negotiating the "horse-drawn" alignment of the remaining section of the Great Sierra Wagon Road.

The latter point of view became dominant as the travel picture changed. Larger cars and increased use of house and camping trailers made the old road a nightmare for many drivers and passengers alike.

The American Automobile Association warned, "It is not unusual to find people . . . unused to mountain roads, who just go to pieces, freeze at the wheel and park their cars in the middle of the road to wait for the Park Rangers or a kindly motorist to drive their cars the rest of the way."[115] And such was the none too happy picture on many a crowded summer day.

The general tenor of the many complaints being received was that the road was not only frightening to drive but was completely unsafe, a trip over it being tantamount to committing suicide. The facts do not bear this out. In actuality accidents on the old 21-mile section were so few that "a statistical analysis is all but impossible. Our records are not complete for the early days of use, but it is believed that no lives have been lost on the narrow highway since automobile travel was initiated in 1915." The primary problems were road jams on steep slopes due to vapor lock, "dented fenders, house-trailers caught between trees, mechanical failures and the overheating of many people's tempers when a speed of 20 miles per hour was alien to their experience on a narrow mountain highway."[116]

Other complaints were more reasonable and to the point. "While perfectly safe (since one must drive it slowly), it imposes undue anxiety on the driver."[113] "I feel this road is . . . unsafe for inexperienced drivers."[114] An experienced driver summed up the general feeling against the road thusly, "These 21 miles are the most exasperating I have ever driven. I will personally guarantee there isn't a trickier road anywhere. It is a good deal like a roller coaster, only rougher! But if your car's in good shape and you are confident of your driving skill; if you are looking for an adventurous route and breathtaking scenery, there's no better place to find them than along the Tioga Pass Road."[115]

If the Tioga Road was to adequately serve the public it needed immediate improvement. Although the routing had been long approved, World War II delayed action and considerable discussion was to ensue before construction began.

During the late 1940s and early '50s, a series of alternate routes were suggested by individuals and conservation groups. One plan, the "high-line" route via Ten Lakes and the northeastern slopes of Mt. Hoffmann was proposed by Superintendent Thomson. The Park Service again sought the advice of foremost experts in the field.

William E. Colby, an esteemed San Francisco lawyer, noted conservationist and Sierra Club officer, in concert with fellow Yosemite Advisory Board members J. P. Buwalda and Duncan McDuffie replied, "This is a subject to which the Yosemite Advisory Board has given very careful consideration over a long period of years. The proposal to route the road north of Polly Dome is, in our opinion, a grave mistake, because it would intrude a road into an area that is now and will remain wilderness in character if the road is not built." The Board endorsed the Park Service's original plan throughout.

Accordingly, it was determined that the 21-mile central section of the Tioga Road would follow the route as proposed by the Service and as strongly endorsed by the Yosemite Advisory Board. There remained, however, the question of standards—what would be the most appropriate construction standards for the new central section and who would be the best qualified person to undertake this study? Director Wirth was able to secure the services of the country's most outstanding authority in this field in the person of Walter L. Huber. Mr. Huber was not only a noted consulting engineer and past president of the American Society of Civil Engineers, but a nationally recognized authority in the field of conservation. He was a former president of the Sierra Club and present chairman of the National Parks Advisory Board. Mr. Huber had often been called to advise State and Federal agencies contemplating construction where esthetic considerations were important.

The Yosemite Advisory Board in 1953 with Superintendent John C. Preston. Left to right, W. E. Colby, F. L. Olmsted, Mr. Preston, and J. P. Buwalda.

After field and office studies Mr. Huber advised, "I feel that the Tioga Pass road is and must remain essentially a park road. For this purpose I consider the 20 foot width of pavement to be satisfactory, i.e., two 10 foot width travel lanes. For the 'Section in Through Fills,' I would recommend that the 3' 0" shoulder on either side of the pavement be widened to 4' 0". I note that this is to be a stabilized base native grass shoulder. I hope this specification will be retained with insistence, otherwise, shoulders are soon coated and from the motorists' viewpoint look the same as pavement;

thus we have in effect a 24 foot pavement without shoulders and once the motorist is over the edge he is often in trouble." He approved the Park Service standards on the remainder of the road, i.e., 2 foot shoulders.[117] These recommendations were accepted by National Park Service and Bureau of Public Roads officials and were incorporated in the final road plans.[119]

Actual construction began in 1957, with contracts let that year for clearing and grading 6 miles on the west end of the 21-mile section and 4.5 miles of the easternmost portion.[121] At that time the total cost of re-doing the 21-mile section was estimated at $4,658,000.[120]

Preservation of scenic values was uppermost in the minds of all connected with the project. If slight realignment would save an unusual natural feature—an ancient juniper, a lodgepole pine grove or glacial erratic boulder—the change was usually made.[121]

At this time Director Wirth pointed out, "There were changes made in the plans for the Tioga Road which took into consideration several of the suggestions made by the conservation people. . . I think the final decision was a good decision which took into consideration the many problems confronting us. No road ever reconstructed in the National Parks has had the detailed study and consideration that has been given to the Tioga Road. The route and standards were under intense study for 31 years."[122, 123] Associate Director E. T. Scoyen summed up, "When the debris of construction operations is cleaned up and the project fully completed, I am sure there will be virtually unanimous approval of this road which is designed to present to the motoring public a sample of high Sierra park wonderland. . . I am sure that hundreds of thousands in future years will be thankful for this opportunity to receive enjoyment and inspiration from superlative scenery."[125]

During the winter with construction halted, plans were completed and bids were let and accepted for the remaining 10 miles of the 21-mile section.[118]

The full 21-mile central section was completed and officially opened to the public on June 24, 1961. The cost was $5,491,000. The cost of the western and eastern sections was $1,450,000, or a total cost of $6,941,000 for the 46 miles from Crane Flat to Tioga Pass.

THE TIOGA ROAD TODAY

The Tioga Road today is the most scenic route in all California and one of the most outstanding park roads in the entire National Park System. It has been carefully designed and built to display the dramatic park values of the Sierra Nevada. The road is the highest trans-Sierra crossing with an elevation of 6,192 feet at Crane Flat and reaching 9,945 feet 46 miles later at Tioga Pass. It is designed for leisure travel (commercial trucking is not permitted), with numerous turnouts and overlooks where the park visitor may stop in safety to enjoy the superb scenery. At each of these vista points, the visitor will find interpretive signs which introduce and acquaint

One of the original interpretive signs at Olmsted Point.

him with that which he views. The interpretive texts, which have been carefully prepared by the park's naturalist staff, have met a hearty welcome from park visitors.

Sections of the old Tioga Road have been retained "as is" for those lovers of the old west who like to get away from the main route. One such section leaves the new road just east of the White Wolf intersection and winds and twists five miles down to Yosemite Creek where the visitor will find the same primitive quality campground which has served travelers on the old Tioga Road since it was first constructed. An additional two mile section of the old road climbs via Snow Flat to the May Lake Trail Junction. Other shorter sections still serve the primitive campgrounds along the old road, all of which have been retained.

What has the visitor's reaction been to the new road? It has been favorable and has drawn expressions such as "Now you can see something," "What a relief," "It's a pleasure to drive it," are common. The greatest number of visitor bouquets is probably received on the numerous vistas and turnouts with their interpretive facilities which help the visitor to understand and appreciate the natural features and park values.

This appendix is a reprint of a special number of *Yosemite Nature Notes* (Volume 40, number 3, June 24, 1961), revised 1975 and 1980.

Sources of Information

SCB – *Sierra Club Bulletin*

YNN – *Yosemite Nature Notes*
 published by Yosemite Natural
 History Association (YNHA)

DFP – *Daily Free Press*, Bodie

Supt Rept – Annual Reports
 of Superintendents and Acting
 Superintendents of Yosemite National
 Park

All other sources are in the
 Yosemite Museum or NPS
 administrative files, Yosemite N. P.

Notes

1. Muir, John, *The Mountains of California* (New York, The Century Co., 1894).

2. Fitzwater, R. J., "Final Report on Two Seasons Excavations at El Portal, Mariposa County, California" (1962).

3. Davis, James T., *Trade Routes and Economic Exchange Among* the *Indians of California* (Berkeley, University of California Archaeological Survey, 1961).

4. Farquhar, F. P., "Walker's Discovery *of* Yosemite" (SCB 27(4):35-49, 1942).

5. Russell C. P., *100 Years* in *Yosemite* (Yosemite, YNHA, 1959).

6. Brockman, C. F., "Development of Transportation to Yosemite, Part I" (YNN 22(6):49-56, 1943).

7. Ibid. Part II (YNN, 22(7):57-63, 1943).

8. Farquhar, F. P., "Lee Vining" (SCB, 13(1):83-85, 1928).

9. Bunnell, L. H., *Discovery of* the *Yosemite* (Los Angeles, G. W. Gerlicher, 1911).

9a. Interview with T. J. Hodgdon by C. P. Russell, 1927.

10. Farquhar, F. P., "Place Names of the High Sierra" (SCB, 12:126-247, 1925).

11. Manuscript, Elmira Parker, no date.

12. Brockman, C. F., "Development of Transportation to Yosemite, Part III" (YNN, 22(10):81-86, 1943).

13. Farquhar, F. P., *Exploration of* the *Sierra Nevada* (San Francisco, California Historical Society, 1925).

14. Manuscript, "Trip across Yosemite in 1869," no date.

15. Russell, C. P., "Early Mining Excitements East of Yosemite" (SCB, 13(1):40-53, 1928).

15a. Hubbard, D. H., *Ghost Mines of Yosemite* (Fresno, Awani Press, 1958)

16. Gondos, V., Jr., to H. L. Bill, 1 Nov. 1954.

17. *Mammoth City Herald*, 3 Sept. 1879.

18. Hubbard, Fran, "Road to Rusting Dreams" (YNN, 34(7):86-91, 1955).

19. DFP, 20 July 1882.

20. DFP, 18 August 1882.

21. Ferretti, J. V., "Surveying the Tioga Road" (YNN, 27(9):109-112, 1948).

22. Report of C. E. Barney, Mining Engineer for the Co., to Thos. Bennett, Jr., President, Great Sierra Consolidated Silver Co., 1 Nov. 1883.

23. Bennett, Thos., Jr., Statement B., Relating to the Great Sierra properties, 15 Feb. 1890.

24. Manuscript, Celia Crocker Thompson, no date.

25. *Homer Mining Index*, 23 June 1883.

26. Morris, F. B., to San Sing Wo (Sun Sun Wo), 11 Aug. 1883.

27. Lord, R. F., Report to Great Sierra Co., 5 Sept. 1881.

28. DFP, 22 April 1882.

29. *Fresno Bee*, 11 Aug. 1958.

30. Smith, Hoke, to John F. Lacey, 5 March 1896.

31. Tuolumne County Deeds, Vol. 24, p. 90.

32. Bill of Complaint, 9th Circuit Court, Northern Calif., (19127).

33. Wilson and Wilson to 9th Circuit Court, (19127).

34. Schlichtmann and Paden, *Big Oak Flat Road to Yosemite* (Yosemite, YNHA, 1959).

35. Private Lands Survey, Y.N.P., Aug. 1931.

36. Manuscript, unsigned and undated.

37. DFP, 1 Aug. 1878.

38. Uhte, R. F., "Yosemite's Pioneer Cabins" (YNN 35(9):134-143, 1956).

39. Ibid., No.5.

39a. SCB, April, 1973:30.

40. DFP, 26 July 1882.

41. Le Conte, J. N., "The Soda Springs Property in the Tuolumne Meadows" (SCB 9(1):36-39, 1913).

42. Stornoway, L., *Yosemite; Where to Go and What to Do* (San Francisco, 1888).

43. Report No. 79, Great Sierra Consolidated Silver Co., 4 Aug. 1884.

44. Barney, C. E., to W. C. N. Swift, 19 Oct. 1884.

45. *Homer Mining Index*, 2 June 1894.

46. Anonymous, "Wagon Trips to the Sierra" (SCB, 3:210-217, 1901).

47. Hutchinson, J. S., "Round About Mt. Dana" (SCB, 3:319-328, 1901).

48. Supt Rept, 1891.

49. Supt Rept, 1895.

50. Supt Rept, 1896.

51. Supt Rept, 1897.

52. Supt Rept, 1905.

53. Reference deleted.

54. McLean, J. T., to Wilson and Wilson, 9 April 1908.

55. Report of the Yosemite Park Commission, Dec. 1904.

56. Supt Rept, 1898.

57. Bill, 56th Congress, 2nd Sesseion, 1 March 1901.

58. S. 3064, 19 May 1896.

59. *Report of the Commission on Roads in Yosemite N.P.,* 8 Feb. 1900.

60. Ise, J., *Our National Park Policy* (Baltimore, Johns Hopkins Press, 1961).

61. Senate Report 863, 5 May 1896.

62. Littebrant, W. L. to Secretary of Interior, 8 July 1913.

63. Anonymous, "Old Tioga Road to be Acquired" (SCB 8:132, 1911).

64. Forsyth, Maj., to Secretary of Interior, 16 April 1912.

65. McClure, W. F., to W. T. Littebrant, 15 July 1913.

66. Wilson and Wilson to Col. S. B. N. Young, 27 Oct. 1896.

67. Thompson, C. C., to D. E. McHenry, 6 Feb. 1954.

68. Affidavit of W. C. Priest to Wilson and Wilson, 22 Oct. 1892.

69. Wilson and Wilson to Maj. H. M. Chittenden, 24 Aug. 1904.

70. Webster, Allen, to Frank Pierce, 12 Dec. 1907.

71. Crocker, Mrs. H. R., to Maj. Benson, 7 Sept. 1907.

72. Crocker, Mrs. H. R. to Maj. Benson, 28 Sept. 1907.

73. Ibid.

74. Dron, A. P., to Mrs. Crocker, 25 Aug. 1908.

75. Crocker, May Hall, Deposition, State of Calif., Co. of San Joaquin, Jan., 1912.

76. Biennial Report, Dept. of Highways, Sacramento, 1899.

77. Supt Rept, 1907.

78. Biennial Report, Dept. of Highways, Sacramento, 1905.

79. Anonymous, "Mono-Tioga Highway" (SCB, 7:195, 1909).

50. Supt Rept, 1910.

81. Littebrant, Maj., to W. F. McClure, 2 June 1913.

82. Littebrant, Maj., to W. F. McClure, 28 June 1913.

83. Sanley, J. N., "Tioga Pass" (Calif. Highways and Public Works 19(7):4-7, 1941).

84. Foley, E. R., to John C. Preston, 7 Feb. 1961,

85. Supt Rept, 1913.

86. Townsley, F. S., "The First Automobile in Yosemite," manuscript dated 1 Dec. 1941.

87. Sargent, Shirley, "The Old Big Oak Flat Road" (YNN, 29(7):68-71, 1950).

88. Shankland, Robert, *Steve Mather of the National Parks* (New York, Alfred A. Knopf, 1954).

89. Colby, W. E., to K. A. Trexler, 17 May 1961.

90. Wosky, J. B., to Director, NPS, 23 Jan. 1936.

91. Report of the General Supt. and Landscape Engineer of NPS to Sec'y of Interior, Washington, D.C., 1950.

92. Supt Rept, 1915.

93. Mather, S. T., "National Parks - The Federal Policy, Past and Future" (SCB, 10:97-101, 1916).

94. Supt Rept, 1916.

95. Sovulewski Construction Reports, 1916 to 1922 (manuscripts).

96. *The California Motorist,* June 1918.

97. Annual Report, Director of National Park Service, 1918.

98. Tioga Road File, Yosemite National Park, 1920, 1930.

99. Yosemite Transportation System brochure, 1923.

100. Lewis, W. B., to S. T. Mather, 28 June 1927.

101. Hall, Ansel F., *Guide to Yosemite* (Yosemite, 1920).

102. Circular letter from W. B. Lewis, 4 June 1924.

103. Supt Rept, 1925.

104. Huber, W. L., to C. G. Thomson, 30 Jan. 1935.

105. Regional Director, NPS Region 4, to Director NPS, 19 Nov. 1958.

106. Supt Rept, 1932.

107. Supt Rept, 1933.

108. Supt Rept, 1928.

109. Park Engineer to K. A.Trexler, 1961.

110. Supt Rept, 1940.

111. Superintendent of Yosemite to Director NPS, 14 Nov. 1942.

112. Kittredge, F. A., to C. D. Boothe, 14 June 1943.

113. Halliburton, G., to Chief Ranger, YNP, 10 Sept. 1958.

114. Frasier, V. M., to Supt. of Parks, Washington, D.C., 12 Sept. 1948.

115. *Travel News Bulletin,* No. 8, 16 May, 1947.

116. Preston, John C., to G. Ballis, 20 July 1954.

117. Huber, W. L., to C. L. Wirth, 4 June 1956.

118. Excerpts from files re Tioga Road controversy, 24 Nov. 1958.

119. Statement of John C. Preston to NPS Region Four Conference, Death Valley, 11 Jan. 1959.

120. NPS Information Service release, 10 July 1957.

121. Tioga Road File, Yosemite NP, 1957, 1958.

122. Wirth, Conrad L., to Pauline Dyer, 3 Oct. 1958.

123. Statement of Director of NPS before Sierra Cub officials, 24 Nov. 1958.

124. *Fresno Bee,* 4 Jan. 1959.

SUGGESTED READING

Albright, Horace Marden and Marian Albright Schenck. *The Mather Mountain Party of 1915*. Sequoia N.P.: Sequoia Natural History Association, 1990.

Bates, Craig D. and Martha Lee. *Tradition and Innovation - A Basket History of the Indians of the Yosemite-Mono Lake Area*. Yosemite: Yosemite Association, 1990.

Bingaman, John W. *Guardians of the Yosemite*. Lodi, Calif.: End-Kian Publishing Co., 1970.

Bunnell, Lafayette H. *Discovery of the Yosemite and the Indian War of 1851 Which Led to That Event.* Reprint of 1911 edition. Yosemite: Yosemite Association, 1990.

Clark, Lew and Ginny Clark. *Mammoth-Mono Country*. San Luis Obispo: Western Trails Publications, 1989.

Cohen, Michael P. *The History of the Sierra Club, 1892-1979*. San Francisco: Sierra Club Books, 1988.

Robert Eccleston *The Mariposa Indian War, 1850-51*. Edited by C. Gregory Crampton. Salt Lake City: University of Utah Press, 1957.

Francis Farquhar, *History of the Sierra Nevada*. Berkeley: University of California Press, 1969.

Fletcher, Thomas C. *Paiute, Prospector, Pioneer*. Lee Vining, Calif: Artemisia Press, 1987.

Gilbert, Bil. *Westering Man – The Life of Joseph Walker*. New York: Atheneum, 1983.

Gudde, Erwin G. *California Place Names*. Berkeley: University of California Press, 1969.

Hartzog, George B., Jr. *Battling for the National Parks*. Mt. Kisco, N.Y.: Moyer Bell Limited, 1988.

Hubbard, Douglass. *Ghost Mines of Yosemite*. Fredericksburg, Texas: The Awani Press, 1958.

Huber, N. King. *The Geologic Story of Yosemite National Park*. Yosemite: Yosemite Association, 1987.

Kimes, William F. and Maymie B. Kimes. *John Muir - A Reading Bibliography*. Fresno: Panorama West Books, 1986.

LaBraque, Lily Mathieu. *Man From Mono*. Reno: Nevada Academic Press, 1984.

Moody, Warren. *Yosemite Ranger on Horseback.* Fresno: Pioneer Publishing Co., 1990.

Muir, John. *My First Summer in the Sierra*. Reprint of 1911 edition. New York and Boston: Houghton Mifflin, 1998.

Muir, John. *The Mountains of California*. Berkeley: Ten Speed Press, 1977.

Olmsted, Frederick Law. *Yosemite and the Mariposa Grove: A Preliminary Report, 1865*. Yosemite: Yosemite Association, 1993.

O'Neill, Elizabeth Stone. *Meadow in the Sky*. Fresno: Panorama West Books, 1984.

Russell, Carl P. *One Hundred Years in Yosemite*. Omnibus edition. Yosemite: Yosemite Association, 1992.

Sanborn, Margaret. *Yosemite: Its Discovery, Its Wonders and Its People*. New York: Random House, 1981.

Schaffer, Jeffrey P. *Tuolumne Meadows*. High Sierra Hiking Guides Series. Berkeley: Wilderness Press, 1977.

Trexler, Keith A. *The Tioga Road - A History, 1883-1961*. Yosemite: Yosemite Natural History Association, 1980.

Williams, John L. *Yosemite and Its High Sierra*. Second edition. Tacoma and San Francisco: self-published, 1921.

Wolfe, Linnie Marsh. *John of the Mountains*. Madison: University of Wisconsin Press, 1979.

INDEX

Page numbers for subject-related illustrations are indicated in bold.